G A R D I N E R S

B A Y

UNITED STATES - EAST COAST

NEW YORK - LONG ISLAND

SHELTER ISLAND SOUND
AND PECONIC BAYS

Mercator Projection
Scale 1:40,000 at Lat. 41° 02'

North American Datum of 1983
(World Geodetic System 1984)

SOUNDINGS IN FEET
AT MEAN LOWER LOW WATER

N O R T H   A T L A N T I C   O C E A N

Shelter Island Sound and Peconic Bays
SOUNDINGS IN FEET · SCALE : 40,000

12358

Nothing Bad
Ever Happens

Nothing Bad Ever Happens

Jim Miller's Life of Hard Knocks, Hard Work, Tough Love, and Joy

by Benedict Cosgrove

Book design by Mary A. Wirth
Frontispiece image © iStockphoto/topten22photo

ISBN 978-1-937650-84-1
Library of Congress Control Number: 2017937260

SMALL
BATCH
BOOKS

493 SOUTH PLEASANT STREET
AMHERST, MASSACHUSETTS 01002
413.230.3943
SMALLBATCHBOOKS.COM

Contents

Introduction

Words are powerful, versatile instruments. They can evoke laughter (*A nun and a penguin walk into a bar . . .*), spark revolutions (*When in the course of human events . . .*), sanctify unions (*I now pronounce you . . .*), and commemorate catastrophes (*Fourscore and seven years ago . . .*).

When trying to sum up a person's life, however—especially a long life, filled with adventures large and small—simply stringing words, memories, and insights together can, quite frankly, feel inadequate to the task. Aren't a person's deeds far more powerful and revealing than any words written on a page? Isn't the impact that a man or woman has on others, and on the world at large, a more accurate gauge of a person's legacy than stories told and memories shared about that impact?

Put another way: Can mere words ever really capture a life?

As it turns out, the answer to that thorny question is both an emphatic and a qualified *yes.* In speaking with family, friends, and colleagues who have known Jim Miller for decades—and, of course, after many enjoyable hours spent with Jim himself as he shared his own memories from his eighty-plus years—I was struck by the way that certain terms and expressions kept appearing and echoing throughout all of those conversations. It was difficult, it seemed—if not impossible—for anyone to speak at any length about Jim without using a number of specific and, as time went on, deeply telling words.

Work. Family. Fairness. Toughness.

Those words—and others that, taken together, suggest a serious but far from somber or joyless life—punctuated pretty much every story or recollection that I heard about Jim Miller. And the more I encountered them, the more these themes or values helped to describe a way of life that Jim not only has embraced but also has in many ways embodied.

That Barbara, his wife of sixty years; his brothers and sisters; his children and grandchildren—that so many others in the Miller clan—share those elemental, "traditional" values indicates that Jim is, in the best possible way, something of a throwback (even if, at the same time, he has also so frequently proven to be something of a visionary, well ahead of his time).

Something else that quickly became clear while I was working on this book was that approaching and trying to relate Jim's life from a purely chronological perspective—as if A always led inexorably to B, which then led to C, without any detours or tangents along the way—could not adequately convey the scope and trajectory of that life, or of the other lives that play their roles here. And so, this narrative has what might best be viewed or described as a *roughly* chronological shape, with side trips, reversals, and even parallel journeys included along the way, in hopes of keeping the larger, central tale from growing stale.

I would like to thank all the people who so generously shared their stories of Jim Miller through interviews and conversations that took place over the course of many months. I also want to thank a sensitive, eagle-eyed editor named Allan Edmands, who helped to hone the end product of these tales.

All this is to say, by way of introduction, that while words are often the pale shadows of deeds, this writer hopes that the words the reader encounters here will do justice to one man's long, extraordinary, and, in many ways, quintessentially American life.

Here's to Jim Miller, the man who said yes.

BENEDICT COSGROVE
Brooklyn, January 2017

Nothing Bad
Ever Happens

Prologue

A midsummer day. The sky is clear—pale blue with a slight haze. A line of thunderheads, white on top, deep gray below, marches across the southern horizon. On the land, the heat comes down like a hammer.

Out on the choppy, greenish-gray waters of Long Island Sound, a humid breeze knocks the temperature down, but only a notch. The air is marginally fresher out on the waves than on the streets of Port Jefferson, New Haven, or New York, but it's still hot enough on one particular lobster boat that the boys who make up the crew—three brothers, not one of them out of his early teens—have been working shirtless for hours.

Today, like every day during the summer months, the brothers awoke before dawn; rode to the dock in a pickup truck, eating buttered rolls and drinking coffee on the way; and were already well out on the water by the time the sun rose over the eastern Sound. Other boats—lobsterers, small trawlers, a handful of private charters—are plying the same waters, the commercial fishermen setting and pulling nets and traps, silhouettes on the charters casting for fluke, flounder, bass, whatever will hit a lure, an eel, or a bunker at this hour.

In the wheelhouse of the lobster boat, the captain—five feet eight, 140 pounds, wiry—throttles back and maneuvers the craft, slowly, slowly, along a buoyed line of traps. As the boys in the boat pull the traps, hauling them up on deck, the energy on board perceptibly shifts. More traps emerge from the waters of the Sound, and the boys glance at one another, smiling. After a while, they're laughing.

This is one of those days, their smiles say. *This is one of those rare days.*

There's not an empty trap along the entire line of thirty; many carry three, four, five lobsters, and some of the creatures are, by Long Island standards, huge. Even before the traps break free of the surface, the boys see claws trying to poke through the water-slick wooden slats, as if the lobsters are waving at them. *Hey! Get us outta here! It's too crowded in this goddamn thing!*

The captain, the boys' father, looks aft at his sons as they haul away, emptying the traps, weighing the lobsters, measuring them, tossing back the little ones under the size limit, checking for roe, rubber-banding thick claws, working tirelessly back there on the open deck in the humid heat.

And that's when the singing starts.

At first, it's just a low, persistent, catchy sort of hum, coming through the open door of the wheelhouse. In the space of a few minutes, the humming has grown, has caught on, and has become a full-throated, four-throated, wordless song. *DUM-de-de-DUM-de-de-DUM-de-de-DUM-de-de-DUMMM-DUMMM!*

The four voices rise from the lobster boat, punctuated by occasional, exultant shouts. On nearby boats, scores of fishermen—some of them on the water for recreation, most of them working the Sound for their livelihoods—cock their heads and listen as the improbable, gradually recognizable theme song from the TV show *Bonanza* fills the late-morning air, drifting from the lobster boat, *Lady Barbara,* like an anthem.

The Miller boys and their father, Jim, are having a good day.

CHAPTER 1

North Merrick: Center of the World

In 1935, Amelia Earhart became the first person to fly solo from Hawaii to California. The world's first parking meters were installed in Oklahoma City. Parker Brothers released the first version of the most popular board game in history, Monopoly. The Gottfried Krueger Brewing Company of Newark, New Jersey, produced the first-ever canned beer. Babe Ruth played in his last major league baseball game. In Germany, the Nuremberg Laws stripped the country's Jews of citizenship. An Associated Press editor coined the term "Dust Bowl" to characterize the horrific storms whipping across vast, drought-stricken stretches of the United States.

Elvis Presley, Julie Andrews, Sandy Koufax, and the fourteenth Dalai Lama were born. Will Rogers, Dutch Schultz, Louisiana's Huey "The Kingfish" Long, and Thomas Edward Lawrence (better known as Lawrence of Arabia) died.

Around the globe, countries struggled in the grip of the Great Depression.

It was into this world that James Miller was born on March 30, 1935, in North Merrick, Long Island.

"I'm the son of an immigrant father," Jim says. "In fact, I'm the third son of a third son of a third son, which is supposedly a good luck charm. My dad, Harry Miller, was born in 1895 in Riga, Latvia, of German parents and left home as a teenager to join the merchant marine. He went to sea early in his career, and he was at sea when World War I erupted. He was captured on multiple occasions—it seemed like the English captured him, the Germans captured him—and every time he was captured, he would say, 'I'm one of you guys!'

"He was on everybody's ship, and he was one of the good guys. That was the story that he told us.

"My mom, Cecelia, was born here in the United States, from English and Irish parents, and her lineage goes back to the beginning of time. Her family was always here. I have three older siblings and three younger siblings."

North Merrick, where Jim spent his earliest, formative years, is a village in south-central Nassau County, New York, not far from the eastern border of the borough of Queens. Merrick—which split into two entities, Merrick and North Merrick, after World War II—was founded in the mid-1600s by settlers from New England. Like a good many towns and regions on Long Island, including Massapequa, Patchogue, Montauk, Manhasset, and others, Merrick's name derives from a Native American term for the area: in this case, Mericoke, roughly translated as "barren land." For centuries after the town was settled, Merrick, like the rest of Long Island, was largely rural—if not downright wild—with virtually all of its residents living off the fruits of the land and, of course, the bounty of the coastal waters of the Sound to the north and the deeper waters of the Atlantic Ocean to the south and the east.

It's no wonder, really, that all the Millers grew up with salt water in their veins and that all of the boys born to Jim and his wife, Barbara—Jimmy Jr., Glen, and Mark (yet another third son)—have spent so much time on and, to a greater or lesser degree, made their living on the waves.

While the region around Merrick in the 1930s and early 1940s—and even more so in the postwar years—was beginning to experience a first wave of commuter-driven development spilling eastward from New York City, it still retained much of the charm that led a *Brooklyn Eagle* reporter to write, a few decades earlier, that "the most beautiful section of the Merrick Road is at Merrick, the village from which it takes its name. Here [the road] runs under a grand foliage of big girthed trees, between glimmering lakes and over rustic bridges spanning picturesque streams. Within sight are the waters of the Great South Bay and the beach."

Beautiful it might have been, but in the midst of the Great Depression, North Merrick—like untold numbers of villages, towns, and cities across the U.S.—was a tough place to make a living, raise a family, and try to get ahead. And just like families everywhere, the Millers worked hard—*very* hard—and found ways to put food on the table, put clothes on their backs, and keep a clean, dry roof over their many heads.

"Those were struggling times," Jim recalls today, gazing back across seven decades at his life as young Jimmy Miller. "We were poor by today's standards, I suppose, but the thing is, you didn't really know it back then. You didn't think about it, because in those days, where we were, everybody was in the same boat."

Then, as is so often the case when telling stories, Jim decides to elaborate—and the details that emerge are fascinating.

"You just lived life that way," he says. "You lived partly off the land, you raised chickens, you had a goat, you had a garden, you grew your own food, hunted your own food. Everybody had dogs—sometimes we'd have as many as four or five beagles for hunting dogs—and we had open woods in the backyard, several acres, so that was a good spot to start out hunting rabbits for supper. Until you were eight or ten years old, you didn't carry a gun, but from the time you were ten years old, you carried a gun in the woods. We got to be pretty good shots with a shotgun, and I remember practicing as a kid with a .22 rifle.

"We'd take tin cans and throw them out in the woods at random, and then you'd walk through the woods and climb over the brambles and everything else, and the second you saw a can, you had to shoot it. We soon found out that if you really, really paid attention, you didn't have to waste the time and bring the gun to your shoulder. You could shoot a .22 rifle pretty well from the hip. After a while, we didn't miss very many. We'd throw the tin cans up in the air and shoot them with a .22, and if you could shoot fast enough, you could actually hit the can a couple of times when it was in the air."

("Pops is still an amazing shot," his son Mark points out, referring to his dad by the affectionate moniker that virtually all of Jim's kids and grandkids use when speaking of him. "In the winter, we all get together and shoot trap, and Pops still regularly hits twenty-three out of twenty-five.")

"Once in a while, you'd shoot a quail or a pheasant," Jim continues, "but whatever you hit, it was all good food. And, of course, absolutely nothing was to be wasted. We also raised rabbits, and we slaughtered them for food. We raised chickens. We raised a pig once and slaughtered that, too. That was a big event, and everybody came by to see how a pig gets slaughtered."

A very slight pause, then Jim continues, offering one more example of how almost unthinkably different his early days were from, say, the way that most kids are raised today. There's nothing in his attitude to suggest that "things were better back then." Instead, he just seems to see things clearly. He's not one to dwell on what can't be changed. *That was then. This is now.* That's his attitude.

"I remember that the telephone was a big thing," he says. "We couldn't afford a telephone, but there was one rich neighbor all the way down the block, and if you had to call somebody, you had to go to the neighbor's house and ask him if you could use the phone.

"It was a big event. And kids did *not* make phone calls. The way I remember it, when we had to use the phone down the block, it was always a message from Mom that was an emergency of some sort. Somebody died, or somebody needed a doctor. The house was on fire. These were not social phone calls. And," Jim says, a slight change in the tone of his voice suggesting that this is a point that really mattered, and is worth stressing, "you had to bring a nickel, because, of course, you had to pay for the call."

Many of Jim's memories of his earliest days, though, center on the outdoors. His keenest pleasure as a boy, he says, "involved just being out in the woods and being in the wild. I guess from around eight years old and up, it was not uncommon for us to sleep in the woods overnight. No bad things could happen to us out there. If you had a good bean shooter, or slingshot, and you were a good shot with that, well, you were set, boy. Sometimes, of course, what with kids being kids, there would be other boys, some younger, some older, who wanted to fight. But that was a bad thing. For them, I mean. You really didn't want to challenge me when I had my bean shooter. Some kids would want to throw rocks, but your rocks up against my bean shooter? Believe me," Jim says, serious and amused at once, "you're going to lose."

It's worth remembering that Merrick, North Merrick, and Nassau County as a whole—and, in fact, much of Long Island during those years, seven decades ago—was still a landscape consisting largely of woods, meadows, marshes, and streams rather than of towns and villages. Utterly unspoiled wilderness? Not quite. But until the postwar push eastward from New York, with thousands— and, eventually, tens of thousands—of families moving to Nassau and Suffolk Counties from the city and from other parts of the Northeast, Long Island was defined more by open space than by sprawl.

"I'd often sleep out in the open," Jim remembers. "Just take a blanket and sleep right out in the open, on the ground. We'd find some straw, throw it down, and sleep there. Look at the stars, build a campfire. Nobody cared."

The unspoken but quite clear counterpoint to the scene that Jim evokes is, of course, the modern mania for safety, safety, safety at all costs and the phenomenon of "helicopter" parenting. Today, parents in pretty much any region of the U.S. would likely be held up for ridicule—if not cited or arrested for endangering the welfare of a minor—if they allowed their kids to go off by themselves and sleep in the woods, unsupervised.

Jim, meanwhile, is caught up in his memories of other adventures in and around long-ago North Merrick.

"There was a farm not far from there. We could always sneak over to the farm and steal tomatoes," he says. "There's nothing better than eating a nice ripe tomato right off the vine. And you could take a half-bushel basket and put some extra tomatoes in there, and they were great to throw at cars. Causing trouble, you know. And if one of the neighbors really caused *you* trouble? Well, maybe his house got some tomatoes, too."

Recalling these bouts of troublemaking sparks another memory in Jim, one that will bring an uncomfortable smile to the lips of anyone who has seen a teenagers-in-the-woods horror flick any time in the past, say, twenty or thirty years.

"There was a lovers' lane around there, too," Jim says, "and there was nothing more fun than harassing some guy who was making love to his girlfriend by going and jumping on the hood of his car and scaring the crap out of both of them."

Abruptly, Jim switches gears, and while the story he tells eventually circles back to one more tale of childhood rowdiness (this time, as it turns out, involving *genuine* crap), he's sidetracked by a concern that is central to his life story: namely, the pursuit of a buck.

"One of the things that became pretty clear early in my life," Jim says, "is that I could figure out how to hustle a dollar. If you were twelve years old, you could get a newspaper route, delivering *Newsday*. Of course, I wasn't twelve yet, but I fudged on my age and I got a route for a while. The paper was three cents a copy, six days a week [*Newsday*, for decades the largest suburban newspaper in the country, would not begin publishing a Sunday edition until 1972], so that was eighteen cents a week per customer. People often gave the newspaper boy a quarter, so that was a seven-cent tip from pretty much everyone along my route. Delivery boys got six cents a week per customer from *Newsday* just for delivering the paper, so with a good-size route and all those tips, a kid could do all right.

"But even before that, we used to help the milkman. You know, back then, the milkman drove around with a truck and with the milk in bottles—in glass bottles—and we'd hang out down at the cow barn and ask, 'Can we go with you in the morning?' And he'd say, 'Well, if you come here at five o'clock in the morning, you can go with me.' So we'd get up early, *early* in the morning, and get dressed, and run down to the farm—he was only about four, maybe five blocks away—and get on the milk truck, and my brother Tommy and I would often go out and deliver milk with the milk-man, and our pay for the day was a pint of chocolate milk, which was a pretty good reward.

"He was usually done by ten, eleven o'clock in the morning, so we were out there for a good five or even six hours. Tommy would run up with the full milk bottles, and I would run up with an empty container and pick up the empties, because every house had to return all the milk bottles they used. We did all the running, and that was fine. There was one occasion I remember so clearly, when I was running alongside the truck and handing up the empty milk bottles, and I stepped in a sand pile, tripped, and fell, and my right leg—not the one I tore up on a goat stake at one point, but the other one—went completely under the rear wheels.

"*Bump, bump*, the truck ran right over the leg, and that was that. My brother saw it, and he's screaming, 'Stop the truck! You ran over my brother! Oh my God, he's there in the dirt!' and all this commotion and whatever else, and the driver stops and comes back, pretty shaken, and he's asking, 'Are you all right? Are you all right? What happened? Let me see, let me see. Can you stand up?' I mean, you could see the tire tracks right across my leg.

"So I move my leg a little bit, and I look up and tell him, 'Yeah, I can stand up. I'm all right, I'm all right. Don't worry, I'm okay.' And the truth was, I *was* okay. The damn truck ran over me, but it was on soft sand, and it sort of squooshed me into the sand and left tire tracks on my leg, and that was that. But that poor guy was all upset. He had to take me home and tell my mother that he ran me over. Oh boy. So for about two days, I couldn't go out with the milkman. But after that, you know, I was right back out there with Tommy. No more running alongside the truck, though.

"But speaking of milk and barns, let me tell you a good story since we're talking about the cow barn. Not far from us, there was a Swiss family—three boys and a girl, and the farmer and his wife. They were old-fashioned Swiss people, and they had a barn, and they had maybe thirty-five milking cows. In the beginning, they milked by hand, and then later, they added a machine for milking the cows. We were allowed to hang out in the cow barn and visit the cows. It was a great place. A hayloft up in the barn, climbing the ladder, jumping out of the hayloft—just a perfect place for boys to play, you know? And any time we wanted, we could go into the cooler house, where the fresh, warm milk was brought in, in buckets, and then dumped into this giant stainless steel vat, where it would cascade across the cooler bars, and out would come this ice-cold milk.

"We'd take a big dip of that, just suck it up, and drink half a scoopful of milk—and whatever we didn't drink just went right back in the bucket. Fresh, raw milk. Or a farmhand would be milking cows, and you'd be looking at him, and he'd squeeze a teat and say, 'Open up,' and shoot a stream of warm cow's milk right into your mouth. It was a lot of fun, that barn.

"Now, in the early spring one year, Mom says, 'Hey, Tom, Jim, take the wagon, go down to the barn, and get some cow manure to put on the garden.' Off we go; it's March or something like that, so most of the snow is gone from the road, but there are still piles of snow along the sides of the road. We get to the barn, grab a pitchfork, and we load up the wagon with cow manure.

"We're pulling the wagon home, and there's a family nearby with a lot of cousins and relatives from Brooklyn, and they're out for the weekend. There's—I don't know—six or eight or ten of 'em, and they had the snow. You see? We're down in the middle of the road with a wagon full of manure, carting it home, and they think that this is pretty silly, these country boys. They think we're a moving target—but a very *slowly* moving target. And, of course, they start pelting us with snowballs and what have you, and down in the road, we've got no snow at all.

"So we're going down what's basically this ravine between a plunging fire of snowballs, and we're getting beat up pretty good. We're outnumbered by about four to one, maybe more. We're trying to hustle through and push the wagon quickly, and keep going. One of the kids from Brooklyn comes out from the side, and he's got a big handful of snow, and he grabs my brother, and he's going to wash Tommy's face in the snow. Me? I got no snow. But I've got a wagon full of cow manure. Then I have a handful of cow manure, and while this Brooklyn kid is washing my brother's face with snow, he's bent over just perfect, and I can mount him like a horse. I somehow get both my feet in his back pockets, and a handful of cow manure—and boy, does he get a dose of it! My brother is free, and he catches on real quick. We've got ammunition now, too.

"The battle changed quickly. They were now the victims and basically covered in manure, and, in a few seconds, they're in full retreat. I guess those city kids didn't like these crazy manurers from the country. Victory that day went to the Millers. To the rubes."

Kids being kids. Some things, it seems, never go out of style.

CHAPTER 2

Save a Leg, Save a Dog

Quick: Think back to your own childhood, and conjure up your first memory. For some of us, that initial memory might be of a seemingly ordinary event that, when recounted, feels decidedly *unmemorable* to the listener—walking in a field with your mom or dad, for example, or standing at the shore with waves lapping at your feet.

For most of us, though, the earliest recollection will be of something so striking—and in a good number of cases, something traumatic—it's hardly surprising that it sticks out as a signature event.

When asked about his own earliest memories, Jim Miller mentions two: one of them similar to the first memories of literally millions of American kids in the early 1940s, the other a distinct memory of an injury that, in its own way, speaks volumes about where Jim and his siblings, the boys and the girls, got their gumption.

"One of my earliest memories," he says, "without question, is from when I was six years old. I very vividly remember a Sunday afternoon in December—December 7, 1941—listening to the radio. We had a big RCA radio in the living room, and I remember my mom screaming out, 'Oh my God! We're going to war!' Then everybody came in and crowded around the radio to hear the bombs falling on Pearl Harbor. My older sister, Pat—her true name was June, but nobody ever knew her as June; she was Pat or Patsy—was dating a soldier, and there was a lot of confusion and concern about where he was supposed to be or where he was supposed to go."

The second vivid early memory Jim recalls is one shared, in kind if not in degree, by an awful lot of kids: namely, an injury sustained while playing hard in the great outdoors. Or in the backyard, as the case may be. But it's really what happens after the injury that helps illustrate the can-do attitude that defines so much about the Millers.

"One other thing I definitely remember from my boyhood is a particular injury I got when I was playing one day with my brother Tommy," Jim says. "He's the next oldest to me among the siblings. We used to hang out together all the time and get into or cause whatever trouble we could find. Of course, that was pretty often, because back then, as long as you were home for supper, nobody really worried about you. You were just outside, and you just lived life—that's all. Besides, we had a very small house there in North Merrick, so there was absolutely no room for us to be in the house doing anything. So in all seasons, we were outside.

"On this one occasion, though, we had a goat, and the goat was tied to a metal stake. There was an apple tree in our yard, and my mom had a set of old stairs, three or four steps, that she used to put her flower pots on in the shade of that apple tree. For some unknown reason—what the hell! I was a kid, maybe five years old—I decided to climb the steps and jump over the stake that the goat was tied to, and one way or another, I jumped short. The stake caught me in the back of the leg and tore open my leg pretty badly.

"I remember that my dad was home, so it was probably a week-end, and off to the doctor's we went. It was a big emergency, but there was no going to the hospital—that was far, far away—so we went to the doctor's office. And I know that there was a big debate: The doctor said, 'Oh, it's badly, badly injured. We're probably going to have to cut it off. It will be the easier way, it will heal faster that way. The tendons are all exposed, so they'll probably be infected. It happened in a farmyard, so probably the best thing we can do is just go forward and take the leg right off.'

"Now, to no one's surprise, my mother was screaming, 'Oh, no! No! It's got to stay on! Even if it's stiff, even if he can't walk, we can't cut his leg off.' There was a big commotion. At the time, they had some type of stainless steel clips that they used, instead of sewing it together with sutures, and somehow or other, they installed those metal clips. There wasn't a lot of anesthesia, either, so there were some uncomfortable moments," Jim says with a wry smile. *Uncomfortable moments.* By which he clearly means, *It hurt like hell. It was absolute agony.* But he moves right along, not dwelling on that aspect of the scene.

"I was terrified, I admit it. Asking the doctor, 'Are you cutting it off, or are you going to glue it on? I mean, what are you gonna do?' But he clamped it together with those metal clips, and somehow or other, I actually recovered from it.

"Now," Jim says, with that change of tone that indicates the real meat of the story is still to come, "maybe a month later, the leg was pretty well healed, and one weekend when my dad was home, he said, 'You know, that leg looks pretty good. We ought to get those clips out—but that means we've got to go back to the doctor. He's going to want three dollars to take them out. I don't think it's a big deal. I think we ought to go ahead and take them out ourselves.'"

Jim widens his eyes, an amused look on his face, as if to say: *You see where I'm going with this?*

"I remember lying on the kitchen table, and they took the clips out, and the big question was: What the hell were we supposed to do with them? So we decided to save them. If nothing else, we could wash them off and save those damn clips. Right? So that was that, and the leg healed and has been fine for the rest of my life.

"But! It wasn't too long thereafter that our favorite dog got into a very, very bad dog fight—we always had dogs around, a lot of hunting dogs—and this dog came home with his jowls all torn out, and he had this big, gaping hole in his throat. We're all looking at him and wondering if he's going to live and how we're supposed to take care of this awful injury to our favorite dog, and after a while, Dad says, 'Well, it's a good thing we saved those clips.'"

Jim Miller shakes his head. Behind his glasses, his eyes are lit up with both pride and amusement—but, in all honesty, there's probably more amusement there than pride.

"We took those clips that had held my leg together, and we used them to clip up that dog's gaping wounds, and he healed, too. He was a good hunting dog for a good number of years after that, I can tell you."

It's always tempting for any reader or listener to read too much into a single story. But in Jim Miller's tale of the apple tree, the goat, the torn leg, and the hunting dog, it's hard not to see in that one narrative a whole slew of themes that run through so many of the stories that Jim tells of his own life and the lives of his parents, siblings, and his own kids. There's the theme of the outdoors—and of endless adventures on the water, in the North Merrick woods, and even in the confines of a backyard. There's the theme of toughness. (*Anesthesia? Who needs anesthesia?*)

And there's the theme of what might be called a kind of tireless, practical ingenuity that appears in story after story told by and about Jim and his family. After all, not only does Jim's father, Harry, see that he can save a few dollars—an amount of money that, in the war years, was nothing to sneeze at—by taking the clips from his son's leg himself. He also has the foresight to hold on to the metal clips once they're removed, on the off chance they might come in handy someday. Which, of course, they did.

The tendency to tackle any task—and the certainty that, once tackled, the task will not only be accomplished, but accomplished right—seems burned into the Miller family DNA. An aptitude for original thinking, a sense of optimism, plain old bulldog tenacity, or stick-to-itiveness: Harry Miller evidently possessed those qualities, and others, to a high degree, and it's clear that he passed them on, in spades, to his third son.

CHAPTER 3

Tough Love

It was a different time.

It's a refrain that echoes through so many of the conversations that children and grandchildren have with their own parents and grandparents everywhere.

"Grandma, how did you manage to take care of so many kids, and keep track of them, and run the household, and balance the budget—and without a smart phone!"

"It was a different time, dear."

"Pop, did you really sleep in a chicken coop? In the winter? With all of your brothers? Just for the fun of it?"

"It was a different time, kiddo."

When Jim Miller talks about his own father and mother, that phrase—*It was a different time*—winds its way through his recollections like an understood, unspoken truism.

"Dad passed away forty years ago," Jim says of his father, Harry. "He left the Brooklyn Navy Yard, where he had worked during the Second World War, after he had a heart attack. It was the late 1940s, after the war, and they were cutting back on staff. So he left the Navy Yard, rehabilitated for six months or so, and recovered enough that he could go back to work. He eventually got a job at the Grumman aviation plant in Bethpage."

Grumman for years was Long Island's largest private employer; in the 1980s, 25,000 men and women worked for the defense and aerospace giant, with the vast majority of those jobs at its sprawling Bethpage facility. Founded in 1929, Grumman Aircraft Engineering Corp. set up headquarters in Bethpage, and by the mid-1940s, thousands of workers were building hundreds of powerful (and today legendary) fighter planes, such as the Wildcat and the Hellcat. Along with the rapidly retooled automotive plants in Detroit that were cranking out bombers and tanks for the war effort—Motor City was dubbed "the Arsenal of Democracy" during World War II—the men and women at Grumman literally helped turn the tide of that war in the Allies' favor. The Bethpage plant also developed the lunar module that landed NASA astronauts on the moon, and throughout the 1970s and 1980s, it continued building ever-more-complex fighter planes as well as critical components for the space shuttle program. For six decades, Grumman was a "heritage industry"—a place where generations of Long Islanders worked while raising families, paying off mortgages, and sending their kids to college.

(In fact, Jim Miller's brother-in-law Bob LaManna—married to Jim's sister Loretta—worked for years at Grumman on Long Island, and today, long after he "retired," Bob is still doing consulting work for the aerospace giant Northrop Grumman in Georgia.)

By 2013, in the face of changing Pentagon priorities and cheaper labor available elsewhere in the U.S. (in Florida, for example), the Bethpage facility that had, in its heyday, employed tens of thousands of people had fewer than 600 workers left.

Harry Miller was there for most of the company's best years and (thankfully, perhaps) didn't live to see the gradual and then rapid decline that both Grumman and Bethpage endured in the early years of the twenty-first century.

"Dad finished his career at Bethpage as a millwright for Grumman, which meant he was an all-around machinist, a role that was part of the maintenance department. He was always very skilled with any sort of machinery, of course, and as a millwright, he kept Grumman's machines running. And he kept the family going."

Despite the fact that his dad had a heart attack when he was only in his forties, Jim Miller recalls his father as "a robust guy. He wasn't a very big guy, but he was tough." There's no mistaking the pride in Jim's voice when he speaks of his dad's mettle. Toughness, after all—mental as well as physical—is a prized trait in the Miller clan.

"He used to scrap," Jim says. "He used to get into fights. And he did drink. He had a short temper, but he was also a very sociable guy. He was a musician. He had a little band, and he could play multiple instruments. He was a good drummer, a trumpet player—and he played the guitar. In those days, the band would organize what they would call a 'racket.' It was a Friday night or a Saturday night racket, and anyone could get all the beer they could drink for two bucks, or whatever, and there was music. They'd rent a hall someplace and literally make a racket! They'd have a party, and that was the social outlet at the time."

Of his mother, Cecilia, Jim recalls that "she was much more private. Her social life, generally, took place on Friday nights. After she went grocery shopping for the week, my mom and dad used to stop at Joe's Bar and Grill, and she would have her usual: two boilermakers. That's a shot of whiskey and a short beer. She'd get a little bit of a buzz on, and she'd be pretty happy. That was Friday night life for my mom."

When it came to other aspects of their lives—something as elemental as disciplining their kids, for example—Harry and Cecilia were, without a doubt, very much of their time.

"Corporal punishment," Jim notes, without rancor or apology, "was an accepted part of life. Did you get a beating? Yeah. You did something wrong, my mom's favorite weapon was a slipper. She was pretty brutal with a slipper, man. Very skilled. It left pretty good black-and-blue marks on your heinie if you got caught doing something wrong. But the ultimate end-all was if Dad had to punish you for something, because he'd punch you, so you didn't want to go there very often. But you know, I was the middle child, and so while the older kids got hollered at, and the younger kids were kind of protected, in a way, I just kind of snuck through life, and nobody bothered me too much."

CHAPTER 4

Caution: Children at Play.
(Seriously. Watch Out.)

The similarities between Jim Miller and his older brother Richard (Richie, or Uncle Richie to most everybody who knows him) are as conspicuous as the stark differences between the two men. They both made their living for years on the water. (Richie, however, is the only Miller brother ever to have had the privilege of taking Helen Keller, *the* Helen Keller, out on a charter fishing trip—an experience he cites as one of the most fascinating and unexpected in a long and full life.) Both Richie and Jim headed up the Long Island Commercial Fishermen's Association during its most politically charged era. When shaking hands, Jim and Richie—now eighty and eighty-six years old, respectively—still both have grips that would do justice to men half their age, the result of decades of hard work and, one suspects, strong genes. Both men are of middling height but appear taller. (This is a trait shared, one finds, by many of the Millers, none of whom tops five feet ten. They all feel somehow *larger* than their physical statistics suggest they should be.)

And, especially when meeting someone for the first time, both Richie and Jim have a look in their blue eyes that is sharply appraising. It's not unfriendly, by any means, or even especially judgmental. But it's a lively, intelligent, measuring gaze: a look indicating that, while they're hoping they've met someone who can keep up with them, they'll reserve judgment—for a while. (The gaze also has something about it that suggests that neither man takes very long to size up a new acquaintance.)

As for their differences, Richie is, by most accounts, a perfectionist. Or, as he says: "I'd put it in slightly different language than that one word. I believe that if you're going to do something, it should be worthwhile doing, and you should do it right and do it once."

Jim, on the other hand, is a proponent of doing things right, doing them quickly, and moving on. A modest distinction, perhaps—but a telling one.

In conversation, Richie is blunt. Again, not at all unfriendly, but impatient with jargon, disclaimers, and other rhetorical flourishes that distract from the matter at hand. (Example: Rather than go on and on about what sort of discrete, nuanced traits might or might not tie the Miller clan together in terms of their approach to work and life, Richie cuts to the chase. "If you're looking for a trait or a trend, just say that for the Millers, the word *can't* doesn't exist.")

And then there's the dynamite.

Asked to think back to his own childhood and find a few instances that helped define his upbringing (and that of Jim and the other Miller kids), Richie doesn't hesitate:

"One day when I was maybe twelve, thirteen years old, and Jimmy was probably eight, my father brings a guy home from the Brooklyn Navy Yard who's an explosives expert. He brings him out to North Merrick because we have a bunch of stumps in the ground in the lot next door to our place, from trees I had cut down to make firewood, and it's time to get rid of those stumps. This guy looks around and says, 'Oh, I can get rid of them easy. I've got it all in the car.' He goes to his car and pulls out a box with Xs on it and a plunger. He points to another box, and—like it's the most natural thing in the world—he tells us, 'That's dynamite in there. We'll deal with those old stumps.' Oh boy, we're going to have some fun here! Then we're handed a great big long bar, and he tells us we're going to have to put holes in the ground. 'I'll show you where,' he says, and he has us poking holes underneath the stumps. 'Don't go too far down,' he tells us. 'The further down you go, the more forceful the explosion's going to be.' We were grinning at that, of course.

"We put the holes in the ground, and he puts skewers in the dynamite and slides it down into the holes. Then he tells us to stamp on the dirt. We know what's down there, so we aren't too quick to stamp on it *too* hard, but we do it just the same. He tells us to back up. 'A little farther. A little farther. Okay. Here we go.' He pushes the plunger down, and out come the stumps. I mean, they come out of the ground in a hurry.

"We were thrilled. We never thought we were going to see something like this, especially right there in our town on Long Island. Even the farmers who lived near us didn't do that back then. They dug them out with a horse and chain.

"We spent all day blowing stumps out of the ground, and we didn't finish the job. At the end of the day, my dad's pal came to me and said, 'I didn't expect to see you boys doing this well. I'm going to leave this stuff here, and I'll come by next weekend and finish it up. In the meantime, if you want to blow up some more stuff, go ahead. I think you can handle it all right.' And off he went. A thirteen-year-old kid with a box of dynamite and a plunger? You can probably see where this is going.

"On Monday morning, we were out in the yard figuring out which of the remaining stumps we were going to blow out first. Pop, he went to work. Jimmy and Tommy and I, we blew stumps out of the ground the whole day. There were a few extra ones here and there that didn't get done, but I had to go to work the next day, so we left them for later in the week—I thought. I went to work, and when I came home, the other two had funny looks on their faces. I knew something was wrong. 'What'd you do?' I asked them. Of course, they said, 'Oh, we didn't do anything.' But no one looks that way when they've done nothing wrong. Finally, they tell me what happened. 'We blew a couple of them out of the ground, but we scared ourselves when we tried to blow one out on the side of the house. We kind of blew the house foundation in, but it's all right, nothing really went wrong. The stump flew off the right way.'

"If it had gone the other way, that stump would have gone through the wall and ended up in the living room. But the real point of this is not only to explain how different everything was back then—not too many kids today are left home with a case of dynamite to play with—but also to kind of give a picture of the sort of kids we were. That guy took a big risk by leaving his dynamite behind. But he did it because we looked so confident, and he'd seen us working with it all day. He figured we could handle it. And for the most part—with the exception of that one stump that Jimmy and Tommy didn't calculate quite right—he was right. We handled it fine."

CHAPTER 5

Seeing Both Sides

Jim Miller is dyslexic, and while today the condition is often seen as a gift rather than a disability—Steve Jobs, Nikola Tesla, Leonardo da Vinci, Jules Verne, and Alexander Graham Bell are just a handful of transformative thinkers and doers reported to have been dyslexic—when Jim was growing up, the disorder was little known and even less understood. ("*Dyslexic* wasn't even a vocabulary word when I was in school," Jim says today. "If you were dyslexic, you were just another dumb kid who couldn't figure anything out.") Who knows how many countless children with dyslexia have been told by teachers, friends, and even family members that they're "slow" or "disabled" when in fact they're very often just as smart as—if not smarter than—those around them?

Jim is matter-of-fact about his dyslexia, as well he should be. He acknowledges it in much the same way as someone else might mention that they're left-handed or color blind: not as an admission of any shortcoming but—in Jim's case—as a possible explanation for why, from a young age, he's been able to literally see things differently from everyone else around him.

He brings it up in a somewhat roundabout but, in the end, perfectly logical way.

"In my early years, I didn't like to be alone at all," he says. "If I came home and nobody was there, I'd go back out again. I wouldn't stay home alone. I wasn't afraid, but I didn't like to be alone. I'm much more of a social person than that. Now, that said, I wasn't one of the guys in the gang. I never fit in any place. I was always different than everybody else.

"Now, all these years later, I've found out that I'm probably dyslexic, and I've always been dyslexic, so therefore I was a lousy student. I never really learned how to spell, and that was a difficult thing for me. When I was writing, there were inverted letters, the spelling was wrong, and I just squeaked by all the time. Then again, to be honest, school wasn't the highest thing in my mom's eyes, so if there was a project at home that had to be done, her attitude was, 'Well, don't go to school today. Take care of the project.'

"At the same time," Jim says, "I was never a go-along kind of a kid. There was no doubt about that. But I believe a large part of that was because of my ability to look at circumstances and understand what the implications were. Say there was a job that had to be done. Even when I was young, just rolling over and doing it because someone said so?" Jim smiles. "Yeah, that wasn't likely to happen. My attitude was, 'Why do I have to do it this way? And what makes you think that that's the only way, or even the right way? It definitely doesn't mean that I have to do it that way. That may be the way you guys do it, but I know a better way to do it.'

"I really don't know if it was to a point where I was being rebellious. It was just that I was seeing things from a different angle than other people were. Later in life, I discovered that dyslexia—which allowed me to see things, solutions, that others simply couldn't see—instead of being this great burden, was instead, to my mind, a tremendous advantage."

Jim holds out his right arm, the palm of his hand facing away from him, fingers spread and pointing toward the ceiling. With his left hand, he points to the right, to the palm itself.

"Everybody sees it this way," he says. "And so do I. I know what's on this side." Then he points to the back of his hand, the side facing him. "And I can see *this* side, too. Other people can't do that. I can see both sides of an issue, so I solve problems quite a bit differently than other people do. It frees my mind to think in other ways to solve problems, not in the standard way everyone else will come up with when looking at the exact same situation."

Jim puts his hands in his lap, smiles, and shrugs his shoulders. He looks, for a moment, almost embarrassed by the obviousness of it all.

"I knew that I didn't see things the same way as everybody else, but I didn't know why. For a long time, if I was looking at a problem and someone else was looking at the same thing, and he came up with a solution that I thought wasn't the best, or most efficient, then I usually thought to myself, 'Well, I don't know what's the matter with this guy. I guess he really isn't too bright.' Because I could see another, better solution so clearly!

"Somewhere along the way, I figured out that the whole problem—which really wasn't a problem at all—was simply that I saw things differently than most other people. There was nothing wrong with any of these other guys—after all, there was a whole bunch of them, and they were all coming up with the same solutions—but I did eventually identify something in the way I saw the world, even if I didn't have a name for it at the time. And I said to myself, 'Okay, Jim, you're going to be different than everybody else. That's just the way it's going to be. Everybody else is going to go that way, and if you're going to live life, you're going to go a different way.'

"So, I found out that you can be different. You can be in the army and march with everybody, or you can stand in front of the army, and they'll follow you—and I found out that people would follow me. I couldn't follow them—I just wasn't able to do it—but it worked out that people were willing to follow me."

Jim's brother Richie can vouch for his younger sibling's unique ability to corral people into helping him get things done—sometimes, in fact, without even having to ask.

"When we were kids, one thing that definitely made me realize Jimmy was a little different than the rest of us involved a task that we all had when we were young fellows," Richie recalls. "We used to raise chickens for food, and periodically, of course, the chicken coops had to be cleaned. For whatever reason, Jimmy always seemed to escape having to take care of it when it was his turn to clean these things. My mother would tell him, 'Jimmy, it's your turn to clean the chicken coop. Take care of it.' He was smart enough even at seven or eight years old not to argue with our mother, so he said yes—and then went on his way, doing whatever it was he'd been doing.

"So of course the chicken coop still needed to be cleaned, until she finally got pretty upset with him and told him, in absolutely no uncertain terms, that she expected that coop to be cleaned *right now*. Well, shortly thereafter, Jimmy went and got a couple of his little buddies down the street, and he somehow convinced them that it was fun—can you imagine that? *fun?*—to muck all the feathers and droppings and all the other crap out of a chicken coop. And he got it cleaned in short order. That," Richie says, "is when I realized that Jimmy was just a little bit different than the rest of us."

It's difficult, of course, to hear that story and not think of Tom Sawyer and the way that Twain's mischievous boyhood hero persuaded a number of his friends to whitewash a fence—a fence *he* was supposed to paint as punishment for skipping school. ("Like it?" Tom says to a friend who passes by and expresses doubts that anyone could enjoy such a toilsome task. "I don't see why I oughtn't to like it. Does a boy get a chance to whitewash a fence every day?" A short time later, not only are Tom's friends painting the fence, but they're paying him with trinkets and other small treasures—including, famously, "a dead rat and a string to swing it with"—for the privilege of doing the work while he sits in the shade enjoying an apple.)

Ultimately, Jim Miller's talent for leadership found its clearest form of expression in one particular word—yes—and in one particular pursuit: building businesses.

"In the businesses we've built and grown—not only the environmental cleanup business but the successful marine businesses that Glen and Jimmy [Jim's sons] now own—customers depend on you to provide service, and that phone call might come in the middle of the night. In fact, it can sometimes feel like those calls *always* come in the middle of the night. The person on the other end of the line is experiencing some disaster, some sort of catastrophe, and their reaction is, 'I don't know what's going on. What are we going to do? We never had this event happen before. Call Miller. He always figures that crap out. He'll send some guys who can figure out something.'

"It starts with the philosophy that the word *no* doesn't exist in our phone conversations. If you call us up in the middle of the night, whatever the time, wherever you are, and you say, 'I have a problem, can you come help me?' the answer is 'Yes.' Before anything else, 'Yes.' Then, once the person on the other end has heard you say 'Yes,' *then* you ask the next question: 'What's wrong?'"

Jim lets that sink in. He's quiet for a while; then he says something that not only doubles down on the philosophy he just articulated but also nicely illustrates his ability to see two sides to every problem.

"*No* is an amazing word," he says, and after all of the talk about the word *yes*, it's more than a little jarring to hear that from him—at first. "Nobody really recognizes the power of the word *no*. That

35

one single word is an instantaneous end to a conversation. Think about it. 'Can you help me?' 'No.' And just like that, the conversation is over.

"But if you start with 'Yes,' then you can have that conversation, you can talk about all the rest of the things that need to be discussed, and ultimately, you can find out what the problem is that started it all. You can learn about what caused the phone call in the middle of the night in the first place. And that's when you can start working on solutions. But none of that happens if you say 'No' right off the bat. It happens only if you say 'Yes' before you say anything else."

CHAPTER 6

The Business of Youth

"I must remind you that Fortune is bald behind. . . . She must be seized by the forelock, since once she is passed there is no clapping on to her hair, at all. . . . She ships none abaft the ears, if you follow me."

—from the Patrick O'Brian novel THE MAURITIUS COMMAND

What most everyone who knew Jim Miller when he was a young man—and even when he was a boy—eventually mentions is the uncanny ability he's always had to see an opportunity to make money, and to seize it. "Fortune is bald behind," the old saying goes, and no one was ever better than Jim Miller at latching on to Fortune before she passed by.

Jim's younger sister Marguerite, for example, remembers that she was roped into helping out her brother on his newspaper route. But in typical Miller fashion, it wasn't just *any* newspaper route.

"Jimmy had the largest paper route of any young kid I ever saw," Marguerite remembers. "And the reason why I know that Jimmy had a paper route that was unbelievably big is because he used to make me help fold the papers. You know, you had to fold it just right, and each one had to be tight enough so he could throw it up onto the lawn or the porch or wherever. And you had to fold in all the extras, too. On Saturday you had the funnies, for example."

Marguerite laughs then, but it's not an entirely mirthful sound.

"Oh, I *hated* to do that. I don't know why I got chosen. Just because I was younger and because I was there, I guess."

"I was around twelve when I started the newspaper route," Jim says. "I remember figuring out early on that getting six cents a week per customer delivering newspapers, plus a seven-cent tip, was okay, but around Christmastime if you had good customers and they thought well of you, you'd get a dollar, and if you had a hundred customers . . . wow! You could really make a hundred bucks?! My God! Then I also realized that if I started out with, say, twenty-five customers, when the weather started to turn bad, other kids would probably say, 'Aw, it's too cold to deliver newspapers. I quit.' So I'd tell the manager, 'Look, I'll take their route, too. It's right next to mine. I'll just take care of it.' So for Christmas, I wound up with a hundred customers. I remember I'd get out of school at three, three thirty, and I'd go home and fold the papers and put them in my bag. I could put maybe thirty papers in there. I had the manager deliver the other papers at two or three different spots along the route for me, so when I was out of papers at one spot, I'd pick up a new batch and continue on, and I wouldn't have to go back home to get the rest. And come Christmastime, I did extremely well.

"At that time, the economics at home were very, very tough. It was right after the war, and the economy hadn't really picked up the way it would in a few years. There was very little money. The family was struggling. But hey! Look here. I wound up with, as I remember it, close to $100, and that was a lot of money at the time. A *lot* of money. It was Christmas for the Miller family, for sure, because I shared half with Mom and bought gifts and presents for my brothers and sisters. That felt great. But man, that was a tough year.

"It was really rewarding to be the big dog at that stage of the game, and it was rewarding to know that I could figure this sort of stuff out on my own."

Jimmy Miller, however, was not destined to become a newspaper mogul.

"Come January first, *Newsday* was raising the price of the paper from three cents to four cents a copy. Now, remember, originally it was eighteen cents a week, which meant I got a seven-cent tip from the quarter that most of my customers paid me, on top of the six cents I got from *Newsday*. The paper tells us that the delivery boys are getting a 50 percent pay raise, from six cents to nine cents a week. That sounds all right—until you take into account that they're raising the cost of the paper to twenty-four cents a week. Most of my customers are still only going to give me a quarter, right? So now I'll only be getting a one-cent tip. Even at that age, I saw that I'd be making less money every week, not more—ten cents per customer, instead of thirteen—even with that 50 percent raise. So I tell them, 'Hey, *Newsday*, you know the hundred customers I have? They're yours now. I quit.'

"And that was the end of my newspaper career," Jim says. "That was life back then."

And how did a twelve- or thirteen-year-old boy in straitened circumstances, in a large family, cope with leaving a job that had recently put a hundred dollars, clear, in his pocket and had allowed him to help put food on the table and presents under the Christmas tree?

Was there, in other words, a *plan*?

"You know, I wasn't that organized yet, in the way I looked at things, to think that far ahead," Jim says—and yet, in the very next breath, he begins a story that illustrates a quality that his friends and family point to again and again as a defining characteristic: Call it a kind of entrepreneurial fearlessness.

"The next job I remember having is one where I delivered packages for a drugstore," Jim says. "I still lived in North Merrick, but I wound up getting a job in Freeport. The drugstore in Merrick, where we knew the druggist, opened a branch in Freeport, and when I applied to the store in Merrick, they said, 'No, no, we don't have any work here, but if you go to Freeport, maybe they'll hire you.' I went to the people at the Freeport store, which was probably four or five miles way, and I got a job. I guess I was fourteen years old then."

("He got me addicted to Jergens hand lotion when he had that job," Marguerite says. "I still use it today. I can't use anything else. He used to bring home the samples. When we heard that the original formula was going off the market, years later, everybody was buying bottles of it—stockpiling them, sort of. I really became addicted. I'm not kidding.")

"So there I was, delivering prescriptions, and anything else that needed doing," Jim says. "In the slack time, you wiped shelves, carried product up from the basement—whatever was needed. After I was there awhile, I started waiting on customers and learned how to run the cash register. And I very much liked interacting with people. I suppose in part it was a level of respect that you got. I was a young kid, but particularly at the cosmetics counter, I thought it was pretty cool that the ladies would come in and they'd buy lipstick and ask me—a kid!—'Do you think this shade works?' And I'd say stuff like, 'Oh, no. That's too dark for you. No, you need a lighter shade, and that will go good with this powder. We have a nice combination package here. You can buy the lipstick, the powder, and the perfume, but if you buy them separately, it's going to cost you $6.00. We have this package here where it's just $3.39 for the lot.' So I could actually be a salesman, and that was a fun thing. The customers liked it, and so did I. And then, of course, there was delivering packages to homes. It was often the same customers that you'd wind up delivering packages to, and I got to know these folks. You know,

Mrs. So-and-So would give you a nickel tip, or a dime tip, for delivering packages. After a while, that adds up. But what I really liked was the personal, face-to-face contact."

It's not so much what went on in the drugstore that really drives this particular story, however, but something that happened while Jim was working in the drugstore that suggests an approach to money-making rather more advanced than that shown by most people in their early teens.

"There was a movie house across the street," Jim says, "and my work hours at that time were 4:00 p.m. to 8:00 p.m., or something like that, so at eight o'clock I would be finished with the drugstore, and I'd go out behind the drugstore to get on my bicycle. In the fall, it was starting to get dark earlier, and people were coming into town in their cars to go to the movies. I saw that in the parking lot next door, there was an old man out there with a flashlight, directing cars to park right there, and after they parked, when they were on their way to the movie, people would give him a tip.

"So I went out in the parking lot behind the drugstore, a car would pull in, I'd wave a flashlight of my own at the driver, and I'd say, 'Hey, there's a parking spot right here, sir. Come right in here.' He'd park in the spot, and it was always, 'Hey, thanks, kid. Thank you very much.' And, of course, I'd run around to the other side and open the passenger-side door for the lady. You've got to remember, these were all Wednesday night dates, so these were dressed-up ladies. And wow! They were pretty girls. So I thought, 'Hey, this is pretty cool, you know?' The guy would park, give you a tip, you'd get a quarter. The whole movie crowd would come in within a half hour, maybe forty-five minutes. They weren't there, and then they were there, and it just so happened that it was about the time that I was out there anyway, right at the end of work.

"You were waving these people in, and man, you'd make five bucks sometimes. Five or six bucks—in less than an hour! I was getting more from the parking lot than I was from my work at the drugstore. That went on for a month or so, and I had this down to a pretty good system, especially on Wednesday nights and Friday nights. And you know, all these guys wanted to impress their date. 'Here you go, young man,' and out came the quarter, like they were big spenders. And I guess maybe there was also a degree of implied intimidation. 'Geez, if I don't give the kid a tip, I don't know how my car is going to be when I come out. This looks like a sketchy kid.'

"So, what it comes down to is, I don't really know *why* they tipped. I only know that they did. But the part of this story where everything changed, and where I learned a lesson, is when the old man in the parking lot next door caught me one day. He says, 'What the hell are you doing?' and I say, 'Hey, I'm just parking cars.'

"'Well,' he says, 'you didn't get permission from me.' And I say, 'Well, I didn't know I had to get permission.' And he says, 'Well, I got permission for this lot here. If you're going to park cars here, you've got to give me half.'

"And of course my reply to that is, 'Oh, crap!' I mean, if that's the rule, that's the rule. Right? What do I know? I'm a kid. He's an old man. He said that's the way it is, that must be the way it is. So for the next couple of weeks, nine o'clock comes around, and the old man shows up.

"'How many did you do?' he asks me.

"'I got four dollars.'

"'Good. Give me two bucks.'

"So I have to split half of what I'm making with him, and that feels bad. I keep thinking, 'This ain't right.' Especially as there's a little restaurant attached to his lot, so his lot is way better than mine. The only thing I get is movie traffic, but he gets restaurant traffic *and* the movies, so he was doing better than me *before* he started taking 50 percent of my money. Anyway, after nine o'clock, I sometimes go over to the restaurant, and I have a cup of hot chocolate there.

Pretty soon, I make friends with the guy who's managing the restaurant, and he asks me, 'What are you doing, kid?' I say, 'Well, parking cars, and I work in the drugstore.'

"He says, 'You're a regular hustler.' But in a friendly way. And that's where the conversation comes around to me saying, 'It would be all right, but I have to give half to the old man.'

"And he looks kind of stunned and says, 'What old man? What for?' And I say, 'Well, he's got permission for the lot, and I've got to pay.'

"Well, he gets pretty hot about that. 'That's crap,' he says. 'The old man is ripping you off.' And next thing I know, he calls the old man into the restaurant. 'What the hell are you doing to this kid? You're ripping the kid off? Okay. Now you work for him. He's got permission for your lot now. If you want, you can go in the back lot, and you've got to give him half of what you make back there.' So the tables got turned completely around."

There's no mistaking the pleasure that the memory of that unexpected development still brings to Jim Miller.

"Oh, the old man is huffing and puffing and hollering and screaming, 'I ain't doing this,' and 'You can't do this to me,' and this, that, and the other. Anyway, it winds up that I tell him to stay where he is. 'If you leave me alone,' I tell him, 'I'll leave you alone. I'm not paying you anything anymore, but you don't have to pay me, either.' And that's how it all worked out.

"The irony of it all is that the drugstore job lasted only another two months or something like that, and they went out of business. So I didn't have a job in the drugstore, and I didn't have a reason to be there anymore, at any time of the day or night."

The lesson of the entire story, though, is far more revealing and more subtle than something as obvious as "Stand up for yourself" or "Don't let people push you around." In fact, one of the key things Jim took away from the entire experience with the moviegoers, the pushy old man, and the restaurant manager was this: There's an awful lot to be said for just sitting down and having a friendly conversation with a stranger.

"I've always had the ability to have a conversation with pretty much anybody, have an exchange and get people to talk about themselves," Jim says. "That's what people like to do anyway, so you just have to have an interest in them, and they'll respond. You've got to participate and contribute something yourself, of course, just like I did with the guy at the restaurant. But you have to recognize that everybody is on a different level, in one way or another, and you have to respect that. The way you would meet and talk to a schoolteacher, for example, is very likely going to be different than the way you'll meet and talk to a laborer, but if you can give the right sort of respect and attention to the laborer, and ask him the right questions, you might just find out that he really knows what he's doing."

These sorts of conversations can wind up being a lesson later on in life. Maybe you didn't know that at the time. There wasn't some grand, overarching plan of how this was going to evolve at the end of the day. But what Jim learned, or was reminded of, with the old guy in the parking lot and the other guy at the restaurant was this: You don't have to accept everything. You can successfully challenge your own—and other people's—assumptions if you put yourself in a position to do so.

CHAPTER 7

The *Pelican* Disaster and a Guardian Angel

S ome events are so seared into the memories of those who experience them that they stand as markers—moments when, as the saying goes, *everything changed*. Pearl Harbor. The JFK assassination. The terror attacks on September 11, 2001. On those dates, the world watched—in disbelief and fear—and those who were witnesses to what unfolded knew that they would never, ever forget.

Other transformative events, meanwhile—perhaps not so cataclysmic that the whole world notices but shocking enough to shake entire regions—generate their own memories, their own legends. The deadly *Pelican* fishing boat disaster is such an event, and September 1, 1951, is such a date. Like thousands of Long Islanders, Jim Miller, all of sixteen years old at the time and a mate on the charter boat *Kingfisher*, clearly recalls that Labor Day weekend and the grim role he played in the midst of a catastrophe that would forever alter the face of charter fishing on the storied East End of Long Island and across the country.

The tale of the *Pelican*—how she capsized in wicked seas and high winds off Montauk Point when two successive, huge rogue waves slammed into her just as the sky began to clear after a brief summer shower; how forty-five passengers and crew, including Captain Eddie Carroll, perished; how the *Pelican* was towed by other boats, for hours, from the open sea to port—has been told many times, and never better than in Tom Clavin's 2005 book, *Dark Noon*. But all these years later, when Jim recounts his bleak experience at Duryea's dock in Montauk, where the foundering *Pelican* finally came to rest, his descriptions are so vivid, his memories so sharp, it's as if the decades drop away, and he is about to experience all over again a cold, dark, miserable night at the edge of the continent that will, in a very real sense, change his life.

"I was sixteen years old," Jim remembers, "and by sixteen, you've earned certain privileges in making your own choices. The previous year, I had fished out of Freeport as a deckhand on a sportfishing vessel, and I'd learned certain skills. I was given an opportunity to go on a fishing vessel that was relocating to Montauk Point for the summer season. I came home and said, 'Mom and Dad, I'm going to go to Montauk to go fishing this year. I'm leaving home.' Of course, that caused a ruckus. 'You're only a kid,' 'You can't do that,' and whatever else. But that's the way life was going to be. I was going. I wasn't asking permission. I was making a statement: I was going fishing, period.

"So off I went to Montauk and spent the summer fishing and working as a deckhand on a charter. At the end of the season, there was the *Pelican* disaster, with tremendous loss of life. I spontaneously responded when I heard about the rescue operations, and I went out on a small commercial fishing vessel and assisted in towing the wreck in, where we finally got it to Duryea's dock in Montauk.

"The *Pelican* was right up against the dock," Jim recalls, "but still mostly submerged, and it was listing something awful. Frank Mundus and Carl Forsberg had towed it for as long as they could. Then the Coast Guard took over and towed it the rest of the way, but it took them hours in those seas. It was late at night, past midnight, by the time the *Pelican* was secured. There were still an awful lot of people hanging around, some of them helping out, doing whatever they could, but most of them just gawking. It was a horrific disaster, you know, and that sort of thing always brings out rubberneckers. Maybe it's inevitable, human nature being what is. I don't know.

"Anyway, I was on the deck of the *Pelican* with a few other guys, and we knew there were still bodies down in the cabin, under the waterline. Maybe there were even survivors. Unlikely, of course, but someone had to go check. It was terrible to think about. It was cold, cold, cold out there, and eerie as hell with the searchlights and smoke from all the cigarettes, hundreds of them, so the idea of swimming down into that black water and looking for anyone, dead or alive, was pretty gruesome.

"A state trooper sergeant, guy by the name of Tom Innes, was the one who eventually went down there. He was wearing white long johns and was able to breathe only because a hose from an air compressor was hooked up to his mask. He dived down in there, into the cabin, and started pushing bodies back along the companionway. I was on the deck, closest to the dock, up to my waist in water, and I'd take these bodies—pretty much all of them weighed a lot more than I did because I was a small guy, and they were ice cold—and I'd have to wrap my arms around the legs or waists and lift them up toward people on the dock. Rigor mortis had set in, so all of the corpses were stiff—which, in a horrible way, was a good thing, because the deck of the boat by then was several feet below the dock, and I don't know how the hell I would have lifted those bodies up if they hadn't been stiff."

Jim's eyes, as he tells this story, seem to widen of their own volition. At times, he seems to be gazing not at the people and things in front of him in the Miller Environmental Group building in Calverton, but back down through the years, to his sixteen-year-old self, manhandling the corpses of strangers in the small hours of the morning. It's hard not to feel a serious chill creep up one's spine as he speaks, knowing that the appalling reality of what he experienced that night, sixty-five years ago, is once again rearing into his mind's eye.

And that's when, with a barely perceptible shift, the tone of the story changes. Something in his voice suggests that, as morbid as his time in that cold, oily water might have been, another memory is pushing to the surface—a memory that brings with it a small grin.

"And then there was the guy with the camera," he says, introducing an unexpected twist to the tale. "I don't know who he was, if he was with the press or was just a ghoul or what, but he had this camera in his hands, he was standing right on the edge of the dock, right above me, and he starts yelling at me and at the guys pulling the bodies up onto the dock, 'Wait, wait! Hold it! Hold it! Let me get a shot!'

"I'm standing there with a dead body in my arms, and this son of a bitch is telling me to wait! But you know what? I'm so exhausted, and freezing, and sort of out of it by that point that I listen to him. I stand there, and he takes a picture, and then the guys on the dock pull the body up, and all of a sudden all the frustration and the anger come crashing down on me, and I gesture to the guy, like, *Hey, come here, I'll get you a great picture.* And as he steps near, I reach out and I grab his ankle and yank on it, and he comes *this close* to falling in the water. And he loses his camera in the bargain."

For a brief moment, the look in Jim Miller's eyes is triumphant.

"Well, he's not happy about that, not one bit, and after he gets his balance, he glares down at me—this is a grown man, angry at a kid who's pulling dead bodies out of a capsized boat!—and he's announcing to anyone who would listen all of the evil things that he's going to do to this punk little kid, by kicking him, beating him up, and whatever else. He's right above me, and suddenly he puts his leg back, and I know he's about to aim a kick right at my head. And I'm so tired I probably won't even be able to get out of the way. And right then," Jim says, raising his voice, "these two enormous creatures step out of the crowd, right behind the guy. I mean, they were *huge*. Two guardians of light came out of the dark—these two giant state troopers. I thought they were eleven feet tall at the time, with their Smokey Bear hats and their spats. The two of them grab the guy who's about to kick me in the face, and they lift him by the elbows like he's a feather, and—*poof!*—he's gone. He just vanishes into the crowd. And that was that."

Jim grins at the suddenness—and the timeliness—of his deliverance.

"They were just a couple of troopers, doing their job," he says. "But to me, right then, they were guardian angels."

As is so often the case with Jim Miller's stories, the tidbit of information that really rounds out the tale feels somehow unexpected, and weirdly inevitable.

"Now, fast-forward fifty years," he says. "I'm in my office here in Calverton, and the local newspaper is reminiscing about the *Pelican*. They print a story on the front page, on the fiftieth anniversary of the disaster, with a picture of the boat at the dock, taken that night. I have the paper sitting there on my desk, and a fellow I met in Riverhead—he and I had become collaborators on installing a migratory fish ladder in the local river, as an environmental project—

he comes in and says, 'Why do you have that paper on your desk?' And I say, 'Well, because the guy in the picture is me.' He says, 'You were there that day? So was I!'

"Turns out, he was out fishing with his uncle, and they were just going past when the boat capsized. They rescued some people, got a couple of live ones, and actually recovered a dead one, and brought him into the dock, and that was that. I say, 'Oh, crap! You were on the other side of the wreck. I was over here,' pointing to the picture. We reminisce, and with that, my secretary comes forward and points to a figure in the photo and says, 'And you see that state trooper there?' I say, 'Yeah, that's my hero.' And she says, 'That's my father.'

"What are the chances? The odds of all those coming together, in one office, fifty years later? Impossible. But it happened.

"I met the trooper a little while after that and got to know him a bit," Jim says of the man who had, for so long, loomed so large in his recollection. "I reminded him about that night, about how he and his partner had pulled that guy away from the dock, and what a memorable moment it was for me."

Then Jim Miller delivers the kicker.

"He didn't remember that incident at all, of course," he says, the look in his eyes suggesting that this is just the utterly improbable way that life sometimes works. A defining moment for one person might be a run-of-the-mill, completely forgettable occurrence for someone else.

"He was just doing his job," Jim says. "It was just like any other night. He said to me, 'Why would I remember something like that? It's like giving out traffic tickets. Why would I remember a blonde-haired girl that I gave a ticket to twenty years ago? I gave out forty tickets a week. Forget it.'"

And with that, Jim holds his arms out wide, as if to say, *Ain't that something?*

CHAPTER 8

South to Mexico and Back Again

By the time Jim Miller was sixteen years old, he'd had it with school, with kids his own age, with trying to just get along. He knew that wasn't him, and he knew what he wanted to do. He wanted to fish. He had no illusions about how hard the work was. After all, he'd been working, in one form or another, all his life and had already spent enough time as a deckhand on a charter to know that, in his words, "it was a job, and it was money. But man, you had to hustle.

"If you hustled, and the customers on the charter liked you, you could make a twenty-dollar tip. That was good money in the early fifties. And remember, at that point in time, the rules were that you split half of what you'd got with Mom. She got ten bucks, and she was happy as hell. That was food for a lot of meals. You went and did a whole week's shopping for ten bucks. The movies were eighteen cents, so figure how much twenty bucks was then. A nickel was money. Penny candy was still around."

"I was sixteen years old in March, so I went in June to Montauk and fished there, and by the time I came back in September, after the *Pelican*, I was pretty upset from having seen and experienced real death and real disaster. I was a little melancholy, I guess, and I went back to school, but I didn't fit in at all there anymore."

In fact, by the time he got back to school, Jim had witnessed even more death firsthand, on top of the horrific memories from those grisly hours spent aboard the barely floating *Pelican*—memories he had tried to fight by getting colossally drunk for three days after the disaster. On his way back to Merrick from Montauk, driving along the Southern State Parkway, he watched as a terrible car crash unfolded in front of him. Pulling to the shoulder and racing to the badly damaged car, which by now was smoking and, for all he knew, about to burst into flames, Jim pulled a young girl from the wreckage. She died in his arms.

At an age when most of his contemporaries were thinking about what to wear to their school prom or where to go on a first date, Jim Miller had seen the face of death and had held the dead themselves in his hands.

"I felt like I was a man," he says, "and I was in school with kids. I had a car, and they didn't have cars. And I guess I looked older than I was, too. I could easily be mistaken for a man at that time, and people treated me like a man. I had the knowledge of a man—as a fisherman—and people respected me, so I didn't relate to the kids at school at all. 'Nah,' I thought to myself, 'this isn't going to work.' So I left school in my senior year."

Did Jim have any qualms about leaving? While he knew in his gut that he didn't belong there, did he nevertheless feel that it was going to be a hard transition to actually leave school for good and enter, as an equal, the adult world?

"No," he says without a second's hesitation. "I knew school was a waste of time—for me. I wasn't learning anything there. They didn't really like me, and I didn't like them. I wasn't an athlete. My oldest brother, Richie, was a much better athlete than I ever was. He was a better wrestler, a better ballplayer, and he played more organized sports in school. But I didn't fit into the social climate. The few kids that I did know, maybe ten or fifteen guys who I knew pretty well, were starting to smoke pot. They were kind of a criminal element. They were stealing cars and stuff. And I said to myself, 'This isn't a good crowd to be with.' So I really didn't feel like I fit in any place—except on the waterfront. I fit in there, and I fished with this Polish fellow, Captain John—or 'Kielbasa John,' as he was known—for a year out of Freeport.

"The following year I wound up getting a job on a commercial fishing boat going to Florida. I joined the crew, and we fished our way on down the coast and went to Fort Myers, Florida, and started shrimp fishing from Fort Myers to the Dry Tortugas."

The Dry Tortugas—so named more than 500 years ago by the Spanish explorer Juan Ponce de León for the turtles (*tortugas*) so abundant there, and later by mariners because of the dearth of fresh water on any of the seven small islands—are in fact part of Monroe County, Florida, located about seventy miles west of the Keys. In Robert Louis Stevenson's classic tale *Treasure Island*, the islands are referred to by the character Billy Bones, a rum-swilling pirate who, early in the book, terrorizes the Hawkins family's Admiral Benbow Inn before dying, in dramatic fashion, of a massive stroke. "His stories," the book's narrator Jim Hawkins recalls, "were what frightened people worst of all. Dreadful stories they were; about hanging, and walking the plank, and storms at sea, and the Dry Tortugas, and wild deeds and places on the Spanish Main."

While Jim Miller's experiences in the Gulf might not have included hangings and walking the plank, they certainly had their share of adventure—and, ultimately, they included his witnessing a kind of government-sanctioned piracy during a fateful week off the eastern coast of Mexico.

At first, though, it was all about the fishing.

"At that time," he remembers, "they were ten-day trips. You would go down to the Keys and farther out, and you'd catch shrimp at night, you'd head them and refrigerate them in chipped ice, and you'd come back in a week or ten days and sell your catch and get paid on a percentage basis. And by any standard, that was pretty good money. I was the youngest guy on the crew, but nobody knew how old I was. That information had conveniently disappeared someplace.

"Besides, no one cared how old I was. What mattered were skills. 'What can you do? Can you pull your weight? Can you fix a winch? How fast can you head shrimp? How are you going to contribute? How are you going to help us make money on this trip?' Those were the things that the rest of the guys cared about. Not whether I was seventeen or twenty-one years old."

On second thought, maybe it wasn't *all* about fishing. Jim Miller was, after all, a healthy young man with money in his pocket. And, as the saying goes, in the spring (and in the summer, fall, and winter), a young man's fancy turns to thoughts of love.

"I had a girlfriend at the time, who I met up in New York," Jim says. "A cute little blonde gal. Her family home was in West Palm Beach, so in between trips to the Gulf, I would commute over there. Visit with her a little bit. It wasn't a serious, serious romance, but she was a pretty girl, and I was just getting to learn about girls. I think I was much more infatuated than she was.

"Anyway, I had a pocketful of money, and I went to visit with her in West Palm Beach. I left her place on a Sunday afternoon to be on the boat in Fort Myers Monday morning because we were going back to sea. I had to be on the boat by six o'clock in the morning, so I took a bus from West Palm Beach to Fort Myers, and we stopped somewhere out in the middle of Florida at some little station, and the driver announced a ten-minute break. 'Everybody off.' You'd run into the station, use the bathroom, then stop at the counter and buy a candy bar or whatever else you might want for the rest of the ride west.

"Well, out I come, and the bus was gone. The bus was *gone*. They left me there. Where the hell was I? You start looking around, and you say, 'Hey, nothing but the bus station here. This is it.' You start looking around some more, and you say, 'Everybody here—I mean everybody—is black. I'm the only white guy. Crap! Wow! It's Sunday afternoon. Wow! Florida . . . in those days, hitchhiking was a bad idea. You'd go to jail if you were hitchhiking. So I ask at the station, 'When does the next bus come?' 'Tomorrow,' the guy says.

"*Tomorrow?*

"And with that, the guy's closing the windows. 'I'm closing,' he says. 'Wake up, kid. You've got to stay outside.'

"Outside? I've got to stay outside? Where am I going to stay? I've got to be on a boat in the morning. I'm in big trouble. How the hell am I going to get out of here? I'm looking around, looking around. I look up the street, and there's a farmhouse up the road, with a bunch of guys sitting on a porch. I figure I'd better give it a shot, man. I'm going to die here, so I might as well try. And I remember thinking to myself, 'Okay, I've got money in my pocket. I'm going to put money in my socks. Wrap it up, and put some money in this sock, some money in that sock, and I've got a little bit of money left in my pocket.'

"Now I'm ready to roll. I go walking up the driveway, and all the black gentlemen on the porch are like, 'Hello, there. Hello, there. Hey, boy, what do you want?'

"I ask if someone would give me a ride.

"They say, 'Yeah? Why?' And I say, 'Well, I'm stuck. I need somebody to give me a ride to Fort Myers. I'll pay.'

"Now they're listening. 'You got money?' 'Yeah, I've got money.' 'How much?' 'I don't know yet,' I say. I don't even know how far it is to Fort Myers. I don't know where the hell I am. I'm out in the middle of no place. 'I've got a couple of boys here who will drive you,' one of the guys says. I ask him how far it is. 'Well, it's going to be a couple of hours to drive there, and these boys gotta have gas money.' Gas is twenty cents a gallon back then. 'It's going to cost two dollars for gas,' he says, 'and we've got to get a soda pop, so that's two and a quarter, and you've got to have two guys, because if you have a flat tire, we've got to be able to fix the tire.'

"So I just ask him outright, 'How much?' He says ten bucks. The bus was only four, but I guess that's not too bad. 'All right,' I tell him. 'I'll give you five dollars now, and five when I get there.'

"One of the other guys says, 'Okay. You get in the back. Don't sit in the front with us.' The obvious message there being, *We ain't going to get in trouble with a white boy up in the front seat with us.*

"Anyway, we made it to Fort Myers, and I got on the fishing boat and ended up going back to sea. But the next trip, I signed on a different boat and went fishing to Mexico. That was a thirty-day trip. We're heading to Mexico, four of us on the boat, and the captain tells me that I'm the cook."

And how did that pan out?

"We survived for a month. There was an arrangement with the local supply store, a supermarket, and you could go in there and say, 'All right, I got a thirty-day trip, a four-man crew.' And they'd ask, 'You want the $100 list, the $125 list, or the $90 list?' Then they'd ask, 'You got any black guys on your boat, or are you all white guys?' This was Florida in the fifties, man.

"Well, we had only white guys on our boat, and we bought the $90 list of food, and they prepared the food for us to take on the trip. Whatever we were going to eat each day was already wrapped up in a package. When we were loading ice—you know, we're loading thirty tons of ice with a big hose—the guy delivering the food would write 'Day 30' on a package, and we'd shove it toward the back, load more ice, and put the package with 'Day 29' in next, and so on. And you built your way out from the back of the hold until you got to 'Day 1,' and you've got a menu every day for thirty days. You looked at the next package in the sequence, and you knew what you were going to eat that day. If there was any question whether anyone could be a cook on a boat, we answered it on that trip. Everybody ate."

A problem-solver by nature and by inclination, Jim makes a point of describing the system the Gulf boats worked out to deal with the logistics—of space, fuel, water, and so on—posed by these thirty-day round-trip excursions.

"In Mexico, we fished nights and slept days, and it was hot, hot, hot," he says. "No air-conditioning, obviously. That didn't exist yet on those boats. We'd fish all night, and then as soon as the sun came up, the fishing stopped, we iced everything and put it away. We cleaned up the nets and fixed whatever we had to fix, and by ten o'clock, we'd go to sleep.

"But the first few days out, it's not easy to move around on those vessels. Boats coming from the home port are fully loaded. They're full of ice, full of fuel, full of water. The crews barely have room to work, so they have a sister boat that's been out there fishing already, and maybe she's on her twenty-first day, running out of water, running out of ice. So you meet up and transfer some ice, some water, and whatever else, and the sister boat heading to port takes the outgoing boat's first six days' worth of fishing back to market. In *that* boat, you're heading in, see, and you have room because you've been out for three weeks and your stores are running out, so you load up with shrimp, shrimp, shrimp, and you take it back with you. Then, later, you work out the repayment with the outgoing boat's crew. It was quite a system. And it worked.

"We were on a sixty-five-footer," Jim continues, "which was a big boat in those days. Of course, we were heading out across the Gulf of Mexico, so we needed a good-size boat. But what I remember, more than anything else, is one particular trip when we got into a little trouble down in Mexico."

A little trouble. Coming from Jim, that phrase suggests that the subsequent story will entail some rough behavior all around.

And it does.

"The Mexican government extended their territorial limit from three miles to *twelve* miles," he says. "They did it arbitrarily. Now, we were Yankees, and we said, 'You can't do that. We're Americans. You can't just push us around.' The best fishing was at four miles out, and they were going to keep it for the Mexicans. So they said, 'Well, we just did it, we declared our sovereign rights, and we've extended the limit to twelve miles. That's now Mexico's water, and if you're in there, you're a trespasser, and we'll arrest you.'

"We go fishing there one night, with a Mexican fishing boat fishing alongside of us, and he announces that he's going to capture us. And we say, 'How are you going to capture us? You're only a fishing boat, we're a fishing boat. What are you talking about?'

"All of a sudden, this guy comes out on deck, and he's got a machine gun. *Bam, bam, bam, bam, bam.* Holy crap! He's shooting tracer bullets at us, and he's got a freakin' Mexican Navy captain's hat on. This is some sort of bad, crazy captain. 'Okay. Okay,' we tell him. 'We'll haul our nets back. You haul *your* nets back.' He's got to go to the left to haul his nets back, and we've got to go to the right to haul our nets back. We hauled back so goddamn fast, man. We never believed we could haul back that quick. When he was as far away as he was going to get, and we were as far away as we were going to get from him, we got the hell out of there. And he was still firing! He really thought he was going to bring us in. He was going to arrest us, but we got away.

"The next day, the American boats are all nestled up again to transfer their catch, and out comes the Mexican Navy, with an announcement: 'All of you guys are arrested now.' We're talking about thirty, maybe forty boats they're aiming to bring into port. This is all happening about four miles off Campeche, in southern Mexico. That's where we always fished. And that really was our attitude. 'We're Americans. You can't push us around. We'll get the U.S. Navy out here. You can't arrest us.' We're on the radio, sending messages back to the United States. 'We're being attacked by Mexicans. Quick, send the Navy!'

"As it turns out, maybe eighteen of the boats get hauled into port, and we sneak out the back door again. We're gone. We ain't going to jail with those guys. We're not going to be part of the protest. In the meantime, the Mexican Navy takes the captains off the American boats they'd seized and puts them all on the Navy ship, and then they order the deckhands to run the boats back into port. And once they tie up, the Mexicans steal each boat's catch. Gotta get those shrimp out, man. Can't let them spoil!"

Jim's laughing, but it's clear that in some ways, the memory still stings.

"Now they've got a bunch of Americans under house arrest on their boats. Unless you have money. If you have money, you're allowed to go ashore. They're happy to have those dollars spent in town, in the bars, the usual places fishermen like to hang out after being on a boat for a while. About the fourteenth, fifteenth day after being arrested, they've run out of water, they're getting bored, they're sitting on the boat all the time. It's hot as hell. One of the American deckhands goes ashore and gets staggering drunk, and when he comes back, he goes after Dick Stearns for some crazy reason. Dick Stearns is a buddy of mine, a big man, six foot eight. A real giant. The drunk guy, a little runt, has got a fish knife in his pocket. He pulls out the knife, and before anybody knows what was what, he's slashing Dick's chest. Dick is bleeding, there's blood all over the place. It's a big commotion, everybody hollering and screaming. A Mexican policeman or sailor or something sees the guy with the knife, and *pow*! He fires his rifle. One shot hits the guy in the arm, and it takes the arm right off. He's dead on the spot. They finally get Dick bandaged up. And at the same time, the American ambassador is taking a tour, and he sees his own Americans getting into this gunfight, and he realizes, 'We better get these guys out of here because this is going to start another Mexican war if we don't stop it right now.'

"At any rate, they all get released within the next couple of days, and Dick winds up coming back home. I finish my own trip, I'm back in Fort Myers, and around Christmastime, my captain says, 'I know where I can buy a mortar. Next time they start shooting at us with bullets, man, I'm going to let them have it. I ain't going to take it.'

"This guy is crazy. I just want to go fishing. I don't like this. Someone is going to really get hurt.

"I'm getting homesick and lonely, and things ain't going all that well in Florida. I'm not getting rich down there, either. Being at sea for thirty days with three other guys? At that point, it doesn't have any appeal for me anymore. That's when Dick comes back, and he's hurting. 'I ain't going to heal down here. How about if we go home?' he asks me. And I tell him, 'Yeah, I'm good with that.'

"So we drive home from Florida. I remember we're coming home on Christmas Eve, and he drops me off at my house, and he comes in and meets my mom and dad. He's still wrapped up with bandages, trying to heal from those knife wounds. He is a towering man. Tall, wide, strong. But a big old teddy bear inside. I remember introducing him to my mom and dad in my house."

Jim pauses, and it's somehow easy, after that vivid tale, to picture the scene: a mother, a father, their teenage son, and his friend, together in a small house in North Merrick. It's cold outside. The boys have driven 1,300 miles, from the Gulf of Mexico to Long Island Sound. It's another world up north. Familiar—but quieter than Jim and Dick remember it. Smaller. Less . . . *varied*.

"Dick eventually wound up buying a boat and fished out of Montauk the rest of his career," Jim says. A moment later, he adds a last observation about Dick Stearns—one that, coming from a man like Jim, carries more than a hint of praise.

"He was a good fisherman."

CHAPTER 9

It's a Dirty Job, But . . .

There's a reason the classic, bare-bones coffee shop, ice cream parlor, or lunch counter so often shows up in American literature, movies, and myths. Think of Hemingway's most famous story, "The Killers," or the legendary discovery of Lana Turner, at age sixteen, in a Hollywood malt shop. After all, the very tone of these places, at once practical and welcoming, seems to reflect something of the American character. They're democratic—or we like to imagine them as democratic—with a lowercase *d*. Walk into an old-school coffee shop or diner in pretty much any town or city in the U.S., and whether it's in California or Connecticut, Nevada or New York, everything feels familiar, from the items on the menu to the chrome-edged countertop, to the booths with their red, green, or blue (and never quite comfortable) vinyl seats.

So picture a coffee shop on the waterfront in Freeport, Long Island, in the early 1950s. At the counter sits eighteen-year-old Jim Miller. His adventures in the Gulf of Mexico are behind him. His future is, at best, uncertain. Living at home with his folks in North Merrick but itching to be out on his own, Jim ponders his next move.

"I was trying to sort through what was the next evolution of my life. What was I going to do now? Go back to fishing? To make any real money, I would have to go offshore fishing, which was a ten-day, maybe a fifteen-day, trip, and scalloping offshore was really hard, horrendous work. That was one opportunity. There was also an opportunity to go skimmer clam fishing, but I wasn't really big enough to be a good skimmer clam guy. The normal day's work was harvesting 150 to 250 bushels of skimmer clams, filling bushel baskets with skimmer clams using a shovel, and then picking them up and stacking them in burlap bags. Then, when you got to the dock, off-loading them. A bushel basket of skimmers was maybe 80 or 90 pounds, so you were hauling and lifting 80 pounds a hundred or two hundred times a day, at a minimum. I probably weighed about 120 pounds at this point—remember, I was a pretty skinny kid—and it felt like skimmer clams were about as big as I was.

"I'd been commercial fishing for a while, on a little day boat. We'd go out every day, come back every night, with Captain John. We were scratching out a living, catching local fluke and codfish and what have you. Not setting the world on fire, just going along, trying to figure out what to do with life. So there I am, sitting in the diner, and by chance this guy comes in who doesn't speak English very well. He's saying he's looking for some boys to go spackling. I say, 'I have no idea what that is. What are you trying to do?'

"He says, 'Construction work.'

"I thought to myself, 'Maybe construction work is something to look into.' You heard stories about guys making some pretty good money doing piecework over in Levittown."

Levittown. The name itself, for Long Islanders of a certain age, conjures the exodus from New York City to the suburbs—and the attendant influx of families, including countless veterans—that forever reshaped the region's landscape in the decade after World War II. Of all the planned communities—with their similarly designed and quickly built homes—that sprouted seemingly overnight outside of major cities all over the U.S., Levittown was the first, the most aggressively developed, and consequently the most famous. Named after a prominent local construction firm, Levitt and Sons—headed by Abraham Levitt and his two sons, Alfred and Bill—which made its money before the war building high-end custom homes, Levittown featured literally thousands of hastily constructed homes sold to young families. Bill Levitt had served in the Navy during the war, and when he came back, he convinced his father and brother, an architect, to adopt the mass-production and uniform-design methods he'd learned while building military housing. By the early 1950s, Levitt and Sons had constructed more than 17,000 homes in and around their namesake community in Nassau County, a virtual stone's throw east of the teeming populations in Brooklyn and the other boroughs of New York City.

"That sort of work was very, very active at the time, all over Nassau," Jim recalls, "and guys were nailing up plywood, doing floors, everything. Piecework was the standard compensation policy in those days, for everybody. At any rate, this guy at the coffee shop convinced me. He was going to pay me a buck-fifty an hour. I said, 'Well, it's better than sitting around doing nothing,' and he said, 'You learn quickly, and then once you learn how to do it, you'll begin to get piecework pay, and then you can make some real money.'"

Jim shrugs as if to say, *What else was I gonna do?*

"I said okay and went to work for him, and I learned how to be a spackler. Oh, it was a filthy job. The spackle was all over me. It was hanging in my hair. And, of course, we were constantly sandpapering everything once the mud dried, so you were full of dust if you were doing that work. At the end of the day, you looked like a ghost. I really didn't think this was the kind of job that I was going to stick with, but he urged me to continue. He told me that I was doing really well after only a month or six weeks. He said I was a very fast learner, and he would increase my hourly rate by a substantial amount. I thought to myself, 'Wow! You work six weeks, and you get a raise. It won't be long before I get piecework, and I'll really make money.'

"Well, a bit later, I was just beginning to do piecework, and he came down and announced to the crew—there were probably six or eight of us at the time—that the government had come after him, and they insisted that he get a contractor's license and that he get an official payroll. Everybody had to be paid wages and be taxed, and he had to get workers' compensation insurance and be a legitimate contractor. All that time he'd been running the business right out of his pocket, so it looked like that was that.

"It turned out that nobody but me on the entire crew—including Andre, the boss, who was Latvian—nobody was American. I was the only American citizen in the whole crew. They were all Latvian fellas, and most of them barely spoke English. Maybe I was adopted by a Latvian crew because it's my father's heritage. Anyway, we were all young guys—I was eighteen, most of the other guys were in their twenties, maybe a couple were in their thirties—and we were gonna be out of work. But we had a whole series of little houses we were building, so we didn't want to stop. At that time, the houses we were working on were 800 square feet—two bedrooms, living room, bathroom, kitchen dinette. They sold for $3,400, and we were getting piecework prices for each segment of the spackling operation. If you were spackling nail heads, maybe you got two bucks. If you were spackling the corners, you got a buck-fifty. If you did the outside corners, there was another price. There was a price for everything. The first coat, the second coat, the finished price, and then so much for sandpapering. No one was really an hourly employee; we were all pieceworkers. But none of that mattered all of a sudden. We were all going to be without a job.

"So, we had a whole range of houses in front of us that needed to be finished, but we had no boss. We went down the list of options. What were we going to do? Andre couldn't qualify as a legitimate contractor. He wasn't a citizen. So we went to Andre's best friend, a guy named Franklin. It turns out he wasn't a citizen, either. We went down the list of six or eight guys, and it finally came to me, and they said, 'Well, Jim, you're the American guy here. You can get a license.'"

More than six decades later, recounting this tale, Jim Miller leans back in his chair, a look of incredulity playing on his face. One can only imagine how much more animated, how intense, that look must have been on the eighteen-year-old Jim Miller.

"I had no idea how to get a contractor's license, or insurance. Who do I call? How do I do it? And all these guys, they start telling me, 'Oh, you call this guy, and he'll get you insurance, and then you call that guy, and he'll tell you how to make a payroll. Jim, come on. You be our boss, and we'll all keep at this piecework, but from now on, when we get sixty dollars for a house, you take five bucks off the top and make piecework for everybody else. You keep doing piecework yourself, of course, but you get five bucks—five whole dollars—for every house that we do.'

"Well. I thought about it for a little while and realized that it sounded like not a bad deal. I became a contractor. Less than six months after starting as an apprentice, I owned a company. And then it evolved. In the beginning, everybody was doing piecework, and that worked fine. My own skills definitely improved to where I could do an entire house—first coat, second coat, finish coat, and whatever else. Then I hired a helper, because if I could get somebody to mix the cement for me, I could do more work in a day. It just evolved little by little, and our reputation grew. People learned that we were reliable, and the quality of the work was pretty good. After a while, we had thirty or forty guys working, and hey! I was a real contractor now—bidding on jobs, giving prices, buying material—and it turned into a real, legitimate business."

Running a contracting business and managing several dozen men while still a teenager hardly incited Jim Miller to rest on his laurels, however. In fact, as Jim's longtime friend Kenny Meyer notes, operating a drywall and spackling business seemed to spur the young Jim Miller to work even harder.

"After he learned the business from his boss, he wanted to do it himself," Kenny says. A retired, decorated Nassau County police detective, Ken Meyer has a ready laugh and a Long Island accent straight out of central casting. When he chuckles in the middle of his storytelling, it sounds like he's gargling gravel. "That was typical of Jim, to want to start his own business. But I really don't think it was a competitive thing. It was more like his reasoning went something like this: 'I can do it, so why should I work for somebody for five dollars an hour when I can do it myself and make ten dollars an hour?'

"So he took me in with him on this business, and we used to do it together. But Jimmy worked nonstop. I mean, *nonstop*. He worked seven days a week if he could—and he did, a lot of times. From first light, all the way up to when it got dark, and beyond"—or, as Jim Miller phrases it, "from you can't see till you can't see."

Kenny chuckles, coughs a hacking cough, and chuckles some more.

"Me, I was interested in girls. And it became something of a problem after a while. So I went back from being a partner—there were no hard feelings at all—to just working for him. Because he was nonstop with it. Nonstop no matter what he did; all his life, he was nonstop."

As for the undocumented immigrants whom Jim worked with during those early years in the sheetrock and spackling business, it turns out that there's a story within a story there, too.

In the years after the war, European émigrés settled in communities all over the U.S., as countless thousands fled the battered continent in search of the peace and economic security—or, at the very least, the economic opportunity—that they believed awaited them in America. That so many of those men, women, and children who left their old lives behind and arrived in the U.S., often with little more than the clothes on their back, actually *did* make productive and prosperous lives for themselves and their progeny speaks volumes about the eagerness of those new Americans to work hard and get ahead. Their stories—of flight, arrival, assimilation, and success—have become a central part of the great American narrative.

Others who left Europe, meanwhile, were understandably less than eager to share the details of what they were running from. After all, not every refugee who made it across the Atlantic in the chaotic years after World War II was a victim. Not every new arrival was a member of a stigmatized minority or ethnicity, fleeing persecution.

"We knew it was a pretty ratty crew," Jim remembers of the scores of Latvians he worked with during his early days in the spackling business in the early to mid-1950s. "At that stage of the game, a bunch of the guys, the Latvian fellas, had made it to the U.S. after they'd been released from German prison camps—or they just kind of filtered in along with guys who were being released from German camps. Some of the guys had been prisoners, and some of them had been guards. And obviously, those guys really didn't want to be recognized. They never wanted to be identified. Now, some of the guys I worked with were real good guys. They became citizens and members of the community. And some of the others were ultimately identified as war criminals and were deported. Everybody wasn't a good guy."

Jim Miller remained in the sheetrock and spackling business for more than a decade. And not too long after he'd started his own company, when he was still in his teens, the trajectory of his life changed forever. He met Barbara Klein.

CHAPTER 10

"Do You, James, Take Barbara . . . ?"

"I met Barbara when I was about nineteen years old," Jim Miller says of his first encounter with the woman who would share his life for the next six-plus decades. "One of the guys in town was dating a girl in Merrick, and he got a call. She wanted him to come over. He said to me, 'Jim, I got this girlfriend, and I want to see her. She's got a drop-dead good-looking friend. I can fix you up with her. Then we can both go over and we can double-date. I can go see my girlfriend, maybe you can hook up with this other girl.' And, of course, my reaction was, 'Get outta here! I ain't got time for your crap.' He just wanted some wheels, and I happened to have a car.

"But he didn't give up. A few days later, he said, 'I got it all set up for you on Friday night. I told her you were coming.' *What?*

"I said, 'I don't care!' So that went on for two or three weeks, us going back and forth about this double date. Finally, a Friday rolled around, and I had nothing to do. 'All right,' I said, 'let's go.' This wound up being on Valentine's Day weekend. We go pick up these two gals. They come out, a tall one and a short one. I say, 'She's so tall, and I ain't tall. Nope. Sorry. Not gonna happen.'

"And my friend says, 'No, no, Jim. The tall one's mine. The shorter one's yours.'

"So I look again, and *boy*! Pretty cute? You kidding me? Jesus! She was drop-dead. This was a home run. She was a doll. I'm telling you, I fell in love the first time I met her. *She* didn't, but I did. I don't think I said to myself, 'This is the woman I'm going to marry.' I didn't think that far ahead. But she was a knockout. I knew I had scored on that blind date."

As with so many stories of young love, however, the details begin to get a bit muddied when the two parties involved share their own recollections.

"I was the type of girl back then who had four boyfriends at one time," Barbara Miller says today. "And here's the sort of man my husband is, the sort of man he has been since he was young. He's not one to let anything get in his way. He found out who I was dating, and then he got hold of my brother and told him that no matter who might call for me at home, he should say I wasn't there. Imagine that! Then he hired my brother to work with him, so he could seal the deal."

It didn't end there, of course. If nothing else, Jim Miller has always shown himself to be thorough when approaching any problem—even if that problem takes the form of rival suitors.

"After he hired my brother," Barbara continues, "he got hold of my other boyfriends, and he offered *them* jobs, too, if they broke off with me. He was born with such a creative mind, you see. So, there was poor Barbara, who was used to dating, and all her dates were gone."

And then, the tone of Barbara's recall undergoes a small but noticeable shift, from a kind of playful banter with herself to something far more pensive. If her voice were a color, it would have moved from, say, a bright blue to a dark gray in a heartbeat.

"But God bless my husband," she says. "He had to teach me how to live, because I lived in a house of horrors, and I didn't know what living really meant." As it turns out, the sweet teenager Jim Miller had fallen for at first glance harbored the same awful secret that countless kids and spouses in seemingly tranquil households everywhere have to keep, and endure: Barbara, her older brother, her stepbrother, and her stepmother (her birth mother was schizophrenic and had been committed to a hospital when Barbara was young) lived in a state of stark, constant fear.

"My wife, when she was young, had a very, very troubled family life," Jim says. "An alcoholic, abusive father, a very dysfunctional family. In public, he was known as Honey. Sweet as can be, and everybody loved him. Behind closed doors, he was a beast. On paper, he was successful. He owned a little home-heating oil company. A stand-up guy. A solid citizen. A well-regarded member of the community. Until we found out who he really was."

Somehow, the matter-of-fact manner in which Barbara recounts her time in that household and the abuse that everyone there suffered at the hands of her father, Edward Klein, makes the reality of the man's cruelties even more chilling.

"I wasn't allowed in the house after school until a grownup was home," she says. "If I didn't have anywhere else to go, like to a friend's house, I would have to stay in the garage until five or six in the evening. In the late fall and winter, that garage was *freezing*. If I had to go to the bathroom, there was a little alleyway between the garage and the next-door neighbor's house, and that's what I used— the alley. My brother Eddie was older, and he took care of me as well as he could. He was like my mother and my father. When I was cold, he would give me his jacket. He'd do things that an older brother would do. But my father? Well, let me give you an example of what we went through at mealtimes. We'd sit at the table, and at that time we had to eat the fat off the meat. And if we didn't eat the fat off the meat, my father had a cat o' nine tails that he would swipe across our faces to make us eat.

"I didn't know anything about life. I thought *that* was life, what I was going through. Years later, when my father was in the hospital dying, there was no way I could go see him. Since then, I've come to believe that he was sick in more ways than one. I don't think that he was just an alcoholic. In fact, I learned later that all of my cousins were frightened to death of my father."

Was Edward Klein a narcissist? A sociopath? Or was he merely, in fact, that bleakest of all stereotypes—a charming guy in public and a depraved, violent drunk behind closed doors? For Barbara Miller, who has had to live with the memories of the way her father verbally and physically abused his wife and his children, the answer is as sordid as it is simple.

"Power," she says. "He wanted power. My father was about the handsomest man on Long Island. And he knew it. He *used* it—to deceive everyone about what he really was underneath it all."

One of the most heartbreaking images that Barbara conjures from her past, however, is not one of violence. It's not a picture of a booze-fueled, towering parent screaming at his cringing children. Instead, it's a quiet portrait of an almost unfathomable despair.

"I don't ever remember being hugged in that house when I was growing up," she says. "I remember we used to have company over, other family members, and when they stood up after sitting in a chair for a while, the cushions were still warm. And I remember so clearly, as a very young child, I used to go over to those cushions and hug them, just to feel the warmth an aunt or an uncle had left behind.

"I had one very, very good friend when I was young, and at one point, when I couldn't take it anymore, I was going to kill myself," Barbara recounts, matter-of-factly. "But of course, I didn't know at that very young age what that meant. I was maybe ten or twelve years old. I was in the woods, and I remember my friend, Janice, calling out to me. She was calling my name because she had an idea that's what I was going to do. So she came looking for me. Oh, her parents were so wonderful to me. They showed me a life I didn't even know existed. They would have me come over on Sunday, and they'd have dessert. I never knew what desserts were! They showed me what a family could be like, or what a home life could be like."

Despite all the brutality and pain of her upbringing, Barbara somehow managed to remain remarkably innocent. Perhaps the dual life she led—abused child inside the home, and smiling youngster outside of it—had some bearing on her ability to simply keep going and not buckle under.

"Barbara wasn't some tough cookie," Jim stresses. "She was just as mild a girl as a guy could hope for. But she really didn't have a clue what was going on in life, really. She was just naïve. She was going through life so quietly, trying not to make waves. She used to spend a lot of time at her girlfriend's house. She wasn't a spectacular student, but she wasn't a dumb lady, either, by any stretch."

(She was also—according to at least one objective, reliable source—a knockout who added a certain style to her boyfriend's previously scruffy image. "Barbara was an absolutely gorgeous blonde at that point in her life," Jim's younger brother, Dave, recalls. "He had this beautiful blonde, and he drove a yellow convertible. They made a pair, I'll tell ya.")

The event that, in effect, freed Barbara from her father's reign of terror highlights her future husband's customary way of dealing with problems. Namely, with a decisiveness that could, at times, border on recklessness.

"We were probably dating for about a year," Jim remembers, "when she and I drove up to her house, and I walked in on a family brawl. We knew something was going on as soon as we pulled up, and I told her to stay in the car. I went inside the house, and *boy*! The father and the stepson were going at it. The father was drunk, of course.

75

Plastered. This was maybe a Sunday afternoon, something like that. I walk in on this disaster, and all of a sudden, I'm refereeing the damn thing. The son, the stepson, the father, the stepmother, all hollering and screaming bloody murder. The police show up, and they separate everybody and cool things down a little bit, and I go out to Barbara, who's still in the car, and I say, 'This is bizarre. These people are all crazy as hell!' Then I tell her to wait, and I go back inside."

"Jimmy went in and grabbed whatever clothes I had in there," Barbara says, "and then he threw them in his car, and he told me, 'You are never going back into that house, ever, because the next person he's going to try to kill is you.' He was right. And I never did. I never went back into that house."

"I knew things weren't good at home for her," Jim says, "but she hid that. Most of the time, I picked her up at her girlfriend's house. She was embarrassed by her family. But when I met them, her dad and stepmother, they were always very gracious and cordial to me. I just didn't realize the reality of what she lived with. So I took her out of there, and she stayed at my brother Tom's house for a month or so. Then I rented a room for her in town, and she stayed there. That was the turning point. We were no longer just dating. I was taking care of her. Her parents didn't protest. I intimidated them. They didn't know who the hell I was. They thought they knew, but they really didn't."

Barbara knew who Jim Miller was, though, and the knowledge—then and now—was a comfort.

"*Reader's Digest* used to have a feature called 'The Most Unforgettable Character I Ever Met,'" Barbara says, "and that's who my husband was. That's who he *is*. He was just unbelievably caring to me. You know, sixty years is a long time to be married, but any congratulations should go to Jimmy because, as they say, I came with a lot of baggage. He became my mother and my father, and he actually had to train me how to live."

· · ·

Time passed. A month. Six months. Jim Miller and Barbara Klein grew closer. Released—physically, at least—from the prison of her father's abuse, Barbara began to imagine what it might be like to really, truly make a life with this man. Imagining the same thing, Jim decided to act.

"We were getting quite serious," he says, "but I don't think we had a sit-down conversation about how serious we really were. Regardless, I'd made my mind up that we were going to get engaged. I think Barbara had *dreamed* that she was going to get engaged, but nothing had come of that for a while. Well, one night we went out on a dinner date. It was her birthday, and I gave her a birthday present. I had bought her a watch. But it was pretty clear that she thought that watch should have been an engagement ring. But she didn't get a ring; instead, she'd gotten a stupid watch. She left the table to go to the bathroom to cry over it, I guess, and when she was gone, I slipped the engagement ring into her drink. When she came back, I thought we should toast our being together. She began to drink her drink, and, of course, she started choking on the damn ring!

"Anyway, it worked out. We got married the following August. Her brother might have shown up, but nobody else from her family was there. Not one person. I was still living at home in North Merrick, and she was living in that rented room in town and commuting to work in Rockville Centre. At that time, there was no living together before marriage. Absolutely not. It wasn't even a possibility.

"It was a small, small wedding. Very informal—and it wound up being in the middle of a hurricane. Perfect."

In fact, Long Island was slammed twice by hurricanes in August 1955—first by Hurricane Connie, a storm that made landfall in North Carolina and plowed its way north through southern New Jersey and Pennsylvania and up to the Great Lakes, where it eventually weakened and died. At almost the same time, Hurricane

Diane caused catastrophic flooding through Pennsylvania, New York, and well up into New England before petering out in late August, south of Greenland. The 1955 Atlantic hurricane season as a whole was a whopper, with thirteen storms leaving more than 1,500 people dead and wreaking havoc on countless properties from the Caribbean to the Gulf of Mexico and throughout the eastern United States.

"Somehow or other, we got word that one of the boats that my dad had at that time was in trouble down in the local marina," Jim explains. "So, on the way to my wedding, we had to stop and fix the boat. And, of course, we ran into all sorts of snags. We couldn't get it tied up properly, or what have you. Barbara was over at her girl-friend's house, getting ready for the wedding, and I was going to pick her up at one o'clock. We were going to get married in Long Beach by the justice of the peace. We had the license. We were all set. Then we were going to come back and have a little reception at my mom's house, and that was going to be it. *But*—the boat took a little longer than we hoped it would, and getting everything in order at the marina kind of dragged out a little bit. So, long story short, I showed up about an hour and a half late to my own wedding. That did *not* go over too good. In fact, from what I could piece together, as it got later and later, there was quite a bit of debate over whether we were going to go through with this thing or not."

Barbara's take on that day's extraordinary events—even if it turned out all right in the end—is succinct.

"He forgot he was getting married," she says, and sixty years after the fact, it's difficult to determine how much of the edge in her voice is genuine and how much is playacting. "When I said 'I do' during that ceremony, I really didn't. Oh, I was *so* mad at him."

CHAPTER 11

Happily Ever After
(Eventually)

Every married couple knows that the life you lead *after* you say your vows is rarely the life you envisioned *while* you were saying your vows. Even clear-eyed realists can get knocked for a loop by the challenges of matrimony. And when the couple in question is quite young, with all the best intentions at heart but little experience of living day by day and night by night with another soul, those realities can quickly begin to chip away at one's illusions about the permanence of domestic bliss.

In other words: Marriage is the hardest work many of us will ever tackle.

For Jim and Barbara Miller, it was no different. That they were in love, and a good match for each other, was rarely in doubt. The fact that they celebrated their sixtieth anniversary in August 2015 suggests that, despite all the ups and downs, they've spent the last six decades doing *something* right.

But for a while there, back in the 1950s and early 1960s, life was tough, and to pretend that financial woes and the growing pains associated with any relationship didn't put a strain on the marriage would be less than honest.

"I was twenty years old when we got married," Jim says, by way of explaining—at least in part—why the early years were something of a challenge. "Barbara was nineteen. We wound up with six kids before we were thirty years old."

Six kids. Three boys, three girls: Jim Jr., the eldest, named for his dad; Barbara, named for her mom; Glen; Mark; Tracey; and Jenniffer. A full house after a while—and a small house at that. But it's the purchase of that first house, and of subsequent properties as investments, that serves as a lens through which we begin to discern the outline and lineaments of the Miller family's lives, individually and collectively, as they take shape.

The way Jim tells it, the single, memorable incident that led inexorably to the purchase of their first home involved a leaky faucet, an ungracious landlord, and an amorous young married couple engaged in the sort of activity that amorous young couples are known for.

"So," Jim says, "within a year or so of starting the spackling company, falling in love, and getting married, we're living in a furnished basement apartment in Lindenhurst, our first apartment as newlyweds. Pretty soon, though, we decided that we didn't like living in a basement, and we had an opportunity to rent an attic apartment, which was an upgrade. We moved into this attic apartment in Copiague, and before long, Barbara gave birth to our first child, we brought the baby home, and there we were, building a family.

"We're young newlyweds at the time, right? So one day I come home early from work—which was an incredibly rare event, by the way, as I was working all the time—and my wife greets me. We're embracing, one thing leads to another, and next thing you know, the damn landlord walks into the apartment—just barges right in without knocking—because he's decided *that* was the perfect time for him to fix a leaky faucet or some such thing.

"I was pretty irate—understandably, I think—and I threw him the hell out. In fact, I seem to recall that I might have told him something along the lines of, 'If you ever come in here again without knocking, I'm going to kick you down the effing stairs.' So we now had this dispute with our landlord. At that same time, I was doing a spackling job in Port Jefferson. There was a small Cape Cod development of twenty homes, and I knew the builder. I was working as a subcontractor to the sheetrock installer, doing the spackling work. The builder and I had a conversation about me purchasing a home from him. Those houses sold for, I think, $10,250 at the time. We needed something like $1,000, half up front and half at the closing, as a down payment. Maybe it was $800. Whatever the exact number was, it's not really significant. The point is that it was a *lot* of money back then. But he and I agreed that I'd buy the house, and since I was working as hard and as fast as I could to accumulate the down payment, I came home to Barbara and told her, 'I bought a house for us.' And of course she says, 'What? *Where?*'

"She didn't have a clue. How could she? It all happened so fast. Anyway, I told her, 'We bought a house. And on Sunday, I'll take you out, and I'll show you what we bought, because I can't take time off from work now to drive over there.' Sunday came, and we drove to Port Jeff, and I showed her the model house, which was exactly like the one we were going to buy. She was very excited, which was a great thing to see. I was twenty-two years old, maybe. Tops."

All this time, of course, Jim was working. And working. And working. Getting ahead, meanwhile—that is to say, actually making enough money to sock some cash away in savings, or to invest in other ventures—was another story.

"Our standard workday," Jim recalls, "was from you can't see till you can't see. From before first light until past sunset. Then, if you got lucky, you found an attic job someplace, and you could set up some lights and work even later. Those were days when we learned to mix the spackle by the headlights of the car, because the sun wasn't up yet and we couldn't see. But the fact is, we were already pretty creative guys. We had pickup trucks, and we'd bring gas generators with us to the job sites so we'd always have a power source—which is something hardly anybody else did back then. Rather than having to try to scrounge around and get five gallons of water on a construction site, we put a fifty-five-gallon drum in the back of the pickup and stuck a spigot through the side, so we had running water on the site. And on top of that, we mixed the spackle with electric drills. We were mechanizing the industry.

"And then there were the stilts. We learned how to work on stilts, which was something of a revelation, because up until then everybody just worked with little stepladders so we could reach the eight-foot ceilings in these Cape Cods. That was time-consuming, though—stepping down, moving the ladder, stepping back up, spackling, stepping back down, and on and on—and when we saw an outfit in California that was advertising a type of stilt that you could wear that would make reaching an eight-foot ceiling a piece of cake, we jumped at it. I learned how to work on stilts, and that increased my productivity substantially. Then, because we were suddenly working at a nonstandard height, we invented a wagon—a kind of modified golf cart—that would hold a spackle bucket where we could gain access to it without much trouble at all. Just constantly innovating, to try to get as much efficiency out of our tools, and ourselves, as we possibly could."

Despite the ingenuity and the ceaseless, can't-see-till-can't-see effort that Jim was putting into his work, the Millers were, each and every month, just scraping by. Business on Long Island was, by most measures, booming in the 1950s and early 1960s, but not much of the enormous money generated by that boom was filtering down to such self-employed, blue-collar guys as Jim. It was, in many respects, the conundrum that has always confronted working-class families everywhere. Namely, there was an awful lot of work for those willing and able to seize it, but the long, long hours and the hard, unceasing labor just didn't translate into a commensurate payday.

"We had a $9,800 mortgage, or something like that, on the Port Jeff house," Jim says. "That'll cost you $87 a month for the rest of your life, you know? *Eighty-seven dollars a month?* Who knows how you can make that much money? And after a while, *boom!* We got a notice in the mail that our mortgage was going up. Taxes were higher, and insurance was higher, and whatever else. The mortgage went from $87 a month to $96 a month. And I remember so clearly sitting at the kitchen table with Barbara and saying, 'We're going to lose this thing. We can't make it.' Nine more dollars a month. That was big money! We'd bought furniture from the Salvation Army. We thought we were being frugal. But a 10 percent increase on the mortgage? Oh boy. This was not good."

So Jim did what he always did when what he had built was under threat. He worked harder.

"I knew I could find jobs. I could do attic jobs at night. I could mix the spackle for the next day's job the night before, so I had it all mixed up for the next morning and could get right to work even earlier than before. Whatever it took to squeeze some more work out of the day, that's what I did."

Eighty-hour work weeks? Yes. Working seven days a week? Sure. Barely seeing his wife and kids (as the family kept growing throughout these years)? Right. Caught in such a relentless cycle, the tendency might be to just keep one's head down, literally and figuratively, and keep plowing ahead. But it seems that Jim Miller is one of those rare folks who can keep his eye on the horizon while putting every ounce of energy into the task at hand. Rather than tossing up his hands and admitting defeat—*I can't keep going on like this forever*—he began to look for a way out of the hardscrabble, if perfectly honorable, life he and his family were living.

"I began to develop a mind-set that I've got to establish an investment pool," he says. "I knew that I had to secrete some money away strictly for investment purposes. Speculation, in addition to the spackling business. Just so that we would have some extra money, or if I came across an investment that seemed especially promising. After that first year of saving up, with this new idea in mind, we had $1,100 in what we called the investment account. Eleven hundred dollars! That was some serious money, man. But you know what? You get up to $1,100, and the engine in the car blows up. Now you're back to 900 bucks. So you're saving and saving again, you're finagling here and there, and before too long, you're up to $1,300. I'd set a goal for myself of $1,500. We're almost there, almost there—and then maybe the baby gets sick, so we're back down again. In the third year of this program, the amount in that account is inching up again, and I get a tax return. A *good* tax return. All of a sudden, not only do I have $1,500, but I have $1,800. I'm over my goal—and I have an idea.

"I knew a guy in town who had a multifamily house that he was trying to renovate and rent out and manage, and he was having a terrible time with it. He'd been trying to make it work, but the tenants were a nightmare, and he'd had his fill of it. So I said, 'Why don't you sell it to Richie and me? We'll take over the friggin' mortgage and give you the difference.' He thought that sounded pretty good—in fact, he jumped at it—and we bought his house for $6,500. There were four families in there, and the rent roll for those four families amounted to $300. Sixty dollars here, seventy-five dollars there. But it was bad. This thing was nowhere near being in compliance with any housing code. They hadn't invented the code yet. It was a slum, really, and it had bad people in there. No wonder the guy jumped at selling it to us. He wound up with fifteen hundred bucks, and we wound up with a $5,000 mortgage and took over his payments.

"So he was gone, and we were the new landlords. Now I had to go down and throw some people out and get this thing shaped up. So the first thing I did is I went down, got myself a gun permit, and strapped on a .38. I went over to the building, introduced myself, and said, 'I'm your new landlord. Now, we can be friends, or we can be something besides friends. You're going to be my friend, or you're not going to be my friend. My friends pay the rent on the first of the month. The people who don't pay my rent on the first are not my friends.'

"There was no wiggle room here at all. I made that plain. 'Rent is due on the first. I'll be here. What time do you get home? I'll be here.'

"Of course, they all thought, 'This guy's crazy. Look at him. He means it. I think he might shoot us.' The first month, they paid rent on time. The second month, trouble started. 'I don't get paid until tomorrow.'

"'I told you I want my rent on the first,' I said, 'and today's the first. I want my rent. You aren't making me very happy. I think you'd better get the hell out of here.'"

Over the next two years, as the troublesome tenants left, Richie Miller remodeled the house, made it safe, upgraded it, and got the rent roll up to $1,000 a month.

"So we're doing a little better now. Things are starting to pay off. We buy another house and start renting there, too. After a while, after we get that first one cleaned up and running, some guy comes by and says he wants to buy it. I say, 'Okay, yeah, for $28,000.' He says, 'Done,' and that was that. Done. Our sixty-five-hundred-dollar house sold for twenty-eight grand.

"'Yeah,' I think, 'you can really make money in this business. This is almost better than spackling, and without all that white crap sticking in your hair.' So I buy some more houses. Renovate them, keep playing landlord for a while. But along that same time, there in the early to mid-sixties, the spackling business is on a little bit of a decline. Collecting money for rents is getting pretty tough. Interest rates are going up, and the building boom of the previous few years, like it always does, is cooling down.

"I had sold the little Cape Cod house that we'd originally bought, and I bought a bigger home—the place we would live in for many years—a farm on Terryville Road in Port Jefferson Station. It was stressful, and on top of it all, I was now getting past my physical peak. I wasn't twenty-nine years old anymore, and spackling was very, very demanding work. You really had to be in good shape, every single day, to operate at maximum efficiency.

"I'll give you an example of seeing the signs that it was time for something else. For some other sort of work. Basically, all the younger guys on my crews were getting to be faster than I was. Now, I was especially proud that I was a very, very fast, skilled spackler. The young fellas had also learned how to work on stilts, and it was not uncommon in those days to be working in similar houses, side by side, and get into a contest with an employee. You know, two guys start at the same time, and the first guy who gets out, who finishes the job—and does it *right*—gets paid for two houses instead of one. It was an athletic contest, and for a quite a while, I had generally won those. But suddenly—or at least it seemed like it happened suddenly—I was picking the guys that I would challenge. There were some guys who were faster than me, and I'd avoid them. And I'm starting to think that maybe, maybe, I need to find another business."

Who could have guessed that the next business that Jim Miller would pursue would present itself, initially, in the form of an unexpected gift from the sea?

CHAPTER 12

Treasure Island

"**G**enius," Thomas Edison once observed, "is 1 percent inspiration and 99 percent perspiration." After all, if an inventor, an artist, or a craftsman sits around waiting for a visit from the muse—instead of courting the muse through tireless, sustained effort—chances of producing anything meaningful are slim to none. In that spirit, the story of the salvaging of the *Diane Janet*, a fishing boat that ran aground in heavy surf off Fire Island in the mid-sixties, might serve as an apt illustration of the adage that hard work makes its own luck.

But another notable characteristic, another personal trait, is in play here, too—a trait that, despite its central role in virtually every conceivable successful endeavor, often gets short shrift. That trait is persistence. Stick-to-itiveness. Plain old bulldog tenacity. Creativity, innovation, the ability to see a single problem from multiple angles—all of those are helpful. All of those are valuable. But without the willingness and the fortitude to see something through to the bitter end—well, it's a bit like a beautiful car that has everything it needs, except an engine: It might look great, but it's not going to get you where you need to go.

The story of the *Diane Janet* is as clear a window into Jim Miller's unique approach to problem-solving and his decisiveness as any that he tells about himself or that anyone else tells about him. And it's powered, in large part, by the man's tenacity.

"I was listening to the marine radio one day," Jim says, "and I heard all this talk about a fishing boat running aground off Fire Island. A fisherman had fallen asleep during the night, and the boat ran aground and got caught in the surf. The men who were on the boat went over the side and were rescued, but this all happened way out, off a desolate part of the coast. I thought to myself, 'Gee, that's kind of interesting. I wonder whose fishing boat it is and what kind of boat it is. Ah, what the hell? I've got a four-wheel-drive Jeep. Let me run down to the beach and see what this is all about.'

"I run down to the beach and pull up, and there it is. A fishing boat in the surf. By then the water isn't very rough. Not a bad day at all. But there's nobody else around. Not a soul. So I'm standing there, looking out at this boat, and before too long, another pickup truck pulls up. A guy gets out. We go through the usual, 'Hey, how're you doing?' and then we start talking about what sort of shape she's in. And the more we look, the more we see that it looks like she's actually in pretty *good* shape. She's listing to one side pretty bad, kind of leaned over a little bit, so she's definitely aground, and we start wondering if we could tow her off of there.

"'I don't know. It'd take a lot of horsepower to get that off.'

"'Maybe you could pull it in. With big winches maybe you could pull it ashore. Get a couple of big tow trucks. What do you think?'

"'It's pretty tough to tow something like that.' Blah, blah, blah.

"Then another pickup pulls up. Now there's a bunch of guys standing around, talking crap with one another, and I remember that there's something I'd heard about salvage: that if there's nobody on the wreck, and it's abandoned, the first guy on it can claim it. Is that possible, I wonder? That boat's got radar, and it has to have all kinds of electronics in the wheelhouse, and I think this thing has to be worth a lot of money.

"It's early May at this point. The water is *cold*. And everyone's got an opinion.

"'You can't get out there, you'll die from hypothermia.'

"'What, are you kidding me? Hypothermia? You're full of crap.'

"'I'm full of crap? You can't go out there, man.'

"'I don't think it's a big deal. Let's go look.'

"We've all got work clothes on, and next thing you know, we're wading out into the ocean. Then the water's deep, and we're swimming out to the damn wreck. We get out there, and we're looking it over, and *man!* it's a nice boat. A beautiful boat, seventy-two feet. And they just left it! And I'm wondering if she's got a hold full of fish—because that would just put a capper on everything. (It didn't.)

"By now, there are more trucks showing up, and there's a police truck with its lights going. Guys waving their arms at us. There's a lot of commotion over there on the beach, and we're afraid that those guys think that they've got to come out and rescue us. That they're going to get the Coast Guard or something and come save us from ourselves. So we jump back over the side and make it back to the beach.

"'What are you guys doing out there?'

"'We just went out to look.'

"'What are you, pirates?' *Pirates!* Can you believe that?

"That's when the insurance guy comes over and says, 'I've got a surveyor here who wants to go out and survey the wreck to determine the condition of the boat.' I tell the guy that we've been out there, that we saw it, that it's making water, but he waves me off. 'No, he's got to go see it. He's a professional.'

"Oh, well . . . if he's a *professional*. Then the insurance guy says that the surveyor can't go out there alone. He asks if we want to go out there with him again. I look over at the guy, and he's dressed in a wet suit. He's got flippers and goggles. He looks like a whale. He can't even walk into the water. He's got to *back* into the water.

"We take him out, and he starts in on what a disaster it is. 'Look at it! It's in bad shape. I gotta get back to the beach. It's dangerous. The water's cold. I'm gonna die out here!'

"Back on the beach, he and the insurance guy decide that the boat—it was called the *Diane Janet*, by the way—the boat's a total loss. It's a wreck. So I ask him what he's going to do with it. He says he's willing to sell it, but who's he going to sell it to?

"I ask him, 'How much are you going to sell it for?' He says, 'How much money you got in your pocket?' Well, how much does anybody have in his pocket? A few hundred bucks? 'That's the price,' he says.

"I can't believe it. I ask him, 'What do you mean, that's the price?'

"'I'll sell it to you for $250,' he says.

"The boat's insured for more than $100,000. And all of a sudden, some guy is tugging at my shoulder. He says, 'That boat's got a brand-new diesel engine in it. All you've got to do is get out there with two chainsaws. You cut down the side, cut across the bottom. It'll expose the engine room. You go in there, it's got wood engine rails. You cut the two engine rails with the chainsaw, and you get a big tow truck over here. You put a cable on it and pull the engine out. You put the engine on the beach here in, say, four hours, I'll give you $1,000 for it.'

"And I'm thinking, 'A thousand dollars for four hours of work?' This could turn into some kind of payday. The electronics in the wheelhouse are cherry. I saw them, and I know they have to be worth money. The cop on the beach and this other guy say they'll go in on it with me. We can do this together, the three of us. We'll salvage it.

"So we buy the wreck, right there, but now it's getting dark, and we're worried that if we leave it overnight, everybody and his brother is going to come and steal anything on the boat that's worth something. So I send word to my wife. 'I ain't coming home tonight.' Because I gotta keep an eye on this wreck I just bought, right?

"The next morning, the sea is a little rough. We're out to the wreck and there's water in the wheelhouse. Things aren't going as easy or as smoothly as we thought they might. At high tide, the waves are breaking over us. There's a hell of an undertow—take your legs right out from underneath you. Now we've got to rig safety lines. Then we start surveying, diving down, getting inside to see what's really in this thing. And what we learn is that this isn't a four-hour job. We work our tails off for a month, and it's clear that what we have here is worth a lot more than whatever that guy on the beach wanted to pay us for the boat's engine. We don't know how much more, but it's a lot more. We've been taking stuff out of the boat, electronics and other gear, and now we have to get at the engine, which is huge.

"We check the phase of the moon. We look at the tide calendars. We see we're going to have a really high tide the next night, and we're going to have a really low tide the day after that at ten in the morning. We've got to be ready to go at seven. We've got to have a big payloader, and we've got to have a bulldozer to save the payloader if it gets in trouble out in the surf. We've got to have big fat cables. We'll cut into the side of the hull facing the beach and pull the side down, so it can act like a ramp. The payloader will pull in, sit on the ramp, and pick up the engine. Then the bulldozer will hook him up and pull him back to the beach. That's the plan.

"Now, I have to call every friend I know to get a bulldozer and payloader. But somehow, we put it all together and time it all just right. The plan gets executed. We get the engine at the exact right time. Out it comes, and it's up on the beach. We get the winch from the boat. We get the generator. We get all the other good machinery that we want to take with us. By then, the tide's coming back in, and the waves are climbing up the bulldozer. So that's it. We get everything off the boat that we can possibly get.

"Now we've got to pay all these other guys who helped out, rented us equipment, all of that. But I'm also thinking that the engine is worth a lot more than a couple of grand if we clean it up and make sure it runs. It's cherry, but it's been underwater now for a month. So now it's time for my partners, or the guys I think are my partners, to step up.

"'All right,' I tell 'em. 'We owe the bulldozer guy $500, and we owe the payloader guy $200. We got oxygen, we got acetylene. That's another $200.' And I tally several other things. 'We're a couple grand in debt here, fellas,' I go on. 'So let's put our money on the table, and let's pay our bills, and we'll go forward with this thing.' And that's when the griping starts.

"'My wife is mad at me because I took two days' vacation off to be down here,' one of them says. 'I haven't been working steady for a month. I ain't seen any money. My wife's a little upset.'

"So I tell him, 'That's your problem, fella. Deal with your own problems. Don't make 'em mine.'

"'I gotta give her some money,' he says. 'I'm in trouble if I don't come home with two hundred bucks to justify what I've been doing here for a month.'

"Two hundred bucks? I give him two hundred bucks out of my own pocket and tell him to go home. We're done. Then I turn to the other guy.

"'What about you?' I ask him. 'You staying, or you going?'

"He hems and he haws; then he says he needs $300. What am I, the banker? I give him $300, and off he goes, muttering, tail between his legs."

In a brief, revealing aside, Jim mentions that he had his family—Barbara and the six kids—there on the beach with him for at least part of the month or so that the salvage operation was under way. Not just visiting during the day, mind you, but *staying* with him: sleeping in canvas army-surplus tents, the boys occasionally helping out with the work. Without making a big deal about it, Jim provides yet another reminder that the way the Millers approached a task, no matter how small or monumental, was often vastly different from the way that most other families would likely tackle the same project.

It might not fit neatly on a bumper sticker or on an ancestral crest, but it's still not a bad motto: *The family that salvages shipwrecks together stays together.*

"So now everything we salvaged off the *Diane Janet* is mine. Lucky me. Not sure what I got myself into here, but let's get her home anyway. So we load it up on trailers and whatever else, and truck it home. We put the engine in the garage back at my house, where we've got heat, we've got lights, and we can work on it.

"I know a good marine mechanic. I call him up and ask him to come over and have a look. 'Well,' he says, 'we've got to take the entire thing apart and clean it. Every single piece of this thing has to be cleaned. She's been sitting in the ocean for a month, but if she runs as good as she looks, she'll be okay. Either way, it's gonna be a couple of weeks' worth of work to take it all apart and put it together again.'

"'All right,' I say. 'Let's go.'"

The mechanic comes by the Millers' place every morning for two weeks. At seven o'clock each day, Jim is ready with the coffee. Spackling? For the time being, that life is left behind. It's forgotten. Jim has a little bit of a cushion in the bank because of the handful of properties he bought, upgraded, and sold, so he spends his days and nights in the garage "playing mechanic," as he puts it, taking the

NOTHING BAD EVER HAPPENS

engine apart piece by piece. He and the mechanic clean everything. They wash all the sand out, replace the gaskets, and put it back together again, shining, freshly oiled, painted green and red, and—God willing—running as good as new.

"Boy oh boy," Jim Miller says, smiling at the recollection, fifty years after the fact. "That thing looked like it just came from the factory. It really did. It was beautiful. And when we started it up after taking it apart and putting it all back together, it ran just like a sewing machine. I mean, it just *hummed*. So we had the engine, a generator, a huge winch, and some other miscellaneous equipment that came off the wreck, and I put an ad in a commercial marine newspaper, something along the lines of, 'Salvaged equipment. Complete supplies and equipment from the fishing vessel *Diane Janet* for sale for $25,000.'

"People started calling up, asking about the engine. 'Is this what you got?' 'Yeah, I got a new 1271 GM.' 'Wow, that's a nice engine. What reduction gear? . . . Yeah? Sounds great.'

"But no one was really ready to buy it.

"Then some guy called up from Halifax, Nova Scotia, and began to interrogate me about the engine, whether I was really in possession of such-and-such an engine with that type of reduction gear and so on. I said, 'Absolutely. I've got it right here in my garage. It looks great, runs great. It's a good piece of equipment.'

"By then, we had a pretty good idea of what we were holding on to. Some people had already hinted that this was a very, very valuable engine, because of its scarcity. This was the Vietnam era, remember, and that particular engine was being utilized in military tanks. There were no new engines like it available for private industry. It was a very, very good modern engine with parts available for rebuild, but you simply couldn't buy it new.

"So this guy from Halifax told me, 'Well, I have a tugboat that I built, and the boat was designed around the engine that you have, but I haven't been able to buy the engine anywhere, and I have a contract to put the boat to work for three years. I just need the engine so I can get working.'

"I said, 'Well, you've got the tugboat. I've got the motor. You've got the money. We can make a deal.' And he said, 'You're my kind of guy.' I said, 'You're my kind of guy if you can put money in my bank. If you can't put money in my bank, you're not my kind of guy.' He asked for my bank information. I gave it to him. He said, 'Go to your bank tomorrow, and you'll find out that I transferred $5,000 into your account.' I said, 'Okay. We'll find out if you're real or not. I mean, you're from Nova Scotia, and I don't know you from Adam, so I don't really trust you. But if your money is there, then I guess you're credible.'

"The next morning I went down to the bank, and there was $5,000 in my account that hadn't been there the day before. I called the guy up, and he said that if everything was good, if it looked like we had a deal, he'd charter an airplane. He would fly down to Long Island, he'd be at my place on Saturday morning at ten o'clock, and if I could start that motor, and it looked and ran as well as I said it did, he'd give me a check for the balance. And of course I said okay. I was confident. So he showed up on Saturday morning, at ten on the dot, and he oohed and ahhed over it because it looked so good, with all the detailing we'd painted on it.

"Then he asked, 'Will it run?' And I said, 'Well, there's the starter button. You have the privilege of pushing it.' He started up the motor, and it ran like a top. 'Happiness,' he said, 'begins today. And I'll give you some extra money if you'll prepare it for shipment. We need a frame around it. We need it loaded on the truck, and if you do that, I'll give you . . . ' I don't know. Whatever it was. Four hundred more dollars? I don't remember, but we crated up his engine for him and called the shipping company and loaded it on the truck, and he paid in full. He wrote me a check for the balance—$20,000—right there. But before he left, he said to me, 'I don't want all the other junk. You can keep that. I'll pay the full price for just the motor.'

"Later on, I sold the winch to somebody for a few thousand dollars, and then I sold the generator to somebody else for a few thousand dollars. It became pretty profitable. I sat down and said, 'Jim, what do you think about this whole deal? You know, you made out pretty good. You made a year's pay, *more* than a year's pay, in a few months with this salvage operation.'

"So I thought about it and came to a decision. That money from the engine—it came from the sea. It should go back to the sea. And maybe I should change my career and go back to fishing. So I went and bought an engine of my own. It's ironic. I bought the engine before I bought the boat, but I found a good, used GM diesel for sale, bought that, and rebuilt it. Then I went down to Cape May and found what later became the *Lady Barbara*, and that was a boat in need of an engine. I bought it for a few thousand dollars and renovated it—made it suitable for the new engine—and then I installed the new engine and other equipment that I thought would be appropriate for fishing in Long Island Sound. In effect, I created a multifunctional fishing boat. It could be a lobster boat. It could be a gillnetter. It could be a dragger. Of course, the fact remained that I had never fished commercially in Long Island Sound in my *life*, so I was sort of sailing by the seat of my pants. I just said to myself, 'Well, I hope it's going to work, but I'm going back to fishing.'"

• • •

And the *Diane Janet*? What became of the rest of the boat that Jim Miller and his soon-to-be-no-longer partners had left there in the waves off Fire Island, after removing the engine, the winch, and other abandoned treasures?

"The night after we'd taken everything we could from the boat," Jim recalls, "we had a big, big high tide, and a hell of a wind came up. Because we'd cut into the vessel with chainsaws and everything else so we could get at its guts, it disintegrated. Disappeared. The next day, it was gone. We never saw it again. It was just gone, gone, gone."

CHAPTER 13

The Storm:
A Son's Memory

"I was probably ten years old, and it was very early in the season," Mark Miller says. Now fifty-four and the president and CEO of the Miller Environmental Group, Mark is thinking back to a time when, working on Long Island Sound with his father and his brothers Glen and Jimmy, he first fully experienced the raw power of a storm on the open water and consciously recognized the limitless trust he had in his father, his siblings, and their boat.

"The weather was iffy, but our gear had to be pulled because the weather window, moving forward from that day, was even worse. In fact, the weather coming our way over the next few days was enough for us to say, 'Yeah, we're going to go out *now*.'

"I remember leaving the dock and clearing the breakwater, making the turn, and it was a little bit snotty but definitely not so bad that we couldn't pull gear. There were plenty of days like that on the Sound. But the sky definitely had a menacing color to it on that particular morning. We started pulling gear. We'd probably pulled only two lines before the weather started really deteriorating.

As we were steaming toward the third line, it got very rough. It was, without a doubt, the roughest water I had seen in my life up until then. There was no way that we were going to pull any more gear at that point, and it was time to get back to the dock. I remember rain was starting, and it was very, very heavy. Thunder squalls were coming through, and Long Island Sound was just white—absolutely covered with whitecaps. The chop of Long Island Sound is notorious. It's not like being out on the ocean, on the Atlantic side of Long Island, where you might have very big waves, but there are these predictable swells, and the period between one wave and another is much longer, and regular.

"The Sound, on the other hand, is notorious for *not* having those long, predictable swells. It's that chop sea, very unpredictable, and the period is very short, so you don't get any relief between waves. I remember, very clearly and precisely, being in the wheelhouse, the doors closed, all four of us tightly packed in there, heading back to Port Jeff. We're in this little thirty-eight-foot wooden trawler, riding up a wave and seeing sky, then as we got to the crest and started aiming down, all you saw was green water. And we were going straight into that. We were taking seas right over the roof of the wheelhouse. We're holding on to the windowsills, and we all had sea legs, of course, so even though it was so choppy, we were able to keep from stumbling.

"And at that moment, I remember thinking to myself, 'I'm not afraid. I'm not afraid. This is so amazing. This is so cool. I have faith in my dad. I have faith in my brothers. I have faith in this boat.' I remember scanning the horizon as we came up to the crest of the next wave, and looking all around and being *so proud* that there was not another boat out on Long Island Sound. For as far as the eye could see, we were the *only* guys out there, pounding our way back to Port Jeff. We were so immersed in nature, and so confident in our understanding of that nature, that we felt we had this unique insight—and we had so much belief in ourselves—that it wasn't a question of whether we should really be out there, because we were okay. And that's when I also thought to myself, 'This is actually kind of fun.'

"It was hard, hard work, always, but there was always a kind of wonderment, too." Mark laughs, and then he says, "Even though we were lobstering, the lobster traps didn't know they were designed only for lobsters. We would pull up all sorts of stuff in the traps. Different kinds of fish, different kinds of critters, and while we were out there, we would see amazing things. I remember the first time we saw a sunfish—just this absolutely huge, weird-looking fish, way in excess of 1,000 pounds—and we thought it was a shark at first because of the fin cutting above the water. We were always so plugged in to our surroundings, and it was just expected that we would have some experience with nature and really come to appreciate what we were exposed to, only because we were taught to be aware. We all became very, very aware of our surroundings at all times, and that's largely because of the natural environment we were in. It was a great thing to be working out there with my brothers and my dad. It was a privilege."

CHAPTER 14

The Trophy:
A Son's Memory

Fairness. Toughness. In the best of times, they go hand in hand.

"My dad was not a big guy when we were growing up," notes Jim Miller Jr., the oldest of Jim's three sons. "He's put on some weight in recent years. But when we were kids, he was lucky if he cracked 135, 140 pounds. He was a skinny little guy, but tenacious. A real tough son of a gun, and he knew how to discipline us. Not in any way, shape, or form was he abusive to us kids. Not at all. But *tough*. And fair. I'll tell you a quick story to give you an idea of what I mean.

"When I was a teenager, I wasn't the most academically accomplished, brightest kid in school, but I had a knack for machinery and equipment. I was into hot rods and stuff like that. I was probably seventeen, and we were starting to do pretty well with the cleanup business. We had a couple of oil spills under our belt by then. My dad had bought this brand-new, 1972 Chevy pickup truck. A nice 350 in it, with dual exhaust, a really nice-looking truck, and it *sounded* great. So we had the brilliant idea to ask my dad, in what we thought was a sort of cleverish way, if we could borrow the truck to go watch the drag races out at National Speedway. He said, 'Yeah, I guess so.' Of course, we never told him our intent was to race the truck.

"So, I saved some money. I went out and bought a Mallory dual point distributor and tuned up the carburetor. We were all pretty handy on anything with an engine. We were absolutely going to register the truck, and we were going to *race* it. We went down to National Speedway and disconnected the exhaust so it was really loud. And it ran great!

"We entered the race, and we actually won our division. The last car we raced was an Olds 442, which is about the same horsepower as our truck. And we won! We got a big trophy for the thing, and I'm thinking, 'You've got to be kidding me!' So we had another brilliant idea—the sort of idea that sounds brilliant only to a seventeen-year-old. 'This is great. Let's go home from Manorville, all the way to Port Jefferson, with open manifolds on the engine'—which is basically driving around with absolutely no exhaust system whatsoever.

"We would be noticed. We would be loud. Really, really loud. And of course we didn't think that anything was going to happen. So I was dropping my friends off in the community, and they were like, 'Yeah, Jim, spin 'em up on your way out!' I revved it up, burning rubber, smoking the tires up. It was almost a brand-new truck, so it was really strong, and I have to say, it really sounded awesome. It sounded like a race car.

"Now, a little bit of background. My dad was very involved with the local community and the fire department. He was a fire commissioner, and he had a lot of friends who did a lot of good for the community. Little did I know that almost everybody in the community that my buddies lived in, all the fathers in that community, were members of the fire department.

"So, here I am, dropping all the guys off, and I'm having a great old time smoking up the tires, proud of my trophy. I turn my corner, and at the end of the street, there is a chain of fathers, arm in arm, blocking the street. My first thought is, 'Oh man! These guys are going to grab me, pull me out of the truck, and beat the crap out of me!' These are big, thirty-, forty-year-old fathers, grown men, and they are not happy. Here's this idiot teenager racing around the development, and he's going to run one of their kids over. I'm a seventeen-year-old kid with long hair who thinks he's cool because he's burning up his dad's truck.

"Okay. I have to stop, and I'm thinking, 'This is not a joke. These guys are going to beat the crap out of you, Jim.' One guy comes over to the window, he reaches his hands in, he looks at me like he's going to drag me out of the truck, and then he says, 'You're Jim Miller's son, aren't you?' I say, 'Yes, I am.' He says, 'Son, you have no idea how lucky you are who you are. We're all members of the Terryville Fire Department. We're all firemen here. We were going to literally drag you out of the truck and beat you until you didn't see daylight. You cannot be running around like this!'

"And of course he was right. Here are all these little kids running around in the street on a quiet Sunday afternoon, and here I am racing around. . . . It was not a good scene.

"He says, 'You drive this truck home and expect your father to receive a telephone call.'

"Oh crap! Of course, he calls my dad, and I'm limping home. My dad's in the driveway with his arms crossed, and I'm positive I'm going to have my freakin' head handed to me. So I grab my trophy, which is about three feet tall with a big racing car on top. I don't think I'm really all that cool anymore. I'm looking at the pavement, and my dad says, 'I got a phone call about five minutes ago.' I said, 'I know, Dad.' And then he asks me, 'So what have you got in your hand there?' So I tell him that we entered the truck in the National Speedway race, and we kind of won in our horsepower division. He looks at me, he looks at the trophy, and he says, 'No kidding. I think that's pretty cool. You know, you did tell me you were going to go to National Speedway, but you didn't tell me you were going to race the truck. And I wouldn't be so mad about that. But did you have to drive the truck through the neighborhood with open headers?'

"And then he says to me, 'You know what? You won the trophy. You had a great time. Just put the exhaust system back on the truck, and let things go at that.' And that was it."

Jim Jr. laughs at the memory, even though it's evident that he still feels a bit rotten, and a little embarrassed, about deceiving his dad.

"He already knew I was disciplined by the time I drove home," he says. "Did he have to beat me to make me see I'd made a mistake? Did he have to yell at me? No. He realized the point was already made the moment I saw those angry fathers in the street. And he knew I'd never forget it. Also, in a way, he thought it was kind of cool what we did. That's just one quick example of how he would discipline us."

CHAPTER 15

Lobstering: The Good, the Bad, the Ugly

Mention *lobster* to most people—perhaps especially to people outside of the Northeast—and Maine immediately comes to mind. That's hardly surprising, of course. Commercial lobstering has been a viable and, in many ways, signature industry along the Maine coast for hundreds of years. That the prehistoric-looking crustacean was once considered "poverty food" might come as a surprise to contemporary gourmands who think of a lobster dinner as a luxury. But in the nineteenth century and earlier, lobster was so abundant and so cheap that it was used as fertilizer on farms and was routinely fed to prisoners and indentured servants throughout northern New England. In fact, in Massachusetts, some servants fought to have a clause in their contracts stipulating that they would not be forced to eat lobster more than three times a week.

Today, lobstering remains a major financial and political force in Maine, employing thousands and generating close to $1 billion a year in a state with fewer than two million full-time residents.

A few hundred miles to the south, the story is quite different. While generations of lobstermen and their families made their living on Long Island Sound—hard, backbreaking work, but a living nevertheless—the past few decades have seen a precipitous and, by almost all measures, irreversible decline. Most everyone points to one year, 1999, as the genuine beginning of the end, when a sudden, massive die-off—by some estimates, close to 90 percent of the Sound's lobster population—gutted the local industry. As a 2007 article in *The Washington Post* noted:

> That year, these picturesque breeding grounds—a gray estuary bordered on the southwest by the glimmering skyscrapers of Manhattan and on the west and north by the grand manses of the Connecticut shore—went barren. In some cases, divers discovered up to a foot of dead lobsters piled on the bottom of Long Island Sound. Since then, the lobster population has continued to erode or languish, with few promising signs of a rebound. The lobstermen here, as well as some marine biologists, have pointed at pesticides that were sprayed on the Connecticut and New York coasts in 1999 to kill mosquitoes during an outbreak of West Nile virus. The lobstermen, in fact, sued Cheminova Inc., makers of one of the most commonly used pesticides, saying that the company did not include enough of the product's environmental side effects on its labels. The company never admitted guilt and it settled out of court this year for $12.5 million—about 10 percent of what the plaintiffs were seeking in damages.

As it turns out, runoff from the West Nile pesticide spraying might well have had an adverse effect on lobsters in the Sound. Both mosquitoes and lobsters are arthropods—animals with external skeletons and jointed legs—and some scientists have argued that their nervous systems are similar enough that what's bad for one could very well be just as bad, if not worse, for the other.

In recent years, however, more and more climatologists and marine biologists are pointing to another, likelier culprit—global warming and rising ocean temperatures generally—as perhaps the key reason that the number of local lobsters remains historically low. The creatures, it seems, are finding their way north, to the colder waters off Massachusetts and, of course, Maine, leaving what F. Scott Fitzgerald famously called "the most domesticated body of salt water in the Western Hemisphere, the great wet barn-yard of Long Island Sound" far behind.

Whether in boom times or lean times, though, lobstering any-where has always been a tough, dangerous pursuit. In the 1960s and 1970s, when Jim Miller was a commercial lobsterman and fisher-man, the Sound was still yielding a remarkable bounty—hundreds of lobstermen plied the waters in those days—but the competition was, in a word, fierce. For a guy who was just starting out, it really was a question of sink or swim, and hoping for help from the boats that had been working the Sound for generations was hardly a win-ning strategy.

"In the beginning," Jim says of his early lobstering, "their atti-tude was just to ignore me. You know: 'This guy's an idiot. He'll kill himself somehow, so don't worry about him. He'll be gone soon. He ain't got a brain in his head. He has no idea what the hell he's doing, and those guys come and go every year.' At that time, there were a lot of part-time lobstermen out there. Schoolteachers and the like who would try to go lobstering in the summertime. They were tolerated, and then they would fail, and they would go away quite quickly."

Not all of the veteran lobstermen on the Sound in those days practiced benign neglect, however. In fact, outright thievery—the despicable crime of stealing from another lobsterman's traps—was not unknown, and Jim Miller was on the short end of that sort of behavior very early on. His solution to the problem, meanwhile, was a classic Millerian setup: direct, creative, and effective as hell.

"I definitely remember this one particular lobsterman who was pretty vicious," he says today. "I mean, my buoy lines would get cut and my gear would get tangled, and this guy would go through my traps when I wasn't there. It took a bit of time for me to figure out who the culprit was, and in the meantime I was getting beat up pretty bad. This guy was taking money out of my pocket. Well, this was still the Vietnam War era, and one of my neighbors was a Vietnam vet, young fella, maybe twenty-five years old. An unusual person. He'd been a sniper in Vietnam, and I got the sense that it affected him pretty deeply. I asked him once how he would pick out who to shoot, and he said, 'Well, you got assigned a hill, and you got assigned a village. You'd sit up on top of the hill and watch the village all day long, and after a while, you'd notice that a guy lived in a particular house, and other young guys would come in and give him gifts and stuff. Then they would leave with rifles and whatever else. So you'd figure out who was the leader of the Viet Cong in that little village, and that's the guy you'd have to get. That was the guy you'd have to pick off.'

"Anyway, this neighbor was a very, very reclusive guy. Nowadays, I guess they'd call it post-traumatic stress, but whatever it was, he was not in great shape. Still, he and I got along pretty well, and one day in the midst of this mess with this other lobsterman stealing my catch and everything, I asked him if he wanted a job. He asked me what I wanted him to do.

"I told him, 'I want you to wear your camouflage clothes like you always do, and I want you to wear those sunglasses like you always do, and we have a little sixteen-foot outboard motorboat. I want you to come down to the town dock every morning about seven o'clock, eight o'clock, and I want you to carry a shotgun over your shoulder with a strap on it, and I want you to get in your boat. And I don't want you to talk to anybody. Anybody asks you what you do, or what you're doing, you don't say anything. You don't have to say anything to anybody. You're not doing anything wrong. It's not against the law to have a shotgun and go out on a boat. You won't have any ammunition in the gun, but you'll have two ammunition belts strapped across your chest in a big X, so that everybody knows you have plenty of ammo. I want you to come down every morning with your gun and your ammo and your shades, and I want you to go out, and I want you to find a particular lobsterman— I'll point out his boat—and then just sit there in the water, about fifty feet off his stern, every single day. Wherever he goes and whatever he says, you say nothing. You don't do anything. You just sit in your boat with a shotgun across your knees, and you don't say a word. He does whatever the hell he wants to do, goes wherever the hell it is he wants to go, and no matter what he says, no matter how much he hollers and screams, you don't do anything. When he finishes lobstering after four or five hours, you just follow him back in again until he gets to his dock and he ties up, and then you head home.'

"Well," Jim says, "that created quite a stir. You know, the local lobstermen were freaked out. 'Who the hell is this guy?' 'I don't know. He's like the lobster watchman.' 'Who the hell is he working for?' Of course, nobody knew. Because the guy wouldn't speak!

"So the guy he was tailing goes to the cops and complains that some guy with a shotgun and sunglasses is following him around, not saying a word. That must be against the law, right? But the cops tell him, 'Nope, it ain't against the law.' 'Is he shooting the gun?' 'No, he's not shooting anybody. But there must be something you can do to stop this!' And the cops say, 'Why? What's he doing wrong? People go out in boats with shotguns all the time. He's a Vietnam veteran. He should be respected and treated with honor.

Leave him alone. That's what he wants to do. If you don't fool with him, he probably won't fool with you.'

"After a while, my traps weren't being messed with. My gear wasn't getting cut or tangled. I was able to go out and do my lobstering and other things, and life was good."

Other things. Did Jim consider himself a lobsterman? Or a fisherman who also pulled up lobsters?

"I was a lobsterman who had a dragger as his boat, because then I could also catch bait. The other lobstermen needed bait for their traps, but they couldn't catch it themselves. Their vessels were straight-up lobster boats, while mine was customized. So I became a supplier. With the dragnet, I would catch a fish called a sundial. It's like a flounder but no good as a food or game fish. It salts very nice, so you can preserve it easily, and it makes a good lobster bait. I would catch thirty, forty, fifty bushels of sundials and sell them to the other lobstermen. I'd get a dollar a bushel for the bait. I'd go out in the morning with my dragnet and catch, you know, bushels of bait and maybe a couple of striped bass and other good fish. The fish I sold to the fish market. The bait I sold to the lobstermen. So it turned out that once or twice a week, I would catch bait and make money with the dragnet, and the rest of the week, I would go lobstering.

"During the wintertime, we would build lobster traps in my garage. We'd go out and cut down some oak trees, bring the wood to the lumberyard, have them cut planks, and then we'd finish the wood into slats and build our own traps instead of buying them from somebody else. We weren't reinventing the trap, though. It turns out that lobsters become acclimated to a particular trap in a particular area, and if you use a trap that's dissimilar to the traps used by local lobstermen, or that's some crazy new design, you won't catch lobsters. If you're in a region where lobstermen have been using a half-round trap for years and doing very well with it, and you suddenly introduce a rectangular trap, it just doesn't work. Over the years, we had trained the lobsters, to a certain extent, to go into our traps. Every two or three days, you'd put a whole bagful of bait in the trap, and all the little lobsters would come into the trap and would eat your bait, and when the trap would begin to shake because you were pulling it up, the small lobsters—those that weren't yet legal size—would slide out an opening on the bottom of the trap. If they were babies, every time the trap would shake, they would escape, and then they would wait until the next time it came down with a full lunch for them—until one day they got too big to escape."

Along with the lobstering, Jim Miller and his eventual partner, a younger fisherman named Nick DeGenaro, began gillnetting in the Sound. A gill net is, in effect, a fence for catching fish—in Jim's case, a 600-foot-long net, perhaps ten feet tall, positioned perpendicular to the shore. As fish migrated along the shoreline, they swam smack into this invisible fence, their heads poking through and their gills catching in the net. The fish couldn't back out, and the thickness of their bodies prevented them from pushing forward. They were trapped.

"It was a very, very good method for catching striped bass and bluefish," Jim says. "At sunset, we would go out with the small boat, and we would set two or three gill nets for the nighttime and then go home and sleep for a few hours. We'd get up at first light and go out and retrieve the gill nets. They were particularly effective in early spring and late fall, during the seasonal runs of striped bass along the beaches. We'd catch a thousand pounds of bluefish and bass and whatever else was running, and we'd come in and unload them. At that time, Nick had a young wife who drove a pickup truck, and we'd load the fish in the pickup truck and take them to the South Shore of Long Island—mainly so the other fishermen on the North Shore wouldn't know that we were catching all these fish over here. It was kind of our secret that we were doing so well, until one of the South Shore gillnetters figured out that we were shipping a thousand pounds of fish down their way for sale every night. Well, they came over, and they started to fish the Sound [the North Shore] instead of the beaches and the shore on the ocean side of the island [the South Shore], and they did very well.

"It was around that time that the tension between sport fishermen and commercial fishermen around Long Island—on the Sound and out on the East End, Montauk, everyplace—was really ratcheting up. An organization called Save Our Stripers was trying to get striped bass identified as a game fish only and to outlaw commercial fishing of that species. To add to the drama of those days—and there was a lot of drama—I was elected president of the Long Island Commercial Fishermen's Association, an industry group trying to manage the litigation and legislation being introduced to basically outlaw commercial fishing in the region. Perry Duryea was a member of the New York State Assembly for years and years, and he was Speaker of the Assembly for a time. He was a resident of Montauk Point, and his family had a long relationship with commercial fishing all around the East End. He owned a dock and was a strong supporter of the commercial fishing industry at the time. Even though the sport fishermen were trying to outlaw us, he supported us. But after a while, we were kind of reduced to just instituting delaying tactics in this fight for our survival. We would offer up some sacrificial part of the commercial fishing industry that didn't impact very many people, and little by little, the sport fishermen gained a little more power until, one day, it came down that Jim Miller, fishing in Long Island Sound, was going to be the sacrificial lamb. The Assembly outlawed gill-net fishing in Long Island Sound from New York out to Shoreham, so that basically ended gillnetting for me."

Not that Jim and his fellow fishermen went down without a fight. In fact, the Millers have a copy of a 1970 issue of the old Long Island weekly *Suffolk Life*, which features a full-page photo of Jim at a hearing about gill-net fishing. In the picture, Jim—in jacket and tie—holds up a nasty-looking, ten-hooked umbrella rig commonly used by sport fishermen, showing by dramatic example the huge number of fish "sportsmen" could catch on what was then considered a single lure. His point, of course, was that sport fishermen sought to effectively outlaw commercial fishermen because, they claimed, the Jim Millers of the region were depleting the fish stocks with their aggressive and irresponsible techniques. At the same time, thousands of sport fishermen were routinely out on the waves armed with umbrella rigs and, in some cases, were catching more fish than the commercial fishermen were hauling in.

"It was hard," Jim says, and for a moment, one hears in his voice just the hint of something highly uncharacteristic of the man: something that sounds like bitterness, or the echo of bitterness. "All this political maneuvering and lobbying meant that another source of income for an awful lot of fishermen was going away. But let me give you an idea of the sort of foolishness we had to contend with out on the water while the politicians were negotiating our livelihoods away. Before a new, restrictive law went into effect, we were allowed to continue fishing, as we had been fishing all along, for the rest of the season. The sport fishermen, meanwhile, who were completely aware that most of us were on the ropes, started to believe that the laws had gone into effect right away and that basically commercial fishermen—and our gear—were fair game.

"So Nick and I come out one morning bright and early, just like we have hundreds of times before, to retrieve our gill nets, and as we're picking up one end of the net, I look across, and there's a sport fisherman on the other end of our net. It's broad daylight—this is not the middle of the night here—and he's pulling my net and harvesting my fish and putting them on his boat. He's even stealing the net itself!

"I'm looking at Nick, and I'm saying, 'This is unbelievable. I mean, he's a thief, right there, stealing from us.' We put our end of the net back in the water, and we motor over to where these other guys are still messing with our catch. 'Guys,' we say. 'What the hell's the matter with you? You're stealing our fish and our net. You can't do that.' And this one loudmouth, he doesn't even bother denying it. 'Oh, eff you!' he says. 'You ain't got no rights here anyway. You're going to be a criminal this time next year. But I'll tell you what I'll do. I'm going to cut off the net, and you can have the other half. We're taking this home with us.'

"Taking it home with them? *Taking it home with them?* I'm not really all that happy about what's happening. So I tell this guy, 'No, you're not taking it home with you. You're going to drop the net and leave.' And he says, 'Yeah, I am. I've got my knife right here. What are you gonna do about it?' And that's when I pull out my pistol, and I sort of point it at him, and I say, 'What am I gonna do about it? Well, I've got a .38 here, and everybody knows it's a bad idea to take a knife to a gun fight. We've got the gun. You've got the knife. So you'd better sit down and shut up, because I'm half crazy right now.'"

It's worth remembering right about now that Jim Miller, while always willing to stand up for himself when he felt he was in the right, was rarely the biggest guy in any situation when he eventually did stand up. At around five feet eight inches and 150 pounds tops before middle age caught up to him, he was not an especially imposing physical specimen—on paper, at least. But as an awful lot of people will tell you, Jim Miller always seemed bigger than his physical stats would indicate—particularly when he was worked up over some perceived slight or injustice, or when he felt someone was, in effect, taking money out of his pocket or food off his family's table. The old expression "It's not the size of the dog in the fight, it's the size of the fight in the dog" comes inevitably to mind.

"So there we are," he continues. "These guys are stealing our fish and our net, and now this one guy is getting all indignant because we're not going to let him get away with it. They're going to call the police, and this and that and the other. Instead, I call the harbor patrol, and I tell them, 'Hey, I've got a guy out here stealing my net and stealing my fish. I want you to come out and arrest him.' 'Well, I mean, Jim, it's a shift change right now,' they tell me. 'The new crew ain't here, and if we go out now, they'll miss the boat, and we'll have to stay overtime, and we can't do that. We're not authorized to have overtime, so we won't be out there until ten o'clock.' And I tell them, 'Well, by ten o'clock, I'll have these guys tied up to your boat. They're coming in with me right now, so you just wait there, and I'll bring them to you.'

"So we put a line on their boat, and we tow them back to the dock. They're yelling and screaming, but we tow them in, and we tie them up, right against the police boat. 'That's my net,' I tell the guy in the police boat. 'Those are my fish. Here are your two thieves. I want you to arrest them.'

"'Wow,' he says. 'That's pretty serious, Jim.' And I say, 'Well, it *better* be serious. I mean, they're thieves. I caught them red-handed with the evidence. What more do you want?' 'Well, Jim, how did you get them in here?' 'I towed them in.' He says, 'But why didn't they just go away?' 'They thought I was going to shoot them.' 'Oh, man. Jim, you can't do that. That's illegal, you know.' 'Well,' I tell him. 'I did it. Here they are. That's that.'

"And the guy looks at me like I'm nutty. 'But Jim, you could be in more trouble than they are.' Which is not what I want to hear. I was pissed before, and now I'm getting even *more* pissed. 'What are you talking about? I mean, these guys are criminals.'

"The cop is really worried now. 'These guys are going to get a fine,' he says, 'but you're going to go to jail. Jim, listen. We like you, but pulling a gun on someone? We've got to do something about that.'

"I've had it. 'Well, call the game warden,' I tell him. 'Tell the game warden to come down here. These guys have an illegal fishnet.'

I know the game warden, of course. He and I are pretty good friends. 'Tell him to come down here. Tell him it's Jim Miller, and he's got some grief here, and he needs help.'

"The game warden comes down. He's on my side. He really is. He understands that these creeps were stealing my net and my fish. That's serious business right there. But when he hears that I pulled my gun on these guys and threatened to shoot them, he's not real happy. He's not happy at all. I tell him I've got a license for the gun. I'm legal. But he's shaking his head, and he says, 'I know, I know, but you can't threaten people with a firearm.'

"Now they've got me terrified. I call my lawyer. The lawyer comes down. 'No, Jim, you're really in bad trouble here,' he tells me. I'm in trouble for catching bad guys! Everything is upside down. This is crazy. But then the game warden says to the guys I towed into the dock, 'Hey, while I'm here, I'm going to do a little boat inspection. Let me see the boat registration.' They don't have a boat registration. 'Okay,' he says. 'That's the first ticket you get, no boat registration. Let me see the fire extinguisher over there. Oh, this is bad. This fire extinguisher is expired. You get a ticket for that, too. Hey, I see you've got a gas can there, and it's leaking. You get a ticket for *that*, too.'"

It's plain to everyone there at the dock—Jim Miller, the lawyer, the warden, and especially the now-very-nervous poachers in the other boat—that the tenor of the conversation has definitely changed over the course of a very few minutes. Jim Miller isn't the guy on the hook anymore. And the warden isn't done—because he hasn't even gotten to the purloined fish yet.

"So," Jim says, "the warden has these guys shaking in their boots. And then he goes, 'This is your boat, right? And those fish in the boat are yours, right? Well, that one right there's too short. That's illegally taken, so you get a ticket for that fish—and that fish, and that fish. Looks to me like they're pretty much all illegal, so you get tickets for all of them. I'll start with a dozen, but as we unload the boat, we'll probably find more. I mean, it looks like there's, what, maybe fifty fish in there? At $100 apiece, that's an expensive day of fishing, wouldn't you say?'

"The look on their faces," Jim says, relishing the memory. "Priceless. Then the warden asks them, 'Are you going to cause any trouble for Miller over towing you in, or over anything else that happened this morning?' Of course, they say no, no, they're not going to cause any trouble. They just want to take their boat and leave. But the warden says, 'I think you better get the hell off your boat, and let Miller take it around the corner of the dock and unload his net. I'll just give you a few tickets, but you better sit here until Miller takes care of your boat properly. He'll put it over on the ramp for you to get later on, but I don't think you should go over there and watch him and harass him, because if he gets pissed off, God only knows what he's going to do to your boat. You just sit here with the police, and we'll think about it for a while.'

"So we unloaded the boat and dropped a few small fish into the gas tank and maybe dreamed up a few other miscellaneous punishments. So they got their boat back and a handful of tickets, and Nick and I didn't get arrested or thrown in jail. And that was the gist of the famous gill-net escapade."

Never let it be said, though, that Jim Miller's time as a commercial fisherman and lobsterman was all toil and strife. His son Mark, for instance, recalls that he and his brothers had so much fun working with their father (above and beyond singing songs to help pass the time on the boat) that they took to referring to Jim by a fond and telling nickname. While the phrase used by any of their peers when discussing their dads was invariably "the old man," the Miller boys found that another moniker made more sense in light of Jim Miller's approach to any job at hand: the Old Boy. He always approached any undertaking with humor and, if possible, as an opportunity to have fun. Thus, his sons saw Jim as an older version of a boy rather than as their "old man."

And in keeping with the Miller family ethos, it wasn't just the boys who played a role in the lobstering business. In fact, Jim's wife, Barbara, and their daughters—from the time they were quite young—set up a floating fish market of sorts, down at the dock to meet the *Lady Barbara* when Jim and his crew brought the boat into port. With an old-fashioned manual cash register ringing out the sales, Barbara Miller and her lively assistants—younger Barbara, Tracey, and Jenniffer—put on something of a show for potential customers and curious passersby, selling live lobsters and more from the day's catch. Part entertainment, part savvy sea-to-table business venture, the work done by Barbara and the Miller daughters right from the deck of their dockside "shop," the *Lady Lobster*, served a dual purpose: It brought in a steady, if thin, stream of always-welcome ready cash while also allowing the entire family to spend time together—even in the midst of notoriously long, grueling days.

In fact, it's in that image of the *Lady Lobster* that one again senses those signature themes of the Miller family's lives weaving themselves together—work, family, toughness, the creative approach to making a buck—along with one last familial attribute that should not get short shrift: an abiding sense of fun.

Looking back at that particular time, though, one also sees signs of real, lasting change on the horizon. Just as the sixties and seventies saw upheaval across the U.S. and across the globe, an evolution was under way, on an admittedly smaller scale, in the lives of the Millers. For example, as telling as that earlier story about the "gill-net escapade" might be—what it says about Jim Miller's refusal to back down, his sense of fair play, his creative way with retribution when he knew he'd been wronged—it also serves as an emblem of a larger, irrevocable transformation in the atmosphere and the attitude on the water during that time around Long Island.

"The handwriting was on the wall at that point," Jim says, "that being a commercial fisherman was going to get tougher and tougher, whether we were gillnetting, dragging, whatever. We became the enemy. We knew that things were going to go poorly in the fishing industry and that we were going to have to start looking around for other ways to make a living, on the water or off. And that's right about the time that I started doing consulting work for researchers in the Sound, starting with impact studies that were being done around the construction of the Shoreham Nuclear Power Plant. That's also around the same time that the oil spill that got us into the cleanup business took place, so we were migrating into these other areas already. At the same time, the relationship between me and Nick was changing, too, because he didn't want to go into the research business, and he certainly didn't think that an oil-spill-cleanup venture would ever amount to anything. We parted ways, and he wound up more focused on lobstering. He moved across the Sound to Connecticut, and he did well over there for quite a few years. But we worked well together while it lasted, and we had some good times, he and I. We really did."

•   •   •

The .38 that Jim put to such effective use when his catch and his gear was being stolen plays a role in more than a few of his stories. (Maybe that's why, if you look closely at the scale-model replica of the *Lady Barbara* prominently displayed in the lobby at the Miller Environmental headquarters in Calverton, you'll see a tiny holster and pistol hanging in the wheelhouse.) But we shouldn't leave this chapter without mentioning one other occasion when the gun played a key role in helping Jim settle a dispute. After all, as Jim points out, "when collecting money, sometimes you have to be creative. This was one of the more creative techniques I ever came up with.

"When I was in the spackling business, we were generally on a weekly pay schedule. My guys got paid on Friday. And let me tell you, you'd better not bounce a check because these are all twenty-something-year-old guys who are going to get their money, no matter what. Bouncing checks wasn't a healthy thing to do. One time, we had finished a certain number of houses, and I gave the bill to the head contractor who was supposed to be paying us. I told him I had to get a check by Friday because I had to meet my own payroll.

"'Yeah, yeah,' he tells me, 'we've got a mortgage coming from the bank, we're getting it approved, and I'll have the money for you on Monday.' All right, so I pay my guys with whatever money I had in my account, expecting him to pay me what I'm owed on Monday. Monday comes, and he's nowhere to be found. Tuesday comes, and he tells me he's getting his money on Wednesday. 'Look,' I tell him, 'last week, I paid the guys out of my own savings. This Friday, I've got to pay them again, and I've got to get your check on Thursday so I can deposit it and it clears. Otherwise, I'm in big, big trouble here.'

"Of course, Wednesday comes, and he's invisible. Now this is really, really bad. I can't pay my guys. I have to get a check, but I don't know what I'm going to do to get the money out of this guy. I go home, take off my spackling clothes, and put on a jacket and tie. And I put the .38 in the jacket pocket. I go down and sit in his office. He finally comes in. 'Hey, Jim, how are you? You're all dressed up.'

"I say, 'Yeah, I'm dressed up. I'm going to die today.' He looks at me like I'm crazy. 'Huh? What're you talking about?' 'Yeah, I'm going to commit suicide.' Now he's all upset. 'Aw, Jim, that's a dumb thing to do. You don't have to commit suicide, that's terrible. Why would you kill yourself?' So I tell him, 'It doesn't make any difference if I commit suicide or go out there on Friday without any money for my guys, because they're going to kill me anyway. I either let them kill me, or I do it myself. Doesn't make any difference.'

"Now he's all worked up. 'Jim, Jim, it's terrible that you even have those kinds of thoughts.' I agree with him. It's terrible. But then I tell him, 'You know, there's one other thing. Before I commit suicide, I can kill you. Because you're the reason that I'm here. But you can save *both* of our lives now, by paying me what you owe me.'

"He's nervous. He's not happy. 'I have to leave to get your money,' he says. And I tell him, 'Uh-uh, you ain't leavin', fella. You figure out how to get the money here. That's how it's going to be. Just start figuring it out.' And you know what? He does just that. He figures it out. I get paid, and he saves both of our lives."

The memory of that particular drama, and of those days in general, brings a smile to Jim's face.

"We were young and wild and stupid," he says. "But he and I did business together for years after that. And he always paid me on time."

CHAPTER 16

Three Aces: The Formidable Miller Daughters

The three daughters in the Miller family—Barbara, Tracey, and Jenniffer (more on that spelling in a bit)—are, in some ways, more distinct from one another than the Miller boys are. That is not to say that Jim Jr., Glen, and Mark are simple men, or mere clones of one another, or carbon copies of their dad. On the contrary, each one of the Miller sons is, literally and figuratively, his own man. But as distinct as the sons' personalities might be, and as successful as they have been in so many of their own business and personal ventures, the shape and the direction of the daughters' lives suggest that, on the female side of the ledger, there might be an even deeper individualistic impulse and, perhaps, a broader, more varied scope of pursuits.

In short, Jim and Barbara Miller's daughters are, in some ways at least, more complicated creatures than their brothers are—a family dynamic, by the way, that makes the Millers much like every other family on the planet. After all, as the lyrics of the classic calypso tune (covered by acts as varied as Harry Belafonte, Rosanne Cash, and the Grateful Dead) long ago pointed out:

> *Let us put men and women together,*
> *See which one is smarter.*
> *Some say men, but I say no,*
> *Women run the men like a puppet show*

Be that as it may, and as singular as each daughter might be, the stories and memories that they relate about their own childhoods—individually and collectively—paint a broadly uniform picture of three women shaped to a remarkable degree by their interactions, as children and as adults, with their parents, Jim and Barbara.

· · ·

Barbara, the oldest daughter, is a practicing pediatrician (her husband is an internist) in a large multispecialty practice in Rhode Island. "I love my work," she says. "I have fun every day. I'm lucky to be doing what I do." The medical school gene appears to have been strong enough to make itself felt in the next generation as well: Barbara's son, the couple's only child, is pre-med at Bowdoin—majoring in English literature, minoring in Asian studies—and he spent the fall 2015 semester in Sri Lanka, learning the language and studying folk medicine while doing an independent research project.

"He's a fairly impressive fellow," Barbara says. "A lovely guy."

Of her own youth, Barbara recounts that, for years, she was "the only girl among boys." On the other hand, the self-awareness that she cultivated from a tender age—perhaps because for years she was the only daughter—pointed her down a path toward independence.

After graduating from high school, Barbara went to both nursing school—where she was valedictorian—and medical school at Stony Brook, just down the road from where she grew up. And how did she settle on a career in medicine? Were there women—teachers? fellow students?—whom she could look to as role models, doing the sort of work she wanted to do?

"Among the people I knew? Not really," she says. "But now that you mention it—have you heard the story of the killing of the pig?"

Wait. *What?*

"We had a pig when I was growing up, and let me tell you, they are not nice. But we had this pig in the backyard, and my brothers would play 'chicken' with the pig. Which is to say, they would jump down into the pig's pen, and the pig would charge them, and they'd jump out. Anyway, it came time to slaughter the pig, for pork. We were all kind of excited about this, you know? We're going to kill the pig, and we're going to *eat* the pig.

"All four kids, my three brothers and I, we go into the backyard, and we're going to kill the pig. We don't know what the hell is going to happen. My father is there, and he has an ax. Apparently, his plan is to whack this pig with the flat end of the ax, and that is going to somehow stun or knock out the pig, or do something to the pig, so that he can then *kill* the pig.

"Okay. So we're all there, he hauls off, and he whacks this pig— who just screams like you've never heard something scream in your life. It is the most horrifying sound you can possibly imagine. Four little kids then also start screaming, and they run away. This whole scenario is suddenly horrifying. Oh, it's a freaking nightmare! But at some point, eventually, the pig gets killed. Now there's this whole other situation, which is that we need to now butcher the pig— which turns out to be a very involved process.

"The pig, after all, is enormous. You pull it up in the air with a block and tackle, and when it's hanging there, you have to gut it, and you take out all the innards. You also have to boil the body so that you can scrape the hair off the skin. Anyway, my father cuts open this pig, and there are its guts, including the heart. I don't know how old I am—maybe seven? I was slightly weird and was fascinated by the guts. In particular, I was fascinated by the heart. I'm looking at it, and I think it's amazing.

"Now, at that point in my life, I had decided that I wanted to make a career doing whatever was the hardest thing in the world that a person could do. I think this was in the days of Dr. Denton Cooley, a heart surgeon who was really famous at the time for performing the first implantation of a totally artificial heart in a human. He was always in the news, and he was the smartest person I could think of. I wanted to be a heart surgeon. And here, right in front of me, was this heart, and I wanted to *see* that heart. I wanted to hold it in my hands. Study it. Examine it. I wanted to get a sense of how it worked. A pig's heart, by the way, is remarkably similar to a human heart. I didn't know that at the time, but it's a pretty weird coincidence.

"Anyway, to my father's credit, he took the pig's heart, and he showed it to me, and then—and this was the really amazing thing— we took the garden hose, stuck it into the heart, and turned on the water to see how blood flows through the heart. And you know, that was a very, very powerful moment for me. That was a very powerful thing. My dad didn't blow me off. He was right there with me. The fact that I was interested in this was something that he obviously responded to. It was intense. And I think it was especially intense because I knew, even then, that there was some recognition that the interest that I had in this heart was valid. It was a worthy interest. And that mattered to me. His acknowledgment—his recognition that what I was interested in *mattered*—was extremely important. Especially to a young child. And I remember it still."

(In fact, according to Mark, their dad had Barbara herself reach in and pull out the animal's organs. "I was standing behind her," he says, "and she was reaching in, pulling out the intestines, asking Dad questions about what went where and what everything's function was. You know, 'That's a kidney, and there's another one over here. It's a filter.' I remember him doing that thing with the water hose and the heart, too. But when he took out the bladder, washed it off, blew it up, and tied the ends off, like a balloon—man, that was memorable.")

Kidneys. Lungs. Intestines. A bladder blown up like a balloon. Water coursing like clear blood through a tough, humanlike heart. Can Barbara point to an event like that—in fact, can she point to *that* event itself, which took place in the backyard of her family home—as the moment when her road to becoming a physician was perhaps first laid out for her, in all its winding complexity?

"I think that's fair," she says, after a considerable pause. "Actually, I do think that's fair. Yes."

And then, in the mysterious way that memories often spark seemingly unrelated recollections, Barbara segues into another story about her father—another tale that, at its core, hints at how moments that appear insignificant or fleeting can, years after the fact, bind families together in large and small ways.

"One of the methods by which my dad made extra money when we were growing up was plowing snow," she says. "He had a truck with what—to me, at the time—was an absolutely huge plow on the front. And as a child, as a very young kid, I recall that every once in a while, my dad would put this hand-painted sign on the front window of the house. THINK SNOW, it said, with a big snowflake on it. We would put it right there on the front of the house, facing the street—and the next day, it would snow! Every single time. I thought that was just magical. I thought it was the most amazing, miraculous, powerful thing in the world that this sign would go up, and then it would snow. And of course, being a kid, I couldn't for the life of me figure out why we didn't put that sign up every day, so that there would always be snow. I just couldn't understand it.

"Needless to say, I was unaware of the science of forecasting at that point in my life. But magic sign or no magic sign, my father did not like to go snowplowing by himself, because it was boring, so he would occasionally take some of us with him. I remember going with him in the truck. It was always sleepy time, and you'd get in there, in the big, warm cab, and he'd be plowing the snow. And to make it more interesting, he would try to plow the snow into people's trash cans. Oh, it was very exciting! And he would accompany this with a kind of play-by-play commentary while driving down the road. He'd see the trash can, he'd aim for the trash can, and when he *hit* the trash can with that huge spray of snow, the trash can would go flying, and everyone would be happy."

• • •

A mom of two girls ("my magnificent, beautiful women") and wife to a prominent East End public official—and former employee at Miller Environmental—Vincent Orlando, Tracey is by pretty much everyone's estimation the Miller child who, if such a contest were held, would clearly be voted "least likely to stop moving."

Whether it's modernizing and expanding the East End Seaport Museum in Greenport, where she serves as a trustee; raising money for the American Legion; helping to organize the annual tribute ceremony at the 9/11 memorial in Southold (the center of which is a massive sculpture made up, in part, of beams from the World Trade Center and topped by a sculpture of an osprey, designed by Roberto Bessin); or any number of other causes—Tracey is a whirlwind.

(Tracey is hardly alone among the Millers in, as the saying goes, "giving back." The entire family, it seems, somehow finds time to contribute time, energy, and, frequently, money to worthy causes and projects close to their hearts. Glen, for example, is deeply involved with the Noble Maritime Collection on Staten Island, and, after Hurricane Sandy damaged the Robbins Reef Light in Upper New York Bay, he provided launch services for work crews repairing the 130-year-old "bug light." Mark and his wife, Içim, serve on the advisory board of the award-winning, not-for-profit East End Arts organization, where Mark is a board member and secretary/treasurer for the Shelter Island–based Perlman Music Program—founded by Toby Perlman, wife of the great violinist Itzhak Perlman—and is a trustee of his alma mater, the University of Charleston. And Jim Sr. has been honored by the North Fork Environmental Council for the fish passage he and a friend designed and built in Riverhead. Examples of the Miller family's generosity and community involvement are legion and speak volumes about the standard that Jim and Barbara set for their kids, their grandkids, and future generations.)

Like so many of the Millers, Tracey likes telling a good story. Sometimes, those stories fall under what one might call the "I love my crazy family" category. Like the time her dad beat the hell out of her brother, thinking he was a burglar. That this sort of stranger-than-fiction occurrence was not especially unusual in the Miller household says something about the 24/7, anything-can-happen atmosphere that Jim, Barbara, and the kids enjoyed—or endured—back in the day.

"I have sleep issues," Tracey says. "My youngest daughter seems to have inherited that from me. I never slept well when I was a kid, and I still don't. I get maybe four hours a night. When we were growing up, it was understood that when all else failed, if any of us couldn't fall asleep or had nightmares or whatever, Mom and Dad's door was open. You would lie down on the floor—on Mom's side of the bed—and you could stay there and try to fall asleep.

"On one particular night, I'm lying there on the floor in my parents' room, fearful about something—I can't remember what—for some little-girl reason. And I swear to God, in comes this . . . *figure*. It's dark, so I can just see this creepy thing coming toward me. It looks like it's wearing a hood or a cowl or something, and I am petrified. I'm lying there, telling myself, 'One more step, and I'm going to scream. I don't know what's going on here. I'm gonna scream. I'm gonna scream!'

"Of course, this hooded figure takes that fatal step—and steps right on *me*. I let out a scream. My dad—who really, really needs his sleep—jumps out of bed. He's not even fully awake, and he's throwing punches, beating the crap out of whatever or whoever it is that just stepped on me. By now my mom is screaming, I'm still screaming. It's chaos. I jump in the bed with my mom. And that's when I hear a familiar voice shouting, 'It's me! It's me!' The hooded figure is Glen. He has trouble sleeping, too, and for some reason, he was walking around in the middle of the night with a blanket over his head. But my father's still pounding away and yelling, 'I don't care! I don't care!' and he keeps punching Glen in the face. Mark rushes in with a tennis racket in his hand. Barbara is there. Jenniffer is there, crying. Everybody is awake, wondering who this person is that we're all going to go kill. Then the lights go on, and everyone can see that it's just Glen. And he's like, 'I *told* you it was me!'

"Yup," Tracey says. "Just another night in the Miller house."

One other particular story of Tracey's, though, illustrates just how far from that small, crowded house all of the Millers—and especially Jim—traveled in their public and private lives over the years. It's a strange tale that, with a few changes in the particulars, might not seem out of place in a Kafka parable.

"My dad was an urban legend before the phrase 'urban legend' was coined," Tracey says, "because there were moments we experienced that, we understand, were not quite believable. But this really happened. It was when my mom and dad lived in Rocky Point, before they moved to the house they live in now, the one not far from Mark's place. The cleanup business was doing well, and Dad was more prominent in the community than ever. Mom and Dad lived on the bluff, overlooking the water, and there was a little tram line, of sorts, that ran down to the beach. One evening, my dad and I were sitting there, watching the sunset. At the time, I had moved back home for a while and was living with my folks. On a regular basis, we would watch the sunset from the deck of the house. But on this particular night, it was just so beautiful that we mixed it up a bit and said, 'Let's go sit on the tram,' which we didn't often do. We went out there and were just sitting in that cable car, watching the sunset, talking about nothing.

"And out of the blue, this gentleman comes walking down the path. There's a walkway from the road to the tram, and it's definitely off the beaten path, so if somebody's there, it's unusual if we don't know him. And we definitely do not know this guy. Neither of us have ever seen him before. But we exchange pleasantries: 'How are you doing?' 'Beautiful night, isn't it?' 'Oh, yes, absolutely.' And we're all sharing the silence a little bit. But it's awkward, too. I mean, we're like, *Who* is *this guy?*

"And then it gets really weird. He tells us, 'I know the guy who lives next door.' Being polite, we say, 'Oh, really?' And he says, 'Yeah, his name is Jim Miller. Oh, he's a great guy. I worked on a lot of jobs with him.'"

At this point in the telling, Tracey has a look on her face that's a cross between amusement and bewilderment.

"I'm sitting there staring at my dad, and my eyes are asking him, 'Are you not going to say howdy-ho to this character?' But he just gives me that official Dad nod that we've all come to know, which means, 'Be still, girl, be still.'

"And the guy keeps talking about my dad like they were the best of pals way back when. 'Oh,' he says, 'Miller was a smart son of a bitch.' He tells us that he and my dad worked together on this job, and on that job, *yadda yadda*. Finally: 'I even helped him build his house.'

"My dad and I are just sort of going along for the ride. Sort of stunned, but fascinated, too. 'Really?' we ask him. 'You helped him build his house?'

"'Oh, yeah,' the guy says, 'it was just a little cottage at one time, and it was my idea to build the house back a bit, and make it bigger. I kind of redesigned the whole thing. Jim might not remember it that way, but yes, definitely, I was fundamentally responsible for that house. Isn't it something?'

"What are we supposed to say? We're just nodding at the guy. 'Mmm-hmm. Yeah, it's something, all right.' And then one of us—I can't remember which one—asks him, 'So-o-o, how did you and Jim meet anyway?'

"'He thought I was so smart,' the guy says, 'when we worked together on this one job, that he asked me to come work with him. I was flattered, but I had to tell him no, thanks, that I was already a huge success on my own. I think Jim was disappointed about that. But I gave him some ideas—sort of pointed him toward some good projects—and he took off with them, and he's had some success in his life. He should really be grateful to me. But you know, that's what friends are for. Right?'"

Tracey pauses again to let the acute weirdness of the story sink in. Then she continues.

"By now, the sunset has gotten even prettier. We're there, all three of us—the best of friends, right?—watching the water. I'm looking at my dad, and my dad's looking at the guy, who is standing there looking out at the horizon. Finally, the guy sort of rouses himself and he says, 'Well, I'm going to get going. By the way, I didn't get your name.' He sticks out his hand to my dad, and pleasant as can be, my dad says, 'Jim. Jim Miller.'

"The guy's face just *melts*. He drops his hand, drops his head, mutters, 'I'm sorry,' and he turns and walks away. As quickly as he appeared, he's gone. Poof!

"We had no idea who this guy was. We never saw him in our neighborhood. He wasn't a friend, or a friend of a friend, but he claimed that he was responsible for Jim Miller's success. He was extremely animated, and if you didn't know any better, you might be convinced that what he was saying was completely true. But refusing the offer to work with my dad? Helping to design the house? Why would anyone claim that? It's a bizarre, bizarre world."

For Tracey, as odd as that encounter was, there's a lesson buried in it that's both quite simple and best not forgotten.

"I always told my kids when they were growing up that if they were ever thinking of doing something that might be questionable, they should really think twice or three times about it. Out here, no one who's part of this family is invisible. That's just the way it is."

· · ·

Jenniffer Wheeler, née Miller, might be a grown woman with a family (a husband, a son, and a daughter), a career (she's a teacher; her husband's a school administrator), and accomplishments and pursuits of her own, but as in virtually any family with more than one kid, *once the baby, always the baby*. And even though the age differences among the three Miller sons and the three Miller daughters is not especially dramatic—all six were born inside a span of ten years—Jenniffer's experience of life in the Miller household differs starkly from that of all the other kids. As Jenniffer herself puts it, in some quite elemental ways, she "did not grow up in the same family" as the one her brothers and sisters knew when they were young.

To take perhaps the most obvious and outwardly evident example, in the course of Jenniffer's childhood—from her earliest years through her later teens—the family's financial situation underwent a striking change. In short, the Millers propelled themselves from an environment where hard, hard work and ingenuity were no guarantee against constant money worries to, as Jenniffer puts it, "something quite different." In contemporary economic terms, the Millers left the ranks of the "working poor" (a phrase and classification, by the way, that encompasses something like ten million

Americans today, across every conceivable racial, ethnic, religious, and gender divide) and transitioned to the middle class and beyond with dizzying speed.

In its purest form, the story of upward mobility is part of America's collective national mythology: The fact that such a myth has its basis in verifiable truth hardly makes it less astonishing. In the Millers' case, though, their story has the feel of the American Dream on overdrive. Many families have a hard time adjusting from hardscrabble times to financial security and even significant wealth when the change occurs over the course of generations. That the Millers managed to hang on and not lose their way as they prospered over the course of just a few short decades speaks volumes not only about how close-knit they are as a family but also about how down-to-earth and unpretentious both Jim and Barbara have remained, even in the face of such great fortune.

But it was not only in pure economic terms that Jenniffer's life differed from her siblings'. After all, as the baby of the family, she was the last child left at home after the other five had moved on—and that meant experiencing the day-to-day reality of the household through a new and unique lens. "By the time I was in high school," Jenniffer says, "I was pretty much an only child, in the sense that I was the only one around. This was a complete contrast to the house I knew as a young child, and the house my brothers and sisters knew. That house was always filled with people—with our own family and uncles and aunts and my dad's employees and our friends and, quite often, complete strangers. Later on, when my siblings were gone and the place emptied out, I could be an observer of sorts."

Perhaps it's that experience—spending time in a household that had grown relatively quiet after years of controlled chaos—that instilled a kind of clear-eyed thoughtfulness in Jenniffer. Or maybe it's her own abiding religious faith, which she first embraced in her teenage years and shares with her equally devout mom. But whatever the source of that observant quality, one gets the sense that, in large part, it's at the root of Jenniffer's quietly adamant assertion that one has to "look the past in the eye honestly, not romanticize it—not think of it as, 'Oh, the good old days, when we were always struggling.'"

For instance, of her dad she recalls that "he was never flashy. In fact, he was pretty suspicious of people who were. He never, *ever* wore designer clothes. If he wasn't working (which he was, almost all the time), he was at home with us, reading the newspaper or watching the news. His drive for success was never about materialism. It was about winning—and, as importantly, about not failing—and money was the scorecard. His life revolved around his work and his family, and the two were woven so tightly together, there was absolutely no division between them."

In the midst of all these memories, meanwhile, the reality of the Millers' modest means is ever-present.

"During dinners at home," Jenniffer says, "Dad would engage us in deep conversations, usually around politics, where each one of us was expected to have an opinion and reasons behind it. Being the youngest, I was included in conversations on topics as far-reaching as abortion, taxes, and the death penalty by the time I was seven or eight years old. In the very early years, these discussions were held at the dining room table—which was really an old door laid on its side. It was big enough for all of us to sit around, and it was cheap."

Then there's the story of a particular red coat Jenniffer had when she was younger and how, in some ways, it serves as an emblem of so much about where the Millers came from.

"In the past, I've described growing up in my family as sort of like the Beverly Hillbillies meet Long Island. We were blue collar, just a hardworking family. To some extent, I think my dad still is. You can hear it in his pride in being 'just a poor fisherman scratching out a living'—a favorite saying of his. As success came, transitions

NOTHING BAD EVER HAPPENS

came with it, but the transitions were usually messy. I remember having this beautiful red winter dress coat. It was a nicer coat than what any of my friends had. At the same time, I didn't have any gloves or any socks without holes. So I'd go to school wearing this wonderful, fancy red coat, but for gloves, I was wearing mismatched socks with holes in them. That's how it was in those years. We were coming out from this struggling place into a place that we really didn't understand yet. But I was never self-conscious about any of it. My dad was so confident, so focused, that there just wasn't any room for insecurity."

What Jenniffer emphasizes again and again in the telling is the need to look at the *entirety* of her parents' lives—including parts of the story that might be unsavory, or even embarrassing. Otherwise, she says, "you can't understand how much they overcame. My mom and dad were a team. A dysfunctional team, maybe, but a team nevertheless. And it's not really possible to appreciate how much success they've created for themselves and for their whole family until you look honestly at where they started. At heart, my parents were undereducated, ill-prepared teenagers who fell in love and got married with no real jobs and no real plans. By the time they were twenty-nine, thirty years old, they had six kids. It was a recipe for disaster. And some of what we lived through as kids was definitely messy. I am sure, for example, that our house did not smell very sweet when I was growing up. It had to smell pretty bad. There were eight of us in a very small house. We had dogs running around that were never, ever bathed. My dad was a chain-smoker. He doesn't smoke now, but he did then. We had workers in greasy clothes in and out of the house all the time. And honestly, my mom wasn't a great housekeeper. But I want to emphasize this: When you look at where she came from, the abuse and violence she had to deal with when she was a child herself, there is no reason on earth why my mother would end up being such a loving person. She *chose* to be a loving person. We knew we were loved when we were young, and that is not a small thing. Those two realities—the drive of my dad, and knowing that our mom really loved us—that changed everything, for all of us."

And the unusual spelling of her name?

"There are two versions of how that came about," she says. "My mom has always said that when I was born, it was in the midst of this huge rush of babies coming into the world, nine months after some electrical grid blackout that I guess kept folks inside in the dark for a few days with nothing else to do. For some reason, a lot of these babies were being named Jennifer, and she wanted to make sure she had the right baby at the hospital, so she spelled my name with an extra *f*, so I'd stand out."

Then Jenniffer, with the extra *f*, laughs fondly and says, "I've always suspected that she just spelled my name wrong, and no one bothered to correct it."

CHAPTER 17

Terryville Road: A Brief History of Controlled Chaos

In all the stories about the early years of Jim and Barbara's family life—the long, long working hours, the six kids, the stress, all of it—the expression "the house on Terryville Road" comes up again and again. It's clear that for the Miller clan and those close to them, the phrase not only describes the location of the home where they lived but is also a kind of family shorthand for the era when they lived there—and the busy, sometimes frantic, never dull atmosphere that defined the place.

Walking farm animals around the interior of the family home in a kind of one-time-only, meet-and-greet ritual whenever a new critter came on the scene? Check. An endless stream of visitors, friends, and coworkers at all hours of the day and night? Check. The incessant sound of tools, vehicles, and machinery—hammers, saws, drills, trucks, backhoes—filling the air in all seasons? Check.

No wonder, then, that some of the Miller kids' friends routinely found their way to the house on Terryville Road, seeing it as a place where, at the very least, they were likely to find some sort of activity under way to help them pass the time—or, failing that, a cup of hot soup.

"Mark and I were in a couple of classes together when we were kids, really early on, like in elementary school," recalls Ken Murphy, who grew up in the same Port Jefferson Station neighborhood and now, decades later, works in the financial district in Manhattan, manages many of the family's investments, and oversees Jim's estate planning. "But we weren't running around together. Not at first. From what I can remember, we might have been fighting each other all the time, beating each other up. But we gradually became good friends. So I was at the Terryville Road house all the time. Our family lived around the corner from the Millers. Three brothers in my family, too, and three sisters. My dad was a Korean War vet, blind, and we had just his government pension, you know? Anyway, back then, Terryville Road was where all of the last old farms in Terryville were. And blue collar, for sure. So the Millers and the Murphys, we knew each other; our sisters were in the same dance classes—that sort of thing.

"But one of the things that struck me when I was a kid—besides the gun cabinet that greeted you when you walked in the front door and the big pot of really amazing pea soup that was always, always there on the stove for anyone who wanted some—was how there were routinely piles of cash on the dining room table. I don't know if it was for payroll or what, but it might have been several thousand dollars out there in the open. I never saw that much money in my life. I said to Mark's mom, 'You've got people running around this house all day and night—kids, strangers. Aren't you concerned about that?' And she said, 'Kenny, if somebody needs to take it, they're welcome to it, because it means they need it more than us.'

"I think what she meant, really, was that she and her family were not going to stop being who they were, and living the way they wanted to live, out of fear."

Jim Miller, meanwhile, recalls another scene involving piles of cash at the Terryville Road house that, in its own way, reflects another aspect of so many of the Millers' adventures that sometimes gets lost amid all the tales of economic woe and familial strife.

"One of the funniest things I remember happening," Jim says, "was the time we had a whole bunch of local kids working for us, cleaning up a local oil spill, and we had a cash payroll. Everyone had to come to the house to get paid, and we hired a guard to stand by the front door, to make it look official. Just like an old-school payroll office on payday. We also cut the screen door in half, so all these guys would come up to the door and stand there, and we'd ask, 'What's your name?'—even when we knew most of them already anyway—and they'd say, 'I'm Woods,' or, 'I'm Jones,' and we'd pass an envelope out the open top half of the door with their pay inside, in cash. It felt like everybody in town had worked for us, and everybody in town had money in their pocket. That was a good time."

Jenniffer, as the youngest in the family, had a slightly different responsibility during the years when the Miller place served as something of a cross between a bus terminal, a farm, a boarding house, a heavy-machinery depot, and a sanctuary for insomniacs.

"It wasn't just the business side of things that kept the energy in the house so high and kept people coming in and out at all hours," Jenniffer says. "It was also because of all the kids who were there all the time. Ours was that house—and every neighborhood has one—where kids seemed to congregate. On Saturday mornings, my job was to go around and count how many people were in the house. It would be my sisters, my brothers, friends, strangers—all these folks milling around, many of them working on some project or other—and it was like, 'Okay, how many people do we have to feed this morning?'"

With so much controlled chaos running through the Miller place, like a constant, low-voltage electrical current, there were certainly times when the younger kids were underfoot rather than serving as helping hands. In Jenniffer's case, for example, that meant making her way to someplace safe for a few hours.

"The secretaries—when my dad could finally afford secretaries— were often my babysitters. If my parents were busy, okay, I'd go sit in the office, taking naps at the feet of the secretaries, under their desks, so they could keep their eye on me—but nobody else knew I was there. And the backyard was filled with all sorts of things that our dad acquired—not with any specific purpose in mind but with the idea that sometime, down the road, these things would come in handy on some job or another. And of course they very often did. I remember my childhood fort in our backyard was the wheelhouse from a World War II landing craft. These crazy things became our toys."

Finally, no discussion of the multipurpose nature of the Miller home would be complete without also citing its role—on top of all its other 24/7 functions for the neighborhood kids, employees, and the family itself—as a kind of unofficial safe house for troubled kids.

"I took in troubled girls," Barbara Miller says, the way someone else might mention that she took up needlepoint or fruit canning. There's no hint of do-gooder pride in her tone. Nor is there any suggestion of the congenital idealist's self-righteous swagger. Instead, one hears pragmatism and empathy, and maybe a hint of doggedness, as if she is still making the case for her actions all these years later. "Jimmy was not thrilled when I used to do that," Barbara says. "He really wasn't thrilled at all. I mean, when I say 'troubled girls,' I mean these were really, really troubled girls. Runaways, girls in bad situations at home—really tough, troubled kids. But it was something I could do because I understood it. I knew what they were going through because of my own struggles when I was younger. Jimmy didn't like it, but I wanted to try to help them if I could."

"Our house was a 7-Eleven," Tracey says, a bit more bluntly. "We never knew who was going to show up, or when, or what their problem was going to be. But there was always, always a pot of coffee on. Not just for my dad, who—once the oil-cleanup business was up and running—was getting calls in the middle of the night, but for my mom and whoever else might be up at some ungodly hour, dealing with a teenager who needed a place to crash. We had kids sleeping under beds, on couches—wherever they could find room. One girl slept in my closet—for two weeks! She had a little bed made up in there with blankets, pillows. Fourteen days she lived in the closet. She had a little shelf for her things. It was like that Seinfeld episode when George is working at Yankee Stadium and he decides to sleep under his desk during the day. This girl had her own tiny little room. But for a few weeks, she was safe. She was safe."

Jim Miller's parents, Harry and Cecilia Miller. "He wasn't a very big guy," Jim says of his dad, "but he was tough." His mother, Jim says, "was much more private. Her social life, generally, took place on Friday nights."

Detail from a 1940 census report, with information about Harry and Cecilia Miller's household at Grand Avenue in North Merrick, Long Island.

SUMMARY OF INFORMATION FROM 1940 CENSUS REPORT

Home owned and valued at $2,500

Head of Household: Harry Miller, age 44
Place of Birth: Riga, Latvia
Education: 9th Grade
Occupation: Machinist
Annual Income: $2,184
Employer: Brooklyn Navy Yard

Other occupants:

NAME	RELATIONSHIP	AGE	PLACE OF BIRTH
Cecilia	wife	40	New York, NY
June Miller	daughter, student, 7th grade	14	Brooklyn, NY
Richard Miller	son, student, 4th grade	10	Brooklyn, NY
Thomas Miller	son, student, 2nd grade	7	Brooklyn, NY
James Miller	son, student, 1st grade	5	Nassau, NY
Marguerite Miller	daughter	1	Nassau, NY

Line	Location	Household Data			Name	Relation	Personal Description					Education			Place of Birth		
1	COURT ST.				FREW IRENE	WIFE	F	W	34	M					Brooklyn		Same House
2					— ROBERT	SON	M	W	10	—					Nassau		
3					— DIAN	DAUGHTER	F	W	8	—					Nassau		
4					— JANET	DAUGHTER	F	W	2	—					Nassau		Same House
5	WASHINGTON ST.	R	40		EASTTY FREDERICK	HEAD	M	W	41	M					Brooklyn		Suffolk
6					— CAROL	WIFE	F	W	40	M					New Rochelle		Suffolk
7					— FREDERICK Jr.	SON	M	W	10	—					New Rochelle		Suffolk
8					— JOHN	SON	M	W	8	—					New Rochelle		Suffolk
9		R	35		DIETZEL HARRY	HEAD	M	W	39	M				90	Brook		
10					— RUBY	WIFE	F	W	39	M				90	Providence		
11					— REGINALD	SON	M	W	15	—					New York		
12					— NORMAN	SON	M	W	11	—					New York		
13	N. MERRICK	O	2500		MILLER HARRY	HEAD	M	W	44	M					Righlatija		Same House
14					— CECILIA	WIFE	F	W	40	M				90	New York		
15					— JUNE	DAUGHTER	F	W	14	—					Brooklyn		
16					— RICHARD	SON	M	W	10	—					Brooklyn		
17					— THOMAS	SON	M	W	7	—					Brooklyn		
18					— JAMES	SON	M	W	5	—					Nassau		
19					— MARGUERITE	DAUGHTER	F	W	1	—					Nassau		
20		O	1500		SWANSON ROBERT	HEAD	M	W	53	M				90	Chicago		
21					— BEATRICE	WIFE	F	W	43	M				90	Freeport		
22					— ANN	DAUGHTER	F	W	14	—					New York		
23		O	2600		GREBE HENRY	HEAD	M	W	52	M				90	New York		
24					— HETTIE	WIFE	F	W	65					90	Penny.		
25	GRAND AVE.	O	1800		CALCAGNINO ALFRED Jr	HEAD	M	W	30	M				90	Belmore		
26					— DOROTHY	WIFE	F	W	25	M				90	St. Albins		
27		O	2800		WORTbing JOHN	HEAD	M	W	49	M				90	Vienna		Same
28					— HELENE	WIFE	F	W	43	M				90	Dortmund		
29					— ROBERT	SON	M	W	20	S					New York Cty		
30					— JURGEN	SON	M	W	15	S					Brooklyn		
31					KNEISEL CAROLINE	MOTHER in law	F	W	67	WD				90	Oberhausen Germany		Same
32		R	20		KING HERBERT	HEAD	M	W	29	M					Brooklyn		
33					— AGNES	WIFE	F	W	21	M					Nassau		
34					— JUDITH	DAUGHTER	F	W							Nassau		
35		O	2350		FRASER GEORGE	HEAD	M	W	77	WD				90	Scotland		
36					— ELIZABETH	DAUGHTER	F	W	32	S				90	Brooklyn		
37		O	500		VERITY GRACE	HEAD	F	W	63	M				90	Nassau		
38		O	1800		VERITY GEORGE	HEAD	M	W	33	M				90	Nassau		
39					— ANNA	WIFE	F	W	25	M				90	New York		
40					— DOROThy	DAUG	F	W	12	—					Nassau		

Line	Name	Place of Birth of Father and Mother		Mother Tongue for Native Language		Veterans	Social Security	
		Father	Mother	Code				
14	MILLER CECILIA	NEW YORK	NEW YORK		ENGLISH			
29	WORThing ROBERT	VIENNA	DORTMUND	15	GERMAN			

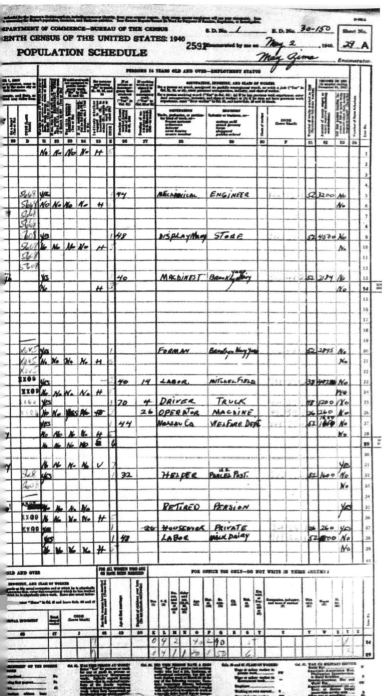

The full census page that includes the Miller family.

The overloaded charter boat Pelican *leaves Montauk, Sept. 1, 1951. A few miles offshore, she was swamped by rogue waves. Forty-five passengers and crew drowned in the worst fishing disaster in the history of Long Island's East End. (Photo by Bill Morris,* Outdoor Life.*)*

The Pelican *after being towed back to Montauk. Seventeen-year-old Jim Miller, who spent hours helping to recover bodies from the half-submerged boat, can be seen on the stern, wearing a white cap. (Photos above and facing page by Yale Joel,* The LIFE *Picture Collection/Getty Images.)*

Sergeant Tom Innes, a state trooper and diver who recovered bodies from the Pelican, *takes a breather from the grim work.*

A father, supported by friends, weeps after identifying the body of his son, a victim of the Pelican *disaster.*

Jim and Barbara Miller on their wedding day, at Jim's parents' house in North Merrick, August 12, 1955.

Jim's older brother and best man, Rich, and Barbara's maid of honor, Faye Hummer, raise their glasses in a toast to the newlyweds.

Jim and Barbara Miller on their wedding day. The car Jim is driving would reappear in Jim and Barbara's lives, in another incarnation, five decades later, as a fiftieth wedding anniversary gift from their children.

Young parents Jim and Barbara Miller with Jim Jr., 1957.

Jim building a snowman in the yard of the house on Joline Road.

Barbara Miller with one of the family dogs outside the Joline Road house.

Jim's Plymouth convertible parked outside the Miller's house on Joline Road.

*Jim and Barbara with five of their (eventually) six kids. With Jim:
Barbara, Glen, Tracey, Mark, and Jim Jr.; with Barbara: Mark,
Glen, Barbara, Jim Jr., and Tracey in the foreground.*

A scale model of the Lady Barbara. A tiny pistol and a holster hang in the model's wheelhouse—reminders of the good/bad old days when Jim Miller was at the boat's helm and often carried a .38 on his hip.

In the late 1970s Miller Environmental moved to Hagerman and purchased South Bay Boatworks on the Patchogue River—Jim's first million-dollar purchase.

The Miller boys (Mark, third from left; Glen, second from right; Jimmy, far right) and friends pose with machetes, trash cans, and other tools of the trade while working the Mount Sinai Harbor oil spill in the 1970s.

The Diane Janet *aground off of Fire Island, 1966. The salvage of this boat was a turning point in Jim Miller's career, and his life.*

The Diane Janet, *now legally Jim's salvage, after Jim and others cut into the hull* *in order to remove equipment, including a valuable, sought-after engine.*

The 1271 GM engine *pulled from the* Diane Janet, *refurbished in Jim's* *garage and later sold.*

The building known as "the Shop" at the Miller house in Terryville. The Shop was a converted barn where the family kept animals like a donkey, pony, sheep, and pigs.

Linda Meyer, who worked with Jim Miller for twenty-one years, in the garage/office, Terryville, 1970s. "I've been out of there for sixteen years," Linda says, "and Jim and I still talk. Who talks to their boss when you haven't worked for them for sixteen years?"

A Miller employee operates a "boatadozer" in a reservoir full of flotsam after torrential rains and flooding, circa 1985. The machine, invented by the Millers, was a converted steelwork boat outfitted with a bulldozer-like sifter bucket, designed to drive through debris fields, picking up and recovering floating waste.

CHAPTER 18

What Work Means

There are several variations on this old saying, but they all mean essentially the same thing: "Find a job you love, and you'll never have to work a day in your life."

It's a wonderful notion, isn't it? A heartwarming, comforting sentiment.

Too bad it's nonsense.

Work is work. That's not to say that everybody necessarily has to hate his or her job. On the contrary, we should all strive for careers in fields that are meaningful to us, for jobs that provide us and our families with a secure livelihood, for work that, in the end, somehow *matters*. But as Brad Warner wrote in his book *Hardcore Zen*, "[even] the best job in the world [is] still just a job. Even Johnny Ramone said that being a rock-and-roll guitar player was a pretty good job, but that, in the end, it also sucked just like any other job."

The point here is that we don't have to love every single minute of every day that we're on the job. In fact, if we worked beside a person who felt that way, we'd probably want to wring his or her neck. But that work is an essential element of a meaningful life, that one should perform a job well because it's the right thing to do, that any job worth doing is worth doing well—those are reflections of certain values, certain attitudes toward work that don't get old.

For the Millers of Jim Miller's generation, of his parent's generation, and of his children and his grandchildren's generations, work is a living, daily reality. In fact, as Jim's son Mark tells it, work is, in many ways, *the* living, daily reality, and a strong work ethic is as intrinsic to a well-lived life as a well-tuned moral compass or a curious, inquisitive mind.

"It wasn't something that was stated outright," Mark says. "It wasn't that my parents pounded it into us, that you have to work, you have to work. I think it was a lot simpler than that. That was just the way that it was. We didn't know anything else. We didn't know any other way of life.

"For example, when we were living on a farm, we had a gang of animals. When we woke up in the morning, the animals had to be tended to. We had to go feed the animals before we were allowed to have breakfast. We didn't think anything about it, because that was just the way that you did it. It wasn't some lesson that we had to be taught. It never felt as if it were a punishment. It was just: You woke up, you got dressed, you went into the barn, you let the animals out, you put the hay out, you fed the rabbits—you just *did* it. Then when those responsibilities were tended to, you headed back into the house, and you had your breakfast. You never imagined doing it in the reverse order. You simply would never think of doing it any other way.

"The concept of responsibility—the idea of taking care of things in the order in which they need to be taken care of, before you have an opportunity to get the rewards of anything—that goes right back to the earliest memories I have. I remember the very first job I had (where I was getting paid) was putting rubber bands on lobsters' claws. When we would go work on the *Lady Barbara*, my dad had Jimmy, Glen, and me as his crew, and he treated us the same way he would treat men. I had my first cup of coffee when I was eight years old. We'd stop off at a deli on the way to the boat, and I got a cup of coffee and a buttered roll, and that was my breakfast. We would sit in the back of the pickup truck, eating our rolls and drinking our coffees—mine was light and sweet back then—and by the time we got down to the dock, the coffee was gone, the buttered roll was gone, and it was time to go to work.

"I remember my dad coming up with this whole compensation scheme. Even though we were little kids, he was paying us the wages that he would pay a man, because we were doing the work of men. He had this whole crazy concept to keep us motivated because, after all, we still were kids. He had to be pretty creative to keep us engaged. Not that being on a lobster boat could ever be boring—there are so many things going on—but he kept us from just being mechanical drones by incentivizing us all the time.

"We would do all kinds of crazy things. We would develop songs and sing to the lobsters as we were hauling gear and the traps were coming up. One brother was cleaning lobsters out, another was baiting the traps, and lobsters would be sliding across the deck to me. I would have to measure them to make sure they were the legal limit, and I would feel their shells to make sure they were hard shell and not soft shell, checking for eggs. Eventually, if it was a keeper, I would have to use this little banding tool, kind of like pliers, to put a rubber band on its claws. And my dad would just create some silly little song. One in particular I remember is 'Hello, Lobsters,' sung to the melody of 'Hello, Dolly.' He would just break out singing, 'Hello, lobsters!' and we would chime in. We would have a lot of fun throughout the day coming up with more and more lyrics to the song. We would just keep each other engaged and happy, and it would be fun. It was a happy boat. That was often key to being successful, because an unhappy boat doesn't catch fish."

It's definitely worth noting here that while Jim Miller's sons might have fond memories of lobstering with their dad, Jim's brother Dave—the baby of the family at seventy-one years old—harbors slightly less rosy recollections. Dave, who lives in North Carolina with his wife, Sandy, worked on a boat for Jim, but for a while, he worked *with* the oldest Miller brother, Richie.

"We were using Richie's boat, and Richie, of course, was the captain," Dave recalls today, "and we were lobstering, and I guess there was a financial deal between Richie and Jimmy. Jimmy owned the traps, and he financed things, and Richie supplied the boat, the knowledge, the skill, and everything else. I was the deckhand and learned the business. That went on for one full year, and the next year, Jimmy suggested that to increase the production, I take his boat and go out lobstering with his sons as my deckhands. I spent a year doing that, and I'll tell you, it was a changing point in my relationship with Jimmy—and with his boys as well—because at the end of that year, I told Jimmy that if I ever had to work with his sons again, I wouldn't stay on with him in the business. I was their uncle, but I was put in the position of having to be their boss, too. I was trying to wear too many hats, and I really got to the point where I hated things. It was just the stress of handling all of it. You know, I had two young children of my own, and I'd come home at night with a chip on my shoulder, and I didn't want to live that way. The little things drove me crazy," Dave says, laughing. "Jimmy Jr. and Mark didn't have belts to hold their pants up. A simple belt. I had to come to the house, get the bait, get them up every morning to go fishing, and they would come out of the house holding their pants up. We would get down in the boat, and I would take out the knife and cut them each a length of lobster pot line. And that was their belt for the day. And I had to wake them up, too. I was there every day at five in the morning, so it wasn't like it was a surprise, right? But I would have to wake them up. You know, it wasn't that I didn't love them. Of course, I did. But those little things really drove me bananas. 'Come on.' 'You're going to work.' 'Put a belt on.' 'Get up on time.'

"And then there was their bickering, which I understood, because even though I'm so much younger, I've heard all of the stories about Richie, Tommy, and Jimmy, and how as young men at home, they bickered, they fought, and they fought with my father—all those things—so to see it in Jimmy's kids, I sort of expected it. But let me tell you, it gets on your nerves, man.

"Fortunately, though," Dave says, "Jimmy was understanding, and he told me, 'Don't worry about it. You want to stay? We're going to be in the spill-cleanup business. I need you to run the boat for me.' That was a great thing. We had contracts to put booms around the tankers coming into Port Jefferson, and we were starting to get into the maritime research business, working with marine biologists and oceanographers. We had a lot of stuff going on, and we definitely had a lot of good times while we were working our tails off. But all these years later," he says, chuckling, "I still get worked up about those damn belts."

All along, whether their pants were held up by belts, twine, rope, or baling wire, Jim Miller's kids were learning. All along, hard and enduring lessons were being instilled in these boys, who were doing the jobs of men.

This is what you do. You keep track of things. You keep a record. You do the job. You do the work right. You get rewarded for it.

"And you do it happily," Mark says, musing on these unspoken but crystal-clear lessons from his youth. "The one time that we didn't do it happily, our dad fired us. We had a fight on the boat. We were on our way back in from a long day of pulling gear. It was hard work. We were working on the lobster boat when most of our friends were at home riding their bicycles and stuff. We weren't envious of them. We actually thought we were getting the better deal; we were having a far better summer than they were. But I remember one day when all the gear had been pulled, we were steaming back to Port Jeff, and the final responsibility was to clean the boat. We were washing the boat down, Dad was steering, and Jimmy, Glen, and I were out on the back deck. There was a whole system for cleaning the boat. I don't remember who started it, but it had something to do with the deck hose, somebody's boots getting full of water, and before you knew it, it was all-out war on the back deck. This rumble was happening, and Dad finally saw what was going on. He looked, the engines slowed all the way back to an idle, he came back, and he yelled a series of very creative expletives. We stopped fighting and started cleaning. We got to the dock, we tied the boat up, we got the lobsters off in the boxes and all the garbage from the day's fishing, and the boat was secured. And he said, 'Okay, you guys done?' We said we were. He said, 'Okay, don't come back. You're fired.'

"He fired us! We thought, you know, 'Dad's just kidding. Tomorrow we'll be here.' No. Overnight he hired a new crew, and we were sitting on the dock, watching the boat leave for the rest of the summer. It was probably midsummer then because, in my mind, I remember that as we were cleaning the boat, we were shirtless. Earlier in the season on the Sound, it was still probably a little too cool to be that way. And I remember in that fight scene, we were all without our shirts. But anyway, there's that dreaded phrase for anybody who is meant to be on the water: 'thrown onshore.' And we were thrown onshore for weeks on end.

"It was horrible, it was so embarrassing, and while I can't speak for my brothers, I know how I felt. That was probably the most horrific punishment that I could imagine, but not because I wasn't making money or anything like that. It was just that I felt like I really blew it. It was such a simple rule that he had, and the three of us violated it. That was the worst part. Having disappointed him and violated a rule that was so basic—and because of that to be missing out on that whole experience. And to imagine that somebody else could actually be on that boat with him, doing our work! Oh my God, that was torturous. That was horrible.

"But those are just a few memories about working and the work ethic. It was not so much a prescribed sort of thing, where our parents sat down and talked with us and told us what was what. It was just how it was. The same way nobody ever taught you that you eat breakfast in the morning. That's just what you do. We just worked. Mowing the lawn, cleaning out the barn, working on the boats. It wasn't an unusual thing for us, and it just became a way of life. It's so ingrained in us that I don't think any of us really understand how to *not* do that—how to *not* get to work when a job needs doing."

CHAPTER 19

Onward, Upward: Voyages of the *Lady Barbara*

"Nothing bad ever happens. There are only missed opportunities."

If a single aphorism could be said to capture Jim Miller's approach to . . . well, to almost everything, his well-known saying about missed opportunities might be it. Certainly during the years when he and his family were transitioning from fishing to other pursuits and other sources of income—including the spill-cleanup business, which would, to a large degree, utterly transform their prospects and their fortunes—Jim never let an opportunity pass by if he could seize it instead.

Case in point: the controversial, ill-fated Shoreham Nuclear Power Plant. Built at a cost of more than $6 billion, the Shoreham facility—which was eventually decommissioned in 1994, more than two decades after construction began in the early seventies—faced massive opposition from elected officials and local communities long before ground was even broken at the site. (Ultimately, the cost of the plant—which never operated at full capacity—was passed on to Long Island electrical utility customers. What ultimately sealed the plant's fate was Suffolk County's determination that residents could not be safely evacuated from the region in the case of a nuclear accident.)

"Very early on," Jim says, "I was approached by some of the folks who opposed Shoreham. As originally conceived, it was going to be a giant facility that was going to cost an outrageous amount of money—more money than anybody had ever spent for a power plant. You know, maybe as much as $100 million, which was an astronomical amount of money. The idea of it costing billions of dollars, as it eventually did, was inconceivable. But it would also provide huge benefits in taxes and everything else—according to LILCO [Long Island Lighting Company] anyway—so it was a gift from the gods. And it would generate electricity for free forever and ever. How could anybody oppose this incredible windfall for Suffolk County, right?

"I was a well-known guy, someone who could speak about the possible threat that the plant posed to marine life in the area. These people who had concerns about the plant asked me if I would sit in on some hearings and maybe even possibly testify. I said sure, of course I would. The big issue, or one of the big issues, being discussed at that time was thermal pollution, or the heated water that would be discharged by the plant. There was a lot of talk about what impact the thermal pollution would have on the marine environment. Would we go from catching codfish in Long Island Sound to catching sailfish, because it was going to become a tropical body of water? Were we going to raise the temperature of the Sound by twenty degrees? Would it be like the Gulf Stream? Would an increase of even a few degrees generate a large, permanent fog bank offshore? There was a whole mess of questions being raised—some of them quite serious and based in real science and others that were just ridiculous and based more in hysteria. But I figured I'd offer whatever expertise I could.

"The utility had hired their own expert—some local professor with an alphabet soup of letters after his name to prove he was a smart guy—to make a lengthy report based on some research and experiments and field studies that he had done, or that he said he had done, near the plant. What his research amounted to was him fishing here and there near the spot where the warm water would be discharged from the plant, and his studies indicated that because he had caught very, very few fish there over the course of however many days or weeks, even if the water coming from the plant *was* ten or twenty degrees warmer than the ambient surrounding water, there were obviously so few fish around—according to him—that the rise in temperature wouldn't have a significant effect on the health of fish that lived or spawned near the discharge pipes.

"Unfortunately for him, I was one of those not-very-bright fishermen who actually kept a logbook. And just by chance, on some of the days that he fished and caught nothing, or very little, I had recorded substantial numbers of bait fish, edible fish, crustaceans, and so on in that very vicinity. The information in my logbook was a 100 percent contradiction of his testimony. He said that he caught a handful of fish—or sometimes even no fish at all—right there where the plant would be discharging warm water after cooling the fuel rods. At the same time, in the exact same place, I had caught thousands of pounds of fish. As a result of that testimony, their marine evaluation was deemed inadequate and had to be done over, in a more rigorous and appropriate way.

"Now, at the same time that this was happening, Perry Duryea was developing the New York Ocean Science Laboratory in Montauk, and that's how I got even more involved with marine studies on the Sound. New York Ocean Science hired me to be their local guy, to tell them where and what and how to go fishing and catch samples for their research, and that developed into a business for me, too. I suppose that maybe part of the reason they hired me is because I knew how to navigate pretty much anywhere around the island. Or maybe it wasn't a consideration on their part. Maybe they just assumed that a local guy wouldn't run into a rock. Regardless, I had the ability to design sampling equipment that would capture the marine species in the area. I built the lobster traps and the gill nets that they used. I designed and built all sorts of equipment for the researchers, and it all fit on my boat, the *Lady Barbara*, so she became the designated research vessel for the laboratory."

One of those researchers was a young marine biologist named Clarence "Corky" Hickey, who for five years in the early 1970s worked on a number of landmark studies of Long Island fisheries. The author of an excellent and ultimately quite moving book, *On the East End: The Last Best Times of a Long Island Fishing Community*, about his time on the Sound with the likes of Jim Miller, Corky Hickey today lives in Maryland, "an hour from Annapolis, which is probably the nearest thing to salt water." Forty years later, his memories of the days and nights he spent aboard the *Lady Barbara* and other trustworthy working boats are both clear and fond.

A native Pennsylvanian who fell in love with the ocean during family vacations on the Jersey shore, Hickey has worked in, on, or near the water (fresh and salt) across five decades. His work and research with NYOSL, meanwhile, "stayed with me and helped me in everything else I've done.

"I have a really healthy respect for, and a little bit of a fear of, the sea," Hickey says, "and I have had a few incidents in my life—as a swimmer, as a surfer, and in boats—that have instilled that. But I'll tell you, I always felt safe on the water with Jim Miller. He was extremely knowledgeable—he was head of the Long Island Commercial Fishermen's Association at that point, and his brother Richie was the association's secretary and, later on, its president—

and Jim didn't take chances. He knew his environment, and you knew where you stood with him when you were on his boat. He was in charge. But we had a kind of mutual respect, I think. For example, I really appreciated it when he entrusted me with taking the wheel when he was doing something else on the boat—running the winches, checking nets or traps, something that took him out of the wheelhouse. When he let me bring *Lady Barbara* in after dark—we often started early and worked long, long days—that was especially memorable. Those were very special times."

It wasn't only the work, though, that Hickey recalls. As he recounts in *On the East End*, he and Jim enjoyed some lighthearted times as well:

> We worked well together, Jim the seasoned captain and fisherman, and me the young biologist still learning. But I got to instruct Jim, once, by showing him how to cook [a meal using the *Lady Barbara*'s hot muffler as a stove], which he really liked. On one subsequent sampling venture, Jim took the lead as ship's steward and brought not only tin foil for the muffler, but lemon, butter, paper plates, and plastic knives and forks. I asked where were the teacups and wine, and we both smiled.

Long conversations with Jim about what Hickey calls "the politics of fishing"—and the difficulties of forming alliances among men as profoundly independent as commercial fishermen—helped him understand that "there was a lot more to studying the fisheries than just gathering data on the fishes themselves. I learned, over time, that environmental problems are really people problems."

CHAPTER 20

Into the Oil

This was also the era when Jim Miller was first introduced to— and immediately grasped the lucrative potential of—the oil-spill-cleanup business. The single, transformative opportunity that presented itself was not especially grandiose, or promising. At least not at first. Instead, at the time, it was yet another in a long line of business openings to which Jim immediately said yes, after which he proceeded to figure out how to get the job done. And that particular yes, on that particular day, has made all the difference over the past five decades.

"It's January 1971," Jim says and, with typical understatement, adds the wry observation that "the weather isn't terribly nice. I'm inbound to Port Jefferson from a day's fishing—which hasn't been very successful. As I enter the harbor, a couple of guys on the oil company dock are waving their arms and shouting, 'Hey! Miller! Come over here!'

"So I go on over, and I ask them what all the shouting's about.

"'Aw, we've got this ship here,' they tell me, 'and she spilled oil.

Look at it—it's in the water. It's everywhere. Can you get some guys with small boats? Get the clam diggers or something and help us clean up this mess? We'll pay you for it, you know. But we gotta get some guys that can stand the cold weather. You and the clam diggers. You're all tough guys. You could do this work. Whaddya say?'

"Well, fishing is lousy anyway, and the guy's promising money, so I figure we'll give it a try. I organize a dozen clam diggers with their boats, and when we're ready to start, everybody sort of looks around and asks, 'Okay, how do you clean this stuff up? It's floating on the top of the water. It's oily, it stinks, it's black and messy. How do we get it out of there?'

"I have a barn with some hay in it, so we go get a couple of pickup truckloads of straw and hay and bring it down to the harbor. But then we stand there, debating. Do we open a bale of straw and toss it in that way, or do we just throw the full, bundled bales into the water on top of the oil? After a while, we figure we have to spread it out across the top of the oil, and it will absorb that way. So we break open the bales of straw and spread it around, and next thing you know, we have the clam diggers pitchforking it out and putting it in garbage bags. After a week or so, we actually managed to get the spill cleaned up. We worked from you can't see until you can't see, and it was cold, cold weather, but everybody worked hard and got it done.

"I was sort of the de facto manager on this project, so all of these guys worked for me. I paid them cash, out of my pocket. When the job was done, they all got paid, and that was that. Then I went up to the oil company guy who was in charge there at the harbor, a Mr. Vandermark, an old Dutchman, as straitlaced as they come and a true gentleman. A very aristocratic, old-school guy. I asked him how I was going to get paid, after I'd already paid everybody else for their time and labor. We'd been so busy with the spill that he and I hadn't had a chance to have a conversation. He said, 'Oh, of course. Just fill out the regular time-and-material rate sheets.' And I had to tell him that we didn't *have* any time-and-material rate sheets. I'd never filled one out in my life."

With that, Jim leans forward in his chair, arms folded across his chest, and hunches his shoulders in an expressive gesture. *What're you gonna do?* Behind his glasses, his eyes are glinting with amusement.

"'Well,' Mr. Vandermark said to me, not missing a beat, 'You'd better go make one up.' So I went home and sat at the dining room table with my wife and a girl from up the street who was a pretty good typist and secretary, and we composed a price sheet for labor and materials and equipment and everything else. So much an hour for a pickup truck, and so much an hour for a boat, and the expense of buying pitchforks, and how much for the hay and whatever else we used on the project. Then we had log entries for the guys who worked on the job, so we converted that information into work-sheets—twelve guys at ten hours a day at this amount per hour, whatever it was—and then we dropped all of that into an invoice.

"We get a manual typewriter from somewhere, and we're hunting and pecking away—and at that time everything is done with carbon paper, so I get three sets of the invoice, the original and the carbon copies—and I bring it up to Mr. Vandermark. And let me tell you, it's *expensive*. Thousands of dollars. I need to get reimbursed, man. I'm hanging out there pretty good. But he starts to review the invoice, and right away he's shaking his head and telling me, 'No, no, no. Jim, this is all wrong. You can't do this. No, this is ridiculous.'

"Of course, I think he's telling me the total is way too high or that I'm charging them for stuff they'll never accept. So I tell him, 'Well, what do you want me to do? We got the damn thing cleaned up, didn't we? I don't know why you're huffing and puffing and getting mad at me.' And that's when he says, 'No, listen to me. You guys worked on Saturday and Sunday. Right? You have to charge overtime for that, Jim. You have to charge time-and-a-half. In fact, for Sunday, it's double-time. And you guys worked more than forty hours. That's overtime, too. And look at this. You're not charging enough for the hay or the pitchforks or anything.'

"So now I go home, and we redo the entire invoice. Now, it's *really* big. We bring it back to him, and he says, 'Yeah, that makes more sense. That's right. Good. Much more fair. That's the way it should look. That's right.' So of course I'm thinking, 'All right. Now we're in business. I'm going to actually make some real money here. This is great.'

"And that's when the other shoe drops. He says, 'I just need a copy for the oil company, and a copy to send to London, and a copy to send to Greece, and we need a copy for you to keep.'

"I tell him I have only three copies. I'm not feeling too good anymore. He says, 'Oh, you've got to send one to the ship owner. He lives in Greece. His insurance company is in London. I've gotta have a copy. We need more copies, and then we'll send them off.'

"By now, I'm absolutely convinced that I'm getting screwed. Sending a bill to Greece, and I'm going to get paid? Yeah, right. Depending on some insurance company in London that has never heard of me? Yeah, sure. And redoing this thing and making more copies? That's going to be another day right there. But he tells me, 'No, you don't have to deal with carbon copies. We have a new device here in the office. We have a special machine. You take the positive paper and the negative paper and the original paper, and you put them on each side, and you feed them into this machine, and it has a special liquid in there, and it goes through the machine and comes out the other end, and everything dries off real quick, and you have a copy. It's a *copy machine*.'

"I say, 'Wow! That's really magic.' I can't believe it. You just put it in, and it comes out the other end, and it's duplicated. We're in a whole new world here. At any rate, we get the invoices out. We ship them off, but by now I'm pretty melancholy. 'Boy,' I think to myself. 'That was a lot of foreplay before getting screwed. It's unbelievable that I'm this dumb and this naïve.'

"Two weeks later, a letter arrives in the mail. It's from Greece. 'Dear Mr. Miller, we are forever indebted to the fine service that your highly skilled organization rendered to our vessel in time of need. We are forever indebted and greatly respect and appreciate the service you gave us. You expedited the departure of our vessel without any unnecessary cost, and if there is ever again a misfortune anywhere in the United States, we will immediately be in contact with you because we've never worked with a group that was so diligent and creative and generous. Enclosed is our check in full. Thank you again. Signed, so-and-so.'

"Holy mackerel! We got paid in full with a nice letter. How about that? We're in Fat City! We went down, put the check in the bank, and it cleared in a week or so. The money was in there. The bills were all paid. We were doing really well. We bought new hay and bought new pitchforks, and we even bought one of those electric typewriters, to replace the manual one. We created letterhead and a price sheet, because in case this ever happened again, we were going to be ready, man.

"We even had enough money that we went down and bought a brand-new Ford four-wheel-drive pickup truck. Walked right into Ramp Motors in Port Jeff Station, looked at a beautiful new blue pickup with a snowplow, and said, 'Man, that's exactly what I want.' I wrote out a check and paid for it in full. And I guess, if you look at it, that really was the beginning. Because a month, maybe six weeks later, a phone call comes in the middle of the night. I answer it, and the voice on the other end of the line asks, 'Is this Mr. Miller?'

"Uh-oh. This can't be good. People don't call a fisherman 'Mr. Miller' when they phone him in the middle of the night.

"Then the voice says, 'This is the United States Coast Guard.'

This is getting even worse. 'Mr. Miller' and 'United States Coast Guard' in the same conversation? How bad is this going to get? 'Mr. Miller, we want to hire the expert organization that you run over there on Long Island.' I'm wide awake now but confused as hell. 'My what? What are you talking about?'

"'The cleanup organization that you have over there. We need to activate those guys. There's an oil spill in Northport. A ship has discharged oil along seventeen miles of beach, and we want you to activate your crew and go over and clean it up. We'll give you a Coast Guard contract to proceed. We call it a basic ordering agreement. We're going to authorize you to spend up to $10,000 to get started, and if you need more money, just tell us, and we'll get it to you.' By now, I'm looking around for another cigarette. I'm smoking two at a time. I call up all the clam diggers. 'Boys, we're going to work.' And by the way, at this point, we still haven't even set up our office, or semi-office, in the garage. We're still working off the dining room table, but we have to organize a whole bunch of people. We have to get payloaders, dump trucks, four-wheel-drive vehicles, and whatever else.

"And this job also really began our education about the logistics of a cleanup operation of any size. Ordering 100 hamburgers from McDonald's. Getting a coffee truck to the beach and paying the owner to stay there, so we could have a Danish in the morning and keep our guys caffeinated. And it was around that time—1970, 1971—when we began to see that this could actually be a business. We incorporated as Marine Pollution Control, and we kept growing from there. We operated as Marine Pollution Control for a good number of years, until we discovered that there was a firm in Detroit, founded by a guy named David Usher, that also went by the name of Marine Pollution Control. It wasn't a trademark issue for fifteen or twenty years, until we started to provide response capabilities and services for major spills around the country. Then we were a national player, and Usher saw us as a genuine competitor. The long and short of it was that after we went to court and both of us spent a lot of money beating each other up over this trademark problem, we came to an understanding. Or the judge on the case made us come to an understanding. Usher kept the name Marine Pollution Control—he still operates out of Detroit, by the way—and we began working as Miller Environmental Group."

Before we leave this particular era in Jim's life—and the lives of Barbara, their daughters, and their sons, all of whom worked with or for Jim when he was still fishing, lobstering, and otherwise making his living on or near the water—we'll just recount one last story from that time. There are, of course, more than a few stories that Jim and his family or friends might tell that highlight the man's unwillingness to get pushed around. An old man trying to shake him down for a percentage of the parking-lot take on movie nights behind the drugstore when Jim was a teen; thieves brazenly stealing his catch and his nets; even *Newsday* and their price hike when Jim was just a kid—a whole cast of characters tried to get the better of Jim through the years, and very few (if any) came out ahead in the end.

But for sheer nerve—fueled, in this case, by a combination of anger and dislike—the tale Jim tells of the time that he stared down the Teamsters in Port Jeff stands out as perhaps the most audacious.

"Around that time," Jim says, "when we were getting established with the cleanup business, our own marine fleet also expanded. For example, we had a wonderful little boat designed, built, and dedicated to oil-boom deployment in Port Jefferson. We named it the 'Pollution Control Boat,' and I guess that people believed that we were government-sanctioned or something—which, strictly speaking, we *weren't*. But all the visiting commercial vessels would call in before entering Port Jeff, and they'd ask for 'Pollution Control.'

They were essentially asking permission to enter the harbor and find out where they were going to berth and everything else, and we would say, 'Certainly, you can come in to the oil company here and tie up, and we'll surround your ship with a boom.' So we became a kind of unofficial keeper of the harbor. But we were just a private entity with a governmental-sounding name.

"At the same time, we also developed into a launch service for visiting oil tankers. They'd remain offshore of Port Jeff, waiting to come in, and if communications were difficult between ship and shore, the oil company would ask me, 'Jim, would you go out to the oil tanker and give them a message?' So in the middle of the night or whenever we were needed, I would take the *Lady Barbara*, sail out to the oil tanker, and gain their attention by banging on the side of the ship with a big engineer's hammer. They'd lower down a bucket, we'd send them a letter and wait for a reply, and then bring it back in to the oil terminal. We became the can-do guys. Whatever the oil company needed, we took care of it.

"There was a time when truck drivers were on strike, picketing at the harbor, and we thought the chances were good that they were going to try to blockade the harbor to prevent the oil tankers from coming in. Captain Jim Stillwaggon, a famous guy in those parts back then, was the harbor pilot, and we had a meeting because he was going to be bringing a ship in, and he thought that the strikers were going to try to threaten the oil tanker or something as it came through the Port Jeff channel. He told us that he figured that they would probably go out with a small boat, and just as the tanker entered the main channel, these guys would pretend to break down and drop anchor right there, claiming they were in distress—that they couldn't move—and the oil tanker would be stuck outside the harbor. The point being that you can't just stop an oil tanker in the middle of the channel when you're inbound. So Captain Jim says, 'Jim, can you stand by in case they pull some shenanigans, and get them the hell out of the way if they do?'

"I tell him, 'Yeah, no problem. Whatever you want us to do, we'll do.' We set up waiting for the oil tanker to come in, and sure enough, four or five guys in an outboard motorboat are cruising around in the harbor. Pretty soon, next thing you know, the tanker is by the breakwater, and these guys in the motorboat make right for the middle of the channel. They throw their anchor over the side, put up a distress flag, and they're waving their arms around—a big commotion. 'We're disabled, and we can't get out of the way, so you have to stop the ship.' Blah, blah, blah. I go sliding right past in front of them, throw my grappling iron, and snatch their anchor off the bottom. And just like that, I tow them away.

"Of course, they don't like that one bit. They weren't expecting *that*. They're screaming and hollering, laying out in detail all the bad things they're going to do to me, but we get under way and get them up on the mud flat, and the oil tanker comes in. And when it's safely in the harbor, we turn these guys loose. That was the end of that—except for the threats. 'We'll get you, Miller! We know who you are! We know where you live! We know what kind of car you've got!' They're gonna do this, and they're gonna do that. The Teamsters at that time were a bad bunch of guys. You know, I couldn't assume that these were idle threats."

This was the era when membership in the International Brotherhood of Teamsters was the highest in its seventy-year history: The IBT counted around two million dues-paying members in the mid-1970s, making it one of the largest, wealthiest, and most powerful labor unions in the world. While the scandal-plagued Jimmy Hoffa era ended in the early 1970s—Hoffa was replaced as Teamsters president by the slightly less notorious Frank Fitzsimmons in

1971—the stink of organized crime still hung heavy over the Brotherhood throughout the decade. For Jim Miller, having Teamsters and those associated with the Teamsters telling him things like "We know where you live" was more than just talk.

"In the early seventies," he says, "they were blowing up trucks in Brooklyn, setting guys' cars on fire. They were bad news, you know. They weren't nice people. So I needed to do something. And this was where my old pal Kenny Meyer fits back into my life. Kenny was a Nassau County detective at the time. I called him and said, 'Kenny, I got big trouble out here with these guys.' I laid it all out for him, describing what happened, the sort of things that were being said—along with solid descriptions of who was making the threats. Kenny didn't hesitate. He said, 'All right, let me check around a little bit. I'll get back to you.'

"Kenny called me the next day, and he said, 'Jimmy, I did a little homework on three of these guys.' Here's this guy's name, he tells me, this guy's name, and that guy's name. Willie Jones, or whatever. 'He lives up in Smithtown, and his wife's name is Gloria. They've got two kids, Frankie and Georgie, and the kids get on the school bus at eight o'clock every morning. Pedro, he lives over there in Port Jefferson, and his wife's name is Mary Lou.' She's a waitress up in such-and-such diner, he tells me, 'and she gets home at eleven every night. She drives a green Ford station wagon. This third guy . . . ' And on he went.

"Now I had three names and some real information that I could use. And not a moment too soon, really, because these guys were already playing nasty. I'm sure they loosened the lug nuts on the wheels of my pickup truck. I drove halfway home one night when the front wheel started flopping around because they'd unscrewed the nuts. That," Jim points out, in one of his classic understatements, "wasn't good.

"So the next morning, there's a gang of these guys in the parking lot, maybe twenty of them, standing around, planning their next bit of harassment, I suppose."

Jimmy, all five feet eight inches and 150 pounds of him, walks over to have a chat.

"Somebody sees me, and he starts yelling, 'Hey, you're Miller, aren't you? What are you doing here?'

"I say, 'Yeah, I'm Miller.' And they get right to it. 'Good,' they say, 'because we're going to beat the living crap out of you.' And I look at them and say, 'I don't think so.'

"That makes them pause for a minute. 'What do you mean, you don't think so? There are twenty of us here, and there's one of you. What are you going to do about it?'

"'Oh, I don't know,' I said, 'But I think I have some friends there in your group.'

"'Bah!' they tell me. 'Who the hell is going to be your friend?'

"'Well,' I said, pointing to one guy. 'You're Willie Jones, aren't you?' 'Yeah, I'm Willie Jones. So what?' 'Well, your wife's name is Gloria, right? You've got two kids? They get on the school bus every day right in front of your house there in Smithtown. And Pedro. Say hi to your wife, who works at the diner, okay?'

"I go on for a while, letting them know that I know as much about them as they know about me. They're all staring at me now, like I'm a crazy man. But they're not yelling anymore. I think I have their attention. 'I just want you to know,' I tell them, 'that you aren't invisible. Not one of you. In fact, I think you guys are now my life insurance policy. Something happens to me? It happens to your own family. It's done. It's all taken care of. This is not bullshit. You want to play the game? I've been out here fishing, lobstering, working on the water all my life. I'm not about to roll over for you punks. See youse all later.' And I walk away."

Jim Miller didn't make any friends that day. But then, he wasn't exactly in a friendly frame of mind, either. He wasn't a man who took kindly to strangers threatening his family, his livelihood, his life. So he decided to do something about it.

(By the way, the strike that started all the trouble? It ended that very night, after the confrontation in the parking lot. Jim has no illusions that his standing up to a group of Teamsters played any role at all in ending the strike. But he does note that the timing was convenient.)

In the end, though, the most telling aspect of that entire scenario is not that Jim stood up for himself and for his family. Countless men and women, when pushed to the wall, would do the same. What's significant is that he dealt with the problem by making a plan. Yes, he marshaled his anger and his indignation. He did not back down. But nor did he go off half-cocked—which, of course, could have simply made things more dangerous for himself. Instead, he looked at the angles, asked an old, trusted friend for a favor, and, face to face, he evened the odds with the people who were messing with him.

In pretty much any time, and any place, that counts as true grit.

CHAPTER 21

Edge of Disaster:
The *Martha R. Ingram*
Breaks in Two

We've all seen variations on this particular adage: "It's not how many times we're knocked down that defines us. It's how many times we get back up."

Of course, just because that particular creed has appeared on countless desktop plaques, inspirational posters, and bumper stickers over the years doesn't make it any less true. How many times we get back up—and *how* we pick ourselves up—after a knockdown blow really does show the world what we're made of.

In 1972, in the early days of the enterprise that would eventually become Miller Environmental Group, Jim Miller brought everything he'd learned up to that point about the oil-spill recovery business to bear on a major disaster in Port Jefferson Harbor and ended up facing the specter of financial ruin. How he managed to survive, and thrive, in circumstances that might have driven a less resourceful man to despair says an awful lot about the famed Miller tenacity and the importance of treating everybody, *everybody*, whom one meets with the respect that is their due—unless or until they prove themselves unworthy of that respect.

The story of the *Martha R. Ingram* oil tanker is still, after more than forty years, one of the more extraordinary tales of maritime disaster—and, for the ship in question, redemption—in the annals of Long Island's storied North Shore. The bare details, meanwhile, are matters of public record: how, on the morning of January 10, 1972, the nine-month-old, $12 million tanker split in half like a monstrous steel egg, as she pulled away from the Port Jefferson dock and then partially sank in the harbor's cold waters.

"I was standing in the pilot house at about nine thirty this morning in the process of undocking," the ship's pilot, Kenneth Johnson Jr., told *The New York Times* on that fateful Monday, "when I heard this tremendous cracking sound. There was a tidal wave of water as the hold split open and the salt water ballast came [pouring] out."

"The 640-foot ship, which carried 280,000 barrels of petroleum products when fully loaded," the *Times* story continued, "immediately sank at both ends into the 32 feet of water at dockside, finally coming to rest as an immense inverted V." (The tanker had already unloaded her cargo of gasoline and No. 2 fuel oil when the ship broke in two, so despite the incredibly dramatic nature of the accident, only about 200 gallons of gasoline spilled into the harbor from the hull.)

In Jim Miller's telling, however, the narrative takes on an immediacy that even newspaper accounts written that very day cannot quite match.

"By 1972, I'd already established a relationship with Consolidated Petroleum in Port Jefferson," Jim says. "I was charged with the responsibility of deploying oil containment booms around all visiting vessels. I had that special vessel built for that, our Pollution Control Boat. We weren't really an official, licensed outfit or anything for that work. We just sort of claimed what you might call a kind of mystical authority over vessels entering the harbor.

"The *Martha R. Ingram* was a new type of vessel at the time, an integrated unit where the tugboat was mechanically fastened to the barge. Prior to that, tugs and barges were separate vessels, with big rubber fenders to insulate them from colliding with each other and cables to keep them both in position during maneuvering. But the *Martha R. Ingram* was one of the very first of its kind—and the first that I ever saw in Port Jeff—where the tugboat was physically locked together with the barge, via these large winglike structures that fit into the hull of the barge. The tug would slide into this huge notch in the back of the barge and lock itself into place with these wings, so that the two were in effect one and the same structure and went up and down simultaneously.

"The economic reward for this sort of innovation was that the *Martha R. Ingram*—a very, very large barge for that time—could carry as much gasoline or oil as a huge tanker with a crew of maybe thirty men. But as a barge, the *Martha R. Ingram* had a tugboat crew of only about ten men. The tugboat crew could also act as the barge crew when it was tied up, and they'd handle the pumping and discharge of the vessel's cargo. I was called early on that winter morning to release the barge from the containment boom, so I went down to the dock, took the containment boom away from the vessel, and left the site.

"I got home a little later that morning, and that's when I heard this huge, awful noise, which seemed to be coming from the harbor, and even from a few miles away, I could feel this enormous vibration under my feet. 'Wow!' I told myself, 'Something really, really bad just happened!' At the same instant, every fire whistle in the entire area went off. I called Consolidated Petroleum to see if they knew what was going on, and the dispatcher there said, 'I don't know, Jim. Some idiot just called me from the dock and said the barge broke in half and sank. But I hung up on the guy, because that's impossible.'

"Well, I figured I'd go check it out anyway, so I drove back to the harbor. I remember coming down the hill, and as I entered the harbor area, I saw the middle of the barge sticking up in the air. I could barely comprehend what I was seeing. I mean, the thing had just cracked in half. What could possibly do that?

"I get to the Pollution Control Boat, and I take it out into the harbor, but before I start putting the oil boom out again around the *Martha Ingram*, I see the tug's pilot. The tug's stern is underwater, and he's up on the second deck, waving at me. I take him back to shore, along with a couple of other guys I pick up off the tug, and then I go out and deploy the oil boom. And that's when I see the police helicopter."

Jim shakes his head.

"This police helicopter shows up, and I guess the pilot decides to really look this thing over. He's hovering right above the hole in the tanker, where you can see the gasoline fumes rising into the air. And I think to myself, 'This guy's going to blow up the wharf! The fumes are right there, and he's going to suck them in, blow up his own helicopter, and fall into the rig. Then that's going to blow to smithereens, and he's going to kill the whole town. He hasn't got a clue what the hell's going on.' I'm waving my arms, he's waving back at me, and the whole time, I'm sure we're all about to be obliterated.

"Somehow or other, we survive. He flies away. By then, fire trucks have arrived, and the Coast Guard and the firefighters are spraying tens of thousands of gallons of high-expansion foam right into the hold of the ship. The harbor is rapidly turning into a full-scale disaster cleanup site."

The disaster itself was a colossal freak accident. Specifically, as the locked-in tug backed away from the dock and turned toward deeper water, its propeller wash sent air bubbles under the tanker's hull, which was ballasted fore and aft. With enormous downward pressure on both the bow and the tug-heavy stern, and with the center of the hull rising like a hinge, the steel plating at the top of the tanker simply ripped apart.

"For the next month or so," Jim says, "I never left the job site. My brothers Dave and Richie came down, and we were there 24/7, bringing people out to the wreck, shuttling supplies here and there, setting booms—whatever needed to be done—and there was never any concern that we wouldn't be compensated. Never.

"We had the *Lady Barbara*, another boat called the *Gannet*, and the Pollution Control Boat, and those three formed the launch service for the whole disaster cleanup. We didn't take on any other work. The tanker job took precedence over everything. Besides, the terminal was closed, because no other vessels could come in while everybody figured out what to do with this enormous tanker half-sunk in the harbor."

Manhattan-based Murphy Pacific Marine got the job to handle the salvage and the wreck removal for the *Martha Ingram*, and as far as Jim knew, he and they were going to have no problem when it came time to pay up. After all, Murphy Pacific engaged Jim's services from the start, and from the time the tanker split and sank until the two halves of the vessel were blown apart by demolition experts and taken to a shipyard—where they were eventually rejoined, by the way—Jim heard nothing but praise from everyone he dealt with at the company. Whatever was needed, Jim and his team handled it, while his own bills (for sandbags, pumping equipment, fuel for his boats, his own and his brothers' time, and a thousand and one other expenses associated with the daily logistics and mechanics of a major salvage operation) piled up.

"This whole salvage operation goes on for about a month," Jim says, "until the two halves of the tanker are completely severed, ballasted, and towed to the Todd Shipyard in Brooklyn. In the interim, the shipyard has already fabricated a new midsection, and when the *Martha Ingram* arrives, they cut off the edges of the damaged halves, winch both halves together with the new midsection, and weld everything together again. In a short period of time, maybe six months, the vessel is back out at sea, and she sails for a good number of years after that."

And when the cleanup work in the harbor was finished, as Jim puts it, "the story got fun. The project was complete, and we put together the invoice for the month's work. It was substantial. We had been there twenty-four hours a day. I think I got home for a shower twice. We were sleeping in a trailer at the dock. Day and night, people were asking us, 'I have to get out to the wreck. I forgot something. Can you take me?' The tanker was only 100 feet from the dock, but unless you could walk on water, we were the only way to get out there. The entire time, we heard nothing but praise from everyone at Murphy Pacific.

"The job's done, and we send them the bill. We don't hear a word from them. I call them up, ask if they got the bill. 'Yeah, we got it,' they tell me. 'Is this some kind of joke?'

"That doesn't sound too good. We worked our butts off for a month, and now they're going to jerk me around on the invoice? 'Hey,' they tell me, 'if you want to come in and talk to us about it, you can. But your invoice is a joke.' What the hell is this guy up to? I go in to lower Manhattan, to their offices on the thirty-third floor of a building near Battery Park, overlooking the harbor. Beautiful offices. The secretaries look like movie stars. This country boy is really impressed. I can see the executive I'm supposed to meet with. His door is open, he's drinking coffee. I'm there at nine in the morning. By eleven, I'm still there, and this joker hasn't had his feet off his desk all morning. He's reading the newspaper, flirting with the girls, drinking coffee, telling stories. Finally, around lunchtime, he deigns to notice me.

"'Come on in here,' he says. 'What do you want?' I tell him I want to get paid. He tells me, 'You're never going to get paid with a bill like that. We don't give money away to dumb fishermen just because they come in here demanding it. We're in the salvage business.' We've worked all over the world, he tells me. We're big, we're smart, we know everything. Blah, blah, blah. 'It ain't gonna happen unless you go home and cut the bill in half. Otherwise, we won't even talk to you.'"

Jim's eyes widen in a perfect reenactment of his long-ago astonishment.

"Whoa! I never could have imagined in a million years that there was going to be any difficulty over this thing. Every day during the job, they told us how wonderful we were. But now it looks like maybe we ain't going to get paid? I have no idea what to do with these guys. I mean, if they were out on Long Island, I could burn their building down, but I don't know how to set fire to a building in New York City.

"This was terrible. I mean, we had spent a lot of money over the past month, expecting we'd get it all back, and it was all on my account. I owed the hardware store, I owed the parts supply place, it seemed I owed everybody in town. We were going to be in really, really bad shape if we didn't get paid everything we were owed. And that's when I remembered that the port captain for Ingram Ocean Systems, the company that owned the tanker, was a great guy. A real Southern gentleman. He and I had spoken every day over the course of the month, and he told me that if I ever had a problem, I should call him.

"I call him up and tell him my tale of woe. 'Ah,' he says, 'they're dirtbags. Real bottom-feeders. I don't know why my company hired them. Listen, can you come down here to New Orleans and see me?' I tell him I can do that. I make copies of the invoice and all the other paperwork, and I fly down to New Orleans.

"Now, Ingram doesn't have a floor in the building. They *are* the building. They own the whole thing. This fellow and I chat for a while; then he asks to see the invoices. He quickly runs through them and says, 'They're all reasonable. In fact, considering how hard you worked, they're *very* reasonable. They should pay this bill in a heartbeat. I don't know why they haven't. Just arrogance, I guess.' Then he tells me he wants to go talk to the boss. He'll be right back. He disappears, comes back in half an hour, and says, 'I want you to meet somebody.' He takes me into another office and introduces me to Mrs. Ingram, a very nice, but obviously formidable, Southern lady.

"She already has a check for me, payment in full, and tells me that they certainly don't want me to think badly of Ingram, the company, or of the Ingrams, the family. The net worth of the Ingram family, by the way, is in the billions of dollars. Their marine division alone operates thousands of barges on inland waterways all over America, and they're a huge name in the publishing industry. This is a big, powerful American family dynasty we're talking about. And here's Mrs. Ingram, telling me that they would never have treated me the way that other company did. Just a class act all the way, you know?"

And what eventually happened to "that other company"?

"Murphy Pacific went bankrupt," Jim says, and he doesn't bother hiding his satisfaction. "They no longer exist. In fact," he adds, "their little tugboat was on charter to me when they went bankrupt, and I foreclosed on it."

At the core of the tale of the *Martha R. Ingram*, Murphy Pacific, and the port captain is Jim Miller's philosophy that it's important to make friends with everybody, from the chairman of the board to the janitor. In fact, one should pay *more* attention to the janitor. Everybody walks past the guy who cleans the bathrooms as if he's invisible, but if you spend a few minutes with him, buy him a cup of coffee, remember his name, it will always be time well spent. At the very least, you'll make the acquaintance of another person.

"But years later, when he's worked his way up and actually runs the company where he used to sweep the floors? When you call, he'll remember you," Jim says. "Nobody else can get to the president of the company then, because he's a big shot and his time is too valuable. But when you call up and say you're so and so, and you shared a cup of coffee with him back in the day, chances are he'll tell you that you can come see him anytime. Because you took the time, years before, to treat him with respect."

· · ·

The final word on the *Martha R. Ingram* belongs to Jim's son Mark, and the story he shares would be laughably improbable if it were told by anyone but a Miller.

"When it finally came time to blow the two halves of the tanker apart," Mark says, "so they could be floated and towed to the shipyard, my dad and his brothers were involved in that, too. They transported all of the plastic explosives and helped the demolition guys set the charges along the hinge, where the two halves were joined. Then there were hundreds and hundreds of sandbags that had to be transported out to the tanker, to cover the explosives. And of course, it became a community attraction because we were going to blow up a ship!

"Dad and Mom brought all of us kids down to the harbor to watch, and when the explosives finally went off, this one piece of steel, maybe a foot across, was blown into the air and landed about twenty feet away from our car. I ran out and grabbed it as a memento of a pretty cool event.

"Now, fast-forward ten years. I spent a year at Sophia University in Japan, and afterward, I wound up taking the long way home. I got on a cargo ship in Yokohama, went through the Sea of Japan, got into the port of Nakhodka, and boarded the Trans-Siberian Railway. This was 1982, during the Soviet era, and I was the only English-speaking, non–Iron Curtain passenger on the train. I spent six weeks going across the Soviet Union. Midway through the trip, we stopped in Irkutsk, near Lake Baikal. And there I am, up on the top deck of a hydrofoil on Lake Baikal, taking it all in, when I hear a woman call out in a Southern accent, 'Oh, Herbert, you just cut that out now, ya hear?' I look over, and I say, 'Hi, you're American?' 'Why, of course, we are,' she says.

"So we're talking for about twenty minutes when I realize I haven't introduced myself. 'I'm sorry, my name is Mark Miller.' And she says, 'My name is Martha. Martha Ingram.' I say, 'Really? Wow! What a weird coincidence! Back in 1972, in Port Jefferson, New York, this huge tanker called the *Martha Ingram* partially sank in the harbor. I was there the day it was blown apart, and a piece of steel flew through the air and landed not far from me. I took it home, and I still have it somewhere.'

"This Southern lady looks me right in the eye and says, 'Sir, my father-in-law named that vessel after me. I am *the* Martha Ingram.'

"Amazed, I looked back at her and I say, 'Well, ma'am. I have to tell you that I have a piece of your bottom.'"

CHAPTER 22

The Rise and Rise of
Miller Environmental

Over the past forty-plus years, Miller Environmental Group, which Jim Miller founded—originally as Marine Pollution Control—and led for decades, has evolved from what was essentially a small family concern tackling oil spills part-time to where it stands today, as one of the industry's premier emergency response companies. With nine facility locations around the U.S., including Pennsylvania, Maryland, Delaware, Virginia, and MEG's longtime headquarters in Calverton, Long Island; a massive fleet of custom vehicles and equipment (often designed by or with critical input from MEG employees and fabricated to the company's specs); hundreds of full-time employees; and the capacity to hire anywhere from dozens up to literally thousands of contract workers in a heartbeat to tackle disasters on any scale anywhere in the world—Miller Environmental is a player to be reckoned with.

And if anyone were to make the perhaps understandable mistake of assuming that Miller Environmental works *only* on major oil spills, it's worth keeping in mind that on any given day, the company has crews responding to literally dozens of incidents large, small, and—occasionally—colossal. Perhaps there's a rail accident in Pennsylvania with a tanker car leaking chemicals from a ruptured jacket. Or a tugboat foundering on the Hudson River somewhere south of Albany. Or an overturned tractor trailer on the Long Island Expressway. Or a subterranean Con Ed fire in midtown Manhattan. Chances are, MEG is there in some capacity—and often in a lead role.

The sheer scale of the company's success, meanwhile, makes a blow-by-blow account of how MEG got to where it is today close to impossible. (A separate book might do that convoluted tale justice; a chapter can't.)

Is it enough to point out that, whenever an environmental or other, similar kind of catastrophe strikes, chances are good that MEG will have a hand in cleaning it up? Or that Miller Environmental is one of the most respected first-response firms on the planet?

Does it make the most sense to point out that Miller Environmental has played a key role in many of Jim Miller's commercial endeavors over the past five decades—ventures that, combined, have generated multiple billions of dollars in revenue?

Or is it especially notable that, even after all of its successes, MEG continues to push the envelope, to innovate, in everything from its approaches to disasters to the machines it employs to get the job done? (Example: Miller Environmental recently unveiled a new training system for an "extraction team" charged with finding and retrieving people or critical gear from a tight, single-entry space: an oil tank, for instance, or a well. Housed in a fifty-three-foot trailer for maximum mobility—per recommendations by one of Richie Miller's sons, a fire department captain in Virginia—the pitch-black, fiendishly inventive obstacle course embodies the challenges and conditions that rescuers might face in, say, a mine disaster or inside a disabled submarine. When all is said and done, Miller Environmental will be the only company in North America capable of training—and certifying—first responders in this sort of mobile, simulated-crisis environment.)

All of those approaches to conveying MEG's origins and its phenomenal growth are, of course, perfectly valid. But in keeping with the methodology employed in the rest of this book—i.e., choosing select examples out of countless possibilities in order to highlight the whole story—let's highlight an especially noteworthy event that helped make Miller Environmental Group not just an industry leader but in many ways a company like no other.

· · ·

By the time the 1970s were drawing to a close, Miller Environmental (or, in the early days, Marine Pollution Control) had responded to countless spills and other disasters, both relatively small and unquestionably colossal. From the St. Lawrence Seaway, 400 miles north of Long Island, to the Hudson River, to tanker groundings, hull breaches, and other catastrophes closer to home, Jim Miller's fast-growing company had established a record of rapid, thorough response to any sort of supersized mess.

But when the 648-foot Liberian-registered tanker *Seaspeed Arabia* grounded in Newark Bay in July 1979, spilling 120,000 gallons of combined No. 2 diesel and No. 6 heavy fuel into New York's Upper Harbor, the cleanup effort was, Jim Miller says, "an absolute turning point for Miller Environmental. We got a call from one of the insurance representatives to respond to the spill in New York. I recollect that I had a salesman by the name of Lenny Krause at the time, and he was still operating out of the chicken coop in the backyard at our Terryville Road house when the call came in. I had a three-acre backyard, and my neighbors in those days were farmers. They had tractors on their land, and I had vacuum trucks. I was just one of the guys. Our main office was in the garage, to give you some idea of the level of the business we were operating at that point. But we were certainly becoming a force in the industry, and for a significant spill in New York Harbor like this one, we would be called by one of the New York Harbor contractors, and we would act as a subcontractor. We wouldn't be hired directly, but we would participate.

"I remember talking to Lenny, who said he'd grown up on Staten Island—which was definitely being affected by the spill. I said, 'Lenny, this is going to be a big spill. This is a big deal. We're going to be working directly for the insurance company, and we've got to have a base of operations. We don't have any place to operate in Staten Island right now, so I need you to drive there right now and capture someplace along the waterfront for us, so we can bring our marine equipment, our land machinery, and everything else.'

"He says okay, he knows Staten Island, he knows everybody there. He'll deal with it. So off he goes to Staten Island, and he calls shortly thereafter. He says, 'Yeah, we have a base of operations. I made a deal with some guys, and I'm going to rent part of a pierhead along the Staten Island shoreline underneath the Verrazano Bridge.'

"This is great! I call all the trucks we have, and we direct everybody to go to this staging area in Staten Island. We quickly overwhelm that particular location when we start to arrive with trucks and personnel and begin to deploy oil containment booms and whatever else, and that's when we see a vacant pierhead adjacent to the place we're renting. You know, it's just an abandoned pier that sticks out into the harbor, and we think, 'Well, what the hell, let's start using that,' and we just commandeer it. We don't have any permission from anyone. We just do it. We take over this pier that's overgrown with weeds and debris—all sorts of nasty stuff. We get a couple of laborers and a little Bobcat, we clear the pier itself, and out on the end of the dock, we establish a beachhead for ourselves. We've got trucks, a little command trailer. It's looking really good.

"We set up radio communications, and we're taking direct orders on how to deploy booms. And as things shake out, we're charged with the cleanup in the area around the bridge and there along the Staten Island shoreline. The other contractors are up in the Kills and in Bayonne—this is a big, big spill—and everybody is working as hard as they can.

"Now they're establishing an incident command post at Governors Island because that's where the Coast Guard is based. The governor, Hugh Carey, is saying we're going to have to start having a regular meeting, and he'd like to schedule a meeting for the following afternoon with all the contractors on the job. But we need a location that's convenient for everybody to get to because getting to Governors Island is time consuming. You have to get on a ferry or have some other way to travel out there. Does anybody have a site we can utilize on Staten Island?

"I say, 'Yeah, well, we're using the pierhead out here, and we've got a big open area. We can meet here.' So he says, 'Okay, that'll be fine. We'll meet there.' Now all the other contractors that are in Staten Island, Jersey, and everywhere else are asking, 'What the hell is this? We're the local guys here. This is a guy from Long Island. What is he up to?'

"These guys know the shoreline, and they think that there's nothing over there where we are. It's all abandoned docks as far as they're concerned. At the time, the woman who is now my daughter-in-law Susan, my son Glen's wife, is one of my secretaries, and she's running the command center. She's a twenty-two-year-old gal, all of about five feet two and 110 pounds. She's talking on a marine radio, coordinating men and supplies and equipment, and I call her and say, 'Susan, I've just committed that we're going to have a contractors' meeting on the site tomorrow afternoon at four o'clock. Go down the street. When I came into Staten Island, I saw a landscape guy down there, and he was selling fifty-five-gallon barrels that he had cut in half and was using as planters for geraniums. I want you to go down there and tell that guy you want four of them, and he's got to bring them over right away. Pay him cash—whatever you've got to do—but you've got to get that right away. Then go out and buy beach umbrellas and six or eight picnic tables with benches. I want an umbrella in every one of them. And you need to buy lots of tall glasses and get a bunch of those little toothpick umbrellas, too, like they put in cocktails. Make sure that you get a bunch of ginger ale, Coke, and ice cubes because we're going to have thirty, forty guys here tomorrow.

"'Finally, I want you to get a couple of laborers and go to the north of our command center. There's a nice, clear place over there. Hire a road sweeper to sweep off that area, get some spray paint, draw a big giant circle, and put an X in the middle of it so it looks like a helicopter landing pad.'

"And all she says is, 'I don't know. You're crazy, but I work for you, so we'll take care of it.' And she does. She organizes the whole damn thing—*while* she's helping to run the cleanup and making sure everybody has lunch and whatever else. But she gets it all done—including moving a big supply truck out of the way of where the helicopter pad is supposed to go. She's on the marine radio with me, telling me she's never driven a truck like that in her life. I say, 'I don't care. Just drive it!' So she jumps in the truck and re-parks it somewhere, and by now the Coast Guard is calling us. 'Where in the hell is this site that you guys are talking about? We're doing fly-overs out here, and we see that there's actually a landing pad out on Staten Island now. Is that you guys?'

"'Yeah, yeah,' we tell them. 'That's us. We figured you were going to come by helicopter, so we made a pad for you.' The next day, all the contractors show up at our job site, at what had been a weed-choked, abandoned pierhead just a couple of days before.

They come out, and there we've got a command center, with a flag-pole, a bunch of picnic tables with umbrellas, big flowerpots. It's crazy.

"And here's Susan, a good-looking young woman, walking around offering everyone drinks with little umbrellas in them. Everybody is scratching their heads, saying 'This Miller is crazy as a bedbug.'

"And just like that, we sort of took command of the cleanup. But we had a confrontation with one of the big local contractors later on. He came over and told us, in no uncertain terms, 'Miller, you've got to get your crap out of here. The spill is over, pack everything up, and get the hell out of New York, because this is our harbor. This is where we work every day. You've got some of the cream on this job, but it's time for you to pack up and go back home. As a matter of fact, if you *don't* take your stuff out of here right now, we're never going to call you again. You'll never work in New York Harbor again.'"

Jim's face, at this point in the story, assumes a look of almost theatrical, innocent surprise.

"Gee! Now we've really upset the apple cart. We pissed off one of the big contractors in the harbor. We were always subordinate to him before, and this time we put ourselves on equal footing. Times had changed, and man, he didn't like it. He was going to run us out of there. He had the power to do it—he thought. And that's when we said to ourselves, 'Well, I guess we're going to have to stay here.'

"That's around the same time that Glen and I made the arrange-ment for him to start the launch service on Staten Island, so we'd have a permanent presence in the harbor. We eventually rented Pier 13 from the city, and it was in the middle of nowhere. We had a trailer, and we built a landing platform and had a barge with a gang-way so we could get on and off the boats. But it was like Fort Apache out there back then. It was in a bad neighborhood. Drug addicts, hoodlums, homeless people living on the pierheads, cars being driven off the ends of the piers. Cops would come by and put divers down to see if there was anybody in there. 'Oh man, there are four other cars down here. The cars seem to be empty, though. No bodies. Guess we better look in the trunk.'

"As far as the business went, for the first couple of spills in that part of New York, we were out-and-out competitors with everyone else. Maybe the guy who told us to leave would get a piece of the spill, and we'd get a piece. But in those days, no one contractor could handle a whole spill anyway.

"That was also a time when we made an arrangement with the insurance company that they would pay us on an incremental basis. They'd pay 80 percent of our invoice at first and then audit it and make adjustments. They had an office in Manhattan, down in Battery Park someplace. They called up and said our first invoices were all approved and asked if we could come to their offices and pick up the check. 'Just stop at the desk and identify yourself, and that will be that.' So I went over there with Glen and Mark. We went by boat from Staten Island to Manhattan and walked up the street to the offices by Battery Park. And we were wearing pretty grimy clothes. I mean, we'd been working on an oil spill. But we headed up to this fancy office tower—just country kids, you know? We're not used to this. We went up to the desk, identified ourselves, and the girl working there handed us an envelope. I remember opening that envelope, and there was a check in there for a million dollars, give or take a few thousand. We walked out of there feeling like kings. I mean, who would believe that three bums in dirty coveralls walking down the street in New York City would be carrying a check for a cool million in their pocket?"

· · ·

Here's an interesting little experiment. Try to think of a darker, more sinister nickname than "the Dragon Lady." Sure, at first it might sound like the moniker of a villainess from one of the lesser-known James Bond movies. But applied to an actual flesh-and-blood person, it assumes an ominous weight. How formidable, disagreeable, and downright bad would a person have to be in order to earn that designation?

For Mrs. Evelyn Berman Frank, who for years headed up a series of notorious, family-run barge, waste-disposal, and tank-cleaning businesses in New York Harbor, the nickname was one part insult and two parts badge of honor. A study in contrasts—foul-mouthed when barking orders to her tugboat captains over the marine radio, but dressed to the nines when driven by limousine to company meetings—Mrs. Frank was the most high-profile of the many idiosyncratic and intensely independent business owners who made a living on the New York waterfront in the rough-and-tumble 1970s, 1980s, and early 1990s. That she and other members of her family were described by critics as "litigious, belligerent, and inclined to cut corners to increase profits" is one thing. That they were eventually taken down by their greed, their blatant disregard for environmental laws, and their incessant flouting of basic maritime codes and conventions is something else entirely.

Jim Miller had crossed paths with Mrs. Frank a few times—"She was a reasonably attractive-looking woman," Jim notes, "until she opened her mouth"—but it was a particular job in the fall of 1990 that left the deepest imprint on the enterprise still called, back then, Marine Pollution Control. (It wasn't until 1992 that the business officially adopted the name Miller Environmental Group Inc.)

The job in question involved a sunken barge; 30,000 gallons of spilled oil; a classic, cynical bait and switch by America's "First Family of Pollution"; and an impromptu trip to the United

Kingdom by a pair of self-admitted "crazy Yanks" hell-bent on forcing the world's most famous insurance market to honor a simple contract.

In other words, just another gig for Jim Miller and company.

"The *Sarah Frank* was a barge berthed at a shipyard in Staten Island that mysteriously sank one September night," Jim says. "We were alerted by the Coast Guard to an oil spill. When we responded, we found a lot of oil in the water, a lot of oil in the area, and we were maxed out in terms of our response capability. A couple of other contractors were on the job as well. Early on, we determined that the barge was owned by the Frank family, and everybody said, 'Oh boy! This is not a good set of circumstances. If we're working for the Franks on this one, we quit.'"

(Incidentally, a few months later, partially in response to the *Sarah Frank* incident, New York State forced the family's sludge and oil barge businesses to close, citing the family for "an unabated record of deliberately illegal conduct and damage to human health and the environment." For her part, in response to the actions by the state, the Dragon Lady adopted the time-honored ploy of deflecting criticism not by stating facts or mounting a coherent defense but by invoking Adolf Hitler and the specter of Nazism. "I can only tell you we're living in Nazi Germany," Mrs. Frank declared at the time. "I have a reputation in this business that's absolutely flawless. They're trying to destroy me. Why?")

"The mere fact that the barge was owned by the Franks meant that they were the 'responsible party,' as it's known in the industry," Jim says of the concerns he and the other contractors shared, "and, therefore, by law, they were obligated to clean up the spill. We were engaged to perform the services, but early on, we said we needed guarantees of payment. Otherwise, we weren't going to work there. The Salvage Association and the insurance surveyor represented to us that even though the Franks owned the barge, they themselves were the insurers, and they would be coming forward with the financing for the cleanup. To which we said, 'Well, it's nice that you're saying that, but we really need some absolute assurances that, down the road, if any of this is contested, you guys are going to be there and taking over payments.'

"So we negotiated an agreement that we would work for the first week, and on the tenth day of the spill, they would provide an 80 percent payment against the first week's invoicing. We agreed to it—as did the other contractors, Ken's Marine and Clean Venture— under those terms because the Salvage Association and the insurer, which happened to be one of the syndicates located at Lloyd's of London, assured us that there was coverage on the vessel. With all those contractual guarantees in place, we went forward and con- ducted the cleanup. Invoicing at the end of the first week was in the range of several million dollars.

"We were assured that they would process it and pay 80 percent of the invoice, subject to audit. On the tenth day, we asked, 'Where's the check?' And that's when the insurer's representatives came for- ward and said, 'Well, we're reserving rights.' I said, 'You can't reserve rights, because that's contrary to our agreement.' They said, "Oh no. The insurer *always* has that right in case there was criminal activity or in case coverage might be invalidated due to fraud.'

"We depended on the Salvage Association and underwriters at Lloyd's to guarantee the payments, and we depended on their good faith. That was no longer there, so we quit. We could not continue to work without payment, so we all agreed to stop work. Eventu- ally, the Coast Guard took over funding the oil spill, but of course the cleanup was basically completed by then anyway, and we wound up with substantial outstanding bills, divided pretty evenly between Miller, Clean Venture, and Ken's Marine. We presented our final invoices, around $5 million in total, to the Salvage Asso- ciation, to LUCRO [London Underwriters Claims and Recovery

Office], and to the Frank syndicate. The insurance underwriters denied coverage on the basis of a warranty that the vessel was to be clean and out of service at the time she was tied up at the dock. But it certainly was *not* clean, because when it sank, it belched oil like Old Faithful.

"It turns out that the Franks, being the Franks, had stored waste oil in the barge. And right about the tenth day of the job, we saw the Franks in their office with boxes full of documents that they were hastily shoving into the trunk of a limousine. The Frank family was bailing out the back door while the FBI was barging in the front. They escaped immediate arrest, for the time being. Just another part of the big, wonderful adventure we had on that job.

"We hired attorneys to try to collect our money. That was a long, drawn-out, unsuccessful approach. They wrote letters, and they talked to people, and they got nowhere. Finally, out of frustration, Mark and I decided to go to London. We showed up at Lloyd's, much to everybody's shock and surprise, because here were these two crazy Yanks in the role of bill collectors. Part of our strategy, if you could call it that, was founded on the fact that after Mark graduated from college, he'd gone to London to study and learn the marine insurance business. He had worked at Lloyd's and still had an expired credential. He had relationships at the insurance market, and with those, we were able to circumvent some of the normal protocols. In other words, we pretty much disregarded the courtesies and formalities that are normally associated with doing business at Lloyd's of London. They were not really accustomed to bill collectors banging on their doors."

Were Jim and Mark in danger of being tossed out on their ears?

"Yeah," Jim admits. "We were. But we also let them know that if they did that, we were going to hold a press conference right there on the sidewalk because Lloyd's and the Salvage Association were the two most respected names in the business at the time, and here they had reneged on the deal. They had absolutely backed away from their guarantee of payment. This very situation was exactly why we had entered into the agreement in the first place, in order to avoid this mess. That was our exposure. That's what we had been protecting ourselves against, because we believed that the Franks' business attitude was immoral and their behavior was borderline illegal, at best, even though we didn't know how circumstances around this particular barge were going to develop. And, as it happened, we were *right*. The barge had been warranted to be clean, so their storage of thousands of gallons of oil in the barge had been illegal. With all that information in hand, plus our contract, we basically browbeat the folks at Lloyd's and the Salvage Association until they gave in. We were there for a couple of days, and in the end, we were able to get about half of the millions of dollars owed to the three of us—the three contractors on the job. At that point, it was a semi-successful attempt to get the money all of us had earned.

"Shortly thereafter, they agreed that they were going to sue the Frank family to try to recoup their funds. If they were successful in their suits, we would be compensated for the rest of what we were owed."

Now, it's important to understand that this was all taking place not long after the Oil Pollution Act of 1990 had been signed into law, in August of that year. The legislation, in part, was a guarantee by the federal government—in order to expedite cleanups of spills—that they would repay response costs if there was no identifiable responsible party. And in order to do that, they would establish a fund of $1 billion, utilizing a tax on the oil industry of a few pennies per barrel.

"So they had put this thing in place, sort of, but the actual steps by which a company or a contractor could apply for those funds—the framework or guidelines by which somebody could be reimbursed—had not been created. By chance, Mark and I were at a spill-control trade association meeting, and the presenter was the future director of the spill fund. During his presentation, he was trying to explain to us that contractors should not hesitate to respond to an oil spill for fear of not being paid, because ultimately if they're not paid, they can file against the federal government, and the feds will pay them for their services. When we asked him how many people had filed against the fund so far, he said they hadn't really codified any rules yet. 'We don't know how to do this yet' was basically his response.

"We said, 'Well, let us work with you and establish a protocol on how to file against the fund because these are the circumstances on the *Sarah Frank* spill that we just worked on.' We hammered things out with the Coast Guard and the federal government, and we were ultimately paid by the government for the whole thing, and so were all the other contractors. Ours was one of the inaugural claims on the spill compensation fund."

CHAPTER 23

Cleaning the Big Black Box

Ome of the signature characteristics of so many of Jim Miller's stories is how visual they are. The landscape or environment in which they're framed—the open ocean, for example—is usually one that most of us can readily picture, even if we haven't spent a single minute hauling pots on the heaving deck of a lobster boat. But even in those stories recounting events that took place in utterly unfamiliar territory—say, in the pitch-dark interior of an enormous oil tank—there's often a kind of cinematic quality to the telling, while the strangeness of the setting often only adds to the adventure's hold on our imagination.

Obviously, none of this is meant to romanticize what was, and what is, difficult, dirty, and often very dangerous work. But the appeal of this particular story is not only that it illustrates Jim Miller's ability to envision and execute singular solutions to seemingly intractable problems but also that it highlights the man's will to *win*. Yes, there was financial gain at the end of it. Yes, this was a job—thornier and more complex than some, and smaller and more straightforward than others, but still, in the end, a job. But it's difficult to listen to Jim Miller recounting the way that he approached this particular challenge and not sense at least a little bit of a competitive fire beneath the matter-of-fact details. Other companies had tried to tackle the problem and had given up. He tackled the problem, and not only did he get the job done, but he took care of it in such a way that left everyone pretty close to awestruck.

Think about it this way: Most people are familiar with the twelve seemingly impossible labors of Hercules, the son of Zeus and a mortal woman, Alcmene, which he performed as penance for having offended the gods and man. (Driven insane by Zeus's jealous wife, Hera, Hercules had killed his wife and children in a blind frenzy. When the madness passed, the guilt-ravaged demigod sought to atone for his sins. Tackling the twelve labors was part of that atonement.) One labor in particular involved Hercules mucking out the colossal—and colossally disgusting—Augean stables, which had not been cleaned in thirty years and housed more than a thousand cattle. Hercules, uncharacteristically using his brain as well as his brawn for this task, cleaned the stables in a single day by rerouting two rivers so that their waters ran through the stalls.

On an admittedly smaller scale, this story is kind of like that.

"We had a tank-cleaning job in Brooklyn when I was in my forties," Jim Miller says. "The tanks belonged to New England Petroleum Company. They were unique tanks because they were square, and they were tanks within tanks. As the industry calls it, it was all monkey bars inside, cross-braced from the inner tank, which held the petroleum, to the space—about six feet—between that inner tank and the tank's outer wall. These tanks were huge. They were about 150 feet by 150 feet by 30 feet high. They were giant pieces of equipment, and the company had upgraded them and painted them, and sand-blasted and welded and fixed and patched and whatever else they had to do.

"It was a tremendous project. The company, NEPCO, calls up and tells me that this project has to be done, it's time-sensitive, and they're looking for a contractor who will guarantee that they can do the job. Would I look at it? They've already been delayed with three previous contractors starting the project, trying to clean the tanks, and failing. They're terribly behind schedule now, and they've got to get this thing over and done with to put the tanks into service. I go down there, look at the job, and see that there's a small manhole to get into the tank—and then pure darkness. We get flashlights and helmet lights, and we go inside the tank, and right away we see that every eight feet or so, there's a crossbar, or brace, blocking the path. And there are *lots* of them.

"We survey a tank, and we go over this crossbar and under that one and over this one to get around the entire circuit, and it just feels like it goes on forever and ever. We finally circumvent the entire tank, but we've seen that this is really a mess. The floor is covered with about a foot of sand and welding rods, lunch bags, beer bottles, and whatever else the guys who were working on these tanks brought in and then left behind. But that's the job: to get those floors clean. That's what we've got to do. We've got to get all of it out of there. And remember, this is time-sensitive. But as we go around the tank, it sort of looks like nobody really worked in there. There wasn't very much done at all.

"My guy Joe Gomer and I look at each other and ask, 'How can we do this job?' You've got to go to the farthest point, and you've got to shovel the stuff off the floor, then you move it eight feet and you throw it to the *next* eight—over the crossbar. But then you have a bigger pile, and you have to go to that eight feet and shovel it and move it eight feet to the *next* pile. You just keep going until you've got a giant pile of sand that's got to get shoveled out of this damn tank.

"Now, if we put a thousand guys in there, we'll be able to put a guy shoveling from here to here, and there'll be a guy there already shoveling to the next guy, and we'll all shovel like crazy—hut, two, three, four!—and maybe that'll work.

"But then there's the problem of lighting all of this. It's pitch dark down there. We could rig up lights and do whatever we have to do to make this thing work. That's *one* way to do it. But if we could get *conveyor belts* in here, on the outboard side of this six-foot space, and we just shovel all this sand and other crap onto the conveyor belt, and the conveyor belt carries it around to the manhole cover, where it all can be emptied out of the tank—well, that might be a smarter way to do it. Conveyor belts are, what, thirty, forty feet long? We can set belts on top of these crossbars, with one conveyor belt dumping onto the next conveyor belt and so on, all the way around the inside of the tank. Right?

"Okay. But how are we going to get them inside? Will they fit? We've got to get everything in through the manhole. How the hell are we going to get the stuff in through the manhole? There are crossbars here, crossbars there—we can't move anything. We have to test it out. What about a ladder? What if we buy a ladder and bring it back and see if we can move a ladder through the tank?

"We go to the hardware store, and we buy a twenty-four-foot ladder, and we bring it back to the tank. We start maneuvering. We can't put it straight in, because it hits the tank, so we have to put it at an angle. If we lift it up a certain amount, we can twist it back, stand it up, move it eight feet, wiggle it around—we can make it work. So with trial and error, we figure out how we can maneuver that twenty-four-foot ladder through the tank space, even with the crossbars and everything else. It's a tight fit, but it will work. That means we can get a conveyor belt in there. We can get several conveyor belts in there. All right. That'll be big savings. We have a couple of conveyor belts in the shop, for some reason, and we know where we can rent some from somebody else. Somehow or other, we conjure up ten or twenty conveyor belts, and we're going to line this thing with conveyor belts. And then we're going to put a bunch of guys in there shoveling sand on the conveyors, and it'll all come out through the manhole. We'll get a payloader and put everything on a dump truck, and it'll be done.

"All right. We've got it figured out how we're going to do the job. But no idea how long it's going to take us to really finish the job. So we go back up to the oil company and ask them what they think this job is worth. They had other guys in here who couldn't get it done. What was it worth it to them to finally have it finished and out of their hair?

"'Ah, this is an expensive job, it's a big deal. Oh my God, we had a deal for fifty grand with this guy and sixty grand with that guy, but they didn't do anything, so we fired them, and we never paid them. But we need this desperately.'

"'Wow!' we say. 'Those are big numbers. Would you pay us fifty grand if we guarantee that we'll clean it?'

"'If you can clean it in thirty days, yeah, it'd be worth fifty grand to us. We're not going to take a chance like we did in the past. If you think you can do it in thirty days, then we're going to put a penalty on anything *over* thirty days.'

"'Well,' I say, 'that sounds fair. I think we can do it in under thirty days."

"'We're going to put a penalty of $1,000 a day.'

"'All right,' I say. 'But if there's a penalty for going over thirty days, then we get a bonus of $1,000 for every day we bring the job in *under* thirty days. Right?'

"'Ha! Yeah sure. Sure. We'll pay that. Anything you get done sooner than thirty days we'll pay you an extra thousand dollars a day. No problem, no problem. But you ain't going to do it in less than thirty days. The other guys were here for three months, and they didn't get anything done.'

"'Well, I think I can do it,' I say.

"'You can say that, but there's $50,000 we're promising to pay you. What are you promising if you don't do it? Put up a bond or something.'

"'I guess I can get a bond. I never had a bond before. It takes some time to do that. How about if I give you a cashier's check for fifty grand? I'm pretty confident I can do this.'

"'All right, you give us a cashier's check. Here's the contract. We'll get punished if you do this; you get punished if you don't do it.'

"I say, 'I don't want any restrictions on what hours I can work because I might work nights.'

"They look at me like I'm crazy. 'We don't care when the hell you work. It means nothing to us. You can work as long as you want. You're inside the tank, who cares?'

"Okay. Off we go. 'When are you going to start? You going to start on Monday?'

"'Oh yeah,' I tell him. 'We'll probably mobilize a little bit before then, though.'

"This is on a Wednesday that we get the job. We start bringing stuff in on Wednesday afternoon. A union guy shows up. 'Hey, what are you doing here? This has got to be a union job, you know.'

"Oh crap! We never planned running into union guys. This ain't going to be good.

"'You're going to need lights, and you need an electrician,' he says. 'You need lights around the clock. You need the electrician around the clock. You've got to put these guys on the job.' Blah, blah, blah. Now this thing's going down the tubes real quick.

"'We're just starting to get set up here now,' we tell him. 'We ain't got this figured out yet. Why don't you come back on Monday, and we'll see how this is all going to come together?'

"Now, we know that we can't use their electric, so we bring in a generator, and our guys run electric cables, and we're hooking up lights, and we've got the whole thing lit up inside like Grand Central.

We've got a big fat cable with pigtails down there for the conveyor belts. We've got this thing coming together real quick, we wiggle these conveyor belts in, and we get them all lined up. We work all night, and Thursday morning, early, we start. We have ten, twelve guys in the tank shoveling, the conveyor belts are running, and the sand is coming out. We've got a payloader there now, and he's loading, and we get a truckload of sand out already in the first hour. It's going gangbusters.

"We've got one old guy, Al Demesco. Al is a retired Rheingold Beer truck driver. Big belly on him. He'd been let go by Rheingold because he was sixty-five years old and it was time to retire. But he's a bull, and he likes nothing better than to work, to get some young buck, some nineteen-year-old kid, and tell him, 'You go quick, go ahead. I go slow, slow, slow, and I'll be here tomorrow going slow, and you'll be passed out somewhere.' Al sets the stage for all the young bucks. 'You just keep up with the old man, slow and steady, shovel for shovel with the old man, and you'll be all right.'

"Sure enough, we're working twelve-hour shifts. There's a diner there, closes at five p.m. I go up, and I tell 'em they can't close at five. I got a dozen guys here, and they're going to need meals, a coffee break every four hours. How much will it cost to keep them open?

"'We never had anybody ask us this before,' they tell me. 'What kind of a crazy guy are you?'

"'What does it cost?'

"'All right. We'll stay open for you. You'll guarantee us you'll pay us $150 for a night shift and $150 for the—'

"'Yeah, it's done. It's done. Absolutely. The guys come in, I just want you to feed them, whatever they want, you just put it on my bill, and I'll pay it.' The guys are excited. 'We're going to *eat*, man. The old man's paying for this.' Some of the guys are really pigs. 'I want four hamburgers.' Okay, eat four hamburgers. I don't care. You'll work that off pretty quick.

"We're there twenty-four hours a day, two crews, twelve-hour shifts. Sunday afternoon rolls around, we're done. The tank floor is swept. Monday morning, the union guys are coming down. 'I guess we're going to get started here.'

"I tell 'em, 'You better come back tomorrow, because we're really busy right now. The boss is going to be here tomorrow. I know he said he'd talk to you guys, but you've got to come back tomorrow.' I go up to the office, and I say, 'You've got my contract?' 'Yeah, we've got the contract. It's all signed.'

"'You know, in the contract, we didn't really talk about how we get sign-off on this thing. Who's going to be the guy to come down and make the inspection and say that it's a done deal?'

"'Oh, I'm going to be the guy who does that. It'll be next month sometime, though, before that happens.'

"And I tell him, 'Well, I really want you to come down today and take a look and see what we did. If you think that it meets your standards, I want to know that.'

"'You started already?'

"'Yeah, we kind of started a little bit. We worked over the weekend. We got some crap done.'

"He gets all huffy. 'We'll see about this. Let's see what kind of work you guys do here.' So he comes down, and we get him in the tank. Guys are sweeping the floor, but the lights are still in place. He's pretty amazed. 'Yeah, it's really done. I have no idea how you did this.'

"'Down on my hands and knees, I ate all the sand myself,' I tell him. 'What does it matter how it got done? Now let's get my money.'

"'Well,' he says. 'We have to go to the comptroller because we don't know how to handle this whole thing.' I say, 'You also have a clause in there that, upon completion, you'd pay the contract price, and there was also a penalty if I went over. Now, today is the first day of the start of the job, and it's already done. In fact, there was nobody here yesterday to sign off, and I was really done yesterday. So which way does it go now?'

"'We don't know,' he says. 'We have to go up to the comptroller now. But we're not prepared to pay you. I'll have to go to the vice president.'

"'I don't care,' I tell him. 'You want me to go with you?'

"Anyway," Jim says, "we got the eighty grand, and everybody on the crew got a bonus and a lot of stories to tell about that crazy couple of days in Brooklyn. But here's the thing: It was all about organizing a crew and having a technique that nobody else saw. Conveyor belts? *Inside* the tank? Nobody else saw that way of solving the problem. I think they all sincerely thought they were going to do the job. But once they got in there, they all saw the same solution—shoveling stuff from pile to pile to pile. But that wasn't really a solution at all, was it?"

CHAPTER 24

From Rocky Point
to the Stars

The commonplace expression "suffer fools gladly" has a long and complex history, dating back almost 2,000 years. The man who would be canonized as Saint Paul famously coined it in his second letter to the Corinthians—" For ye suffer fools gladly, seeing ye yourselves are wise"—and men and women who have made hobbies and even careers out of studying idioms have been puzzling over it ever since. Is it an ambiguous compliment? Are we supposed to admire people who *don't* suffer fools gladly? Or should we consider them impatient, pretentious, and impolite egomaniacs?

Perhaps a more constructive question to ask, however, is this: What's the obverse of that old saying? How do we describe the man or woman who, regardless of how he treats the occasional fool in his life, is perpetually seeking out and spending time with people who challenge his assumptions about the world, who is willing to engage in vigorous and well-informed debate, and who is thrilled to converse with the brilliant and the accomplished about everything under the sun?

Throughout his life, Jim Miller has enjoyed meeting and holding long conversations with men and women of formidable intellect. Perhaps the finest example of that sort of relationship can be found in the many hours that Jim spent with his neighbors Zvi and Temima Gezari, when he and Barbara lived on the bluff at Rocky Point.

Zvi Gezari was a Polish émigré and a renowned industrial engineer and metallurgist. His wife, Temima, was a Russian-born, Brooklyn-raised artist, activist, and educator. For years, the Gezaris lived in the house that Zvi built atop a bluff in Rocky Point, overlooking Long Island Sound. Temima worked for decades in the sculpture studio that Zvi had designed and built for her on their property. (Temima, who knew and worked with such great artists as Diego Rivera and was a lifelong advocate for arts education, died peacefully in the Rocky Point house in March 2005. She was 103 years old. Zvi died in the late 1980s.)

As it turns out, Zvi Gezari was the driving force behind conceiving and building the tram that for years carried people up and down the bluff—the same tram that served as the setting for Tracey Miller's tale of the mysterious stranger who appeared one night out of the blue, claiming a longtime acquaintance with her dad. The other person involved in the conception of the tram was one of Zvi's longtime friends, a fellow European émigré and theoretical physicist named Albert Einstein.

One day (the story goes), Albert and Zvi were walking along the beach in Rocky Point, chatting about sundry topics, as friends often will. When it came time to head back to Zvi's house on top of the bluff, however, the two men had to literally pull themselves up the sandy, 200-foot slope, hand over hand, by way of the knotted towing hawser that ran down to the beach.

When they made it back to the top, huffing, puffing, and completely worn out, the two held a brief conversation—once they had finally caught their breath—that went something like this:

ZVI: Albert, we're a couple of pretty smart guys.

ALBERT: Yes, we are.

ZVI: We should be able to figure out a way to get back up here from the beach that doesn't involve pulling ourselves up by a rope.

ALBERT: Yes, we should.

ZVI: I think I'll design and build a tram.

ALBERT: That's a good idea.

ZVI: Let's go inside and sit down.

ALBERT: That's a very good idea.

A few years later, a tram capable of carrying six passengers up and down the bluff was in place and running smoothly. Decades later, Jim and Barbara Miller moved into their house at Rocky Point—a house that was just steps from the tram's upper terminus. In short order, Jim Miller joined Zvi, who was in his sixties by that point, in maintaining the tram—which had fallen into something close to disrepair—and making sure it was running reliably and safely from the bluff head to the beach and back again.

"I remember the two of them out there," Mark Miller says, "on their hands and knees inside the winch shed, both of them covered in grease and as happy as could be, with their tools scattered all over the place."

One of Zvi Gezari's abiding passions was astronomy. In fact, he is still remembered today as the man who built, from scratch, a six-foot-long, quarter-ton Newtonian telescope for Einstein, right down to the eight-inch lens that he hand-ground at the Hayden

Planetarium in New York and that was, he assured his friend, accurate to one-millionth of an inch.

"All my life I have worked with my head," an admiring Einstein said when Zvi and Temima presented him with the telescope at his Princeton home in May 1954, just a year before his death. "But I have never built anything with my hands."

The telescope's slow-motion drives and finely tuned sights were constructed from parts of German artillery pieces. "It has always been my ambition to turn swords into plowshares," Gezari told Einstein, according to *The New York Times*. In reply, the Nobel Prize–winning physicist, antiwar protester, and civil rights activist (Einstein was a longtime member of the NAACP) "nodded approvingly."

Zvi's interest in astronomy informed what Mark Miller calls an unforgettable—and characteristically enlightening—conversation that he and Zvi had one day on the deck of Jim and Barbara's Rocky Point home.

"Like so many smart, curious people often are, Dad and Zvi were naturally drawn to each other," Mark says. "On weekends, Zvi loved to visit my dad and sit on the deck of the house that was cantilevered over the bluff, drink coffee, and get into these long, deep, intellectual conversations. They would talk about anything and everything, and I'll never forget one particular discussion that I sat in on. Zvi would often bring up topics that he'd been mulling over recently, and this time he brought up the idea of whether there might be life in outer space. He asked me if I believed in extraterrestrials, and I just laughed. I told him that was crazy—the sort of stuff that Area 51 conspiracy nuts believed in.

"He looked at me with surprise, and then he said, 'You're someone who understands a little bit about numbers, Mark. So let's think about this for a minute. What do you think? Is it probable that life might exist somewhere on one of a million other planets? How about on one of a billion other planets in our own galaxy? Or on one of *500 billion* other planets?'

"I remember getting a little nervous then, because he was really hammering away at this probability angle. Then he said, 'Stop thinking about our one, single solar system. You have to think about the universe, and the billions and billions of stars out there, and the hundreds of billions of planets orbiting those stars. In fact, if we accept the proposition that the universe is infinite, then the probability of life beyond our solar system is infinite as well. Personally, I would take those odds any day.'

"When he put it like that, I just sat back and said, for the first time in my life, 'I guess other life probably has to exist out there after all, in some form or another.'

"That's just one, small example of the kind of conversations my dad had on his deck with Zvi all the time—and with other people, too. The two of them really enjoyed each other's company, and Temima was just as brilliant. There's a reason that Zvi and Dad became very close friends. I think each one saw a bit of himself in the other. They were from totally different backgrounds but were similar where it mattered—the intelligence, the curiosity, the unique way each of them had of looking at and learning about the world. They just respected each other on a very deep level. And Dad has had relationships like that with all sorts of people throughout his life."

CHAPTER 25

Big Bird: A Battle for Art's Sake

If one were looking for a single story that manages, in all of its particulars, to serve as an illustration of Jim Miller's tenacity, his
unwillingness to be cowed, and—crucially—his understated but
unmistakable sense of humor, the strange but true tale of a forty-
foot-tall, two-ton steel heron overlooking Long Island's Peconic
Bay would do the trick.

Designed and sculpted by the renowned Venezuela-born artist
Roberto Julio Bessin, the monumental heron—crafted of gracefully
bent, three-eighths-inch steel bars covered in white epoxy, its perfectly lifelike beak pointed skyward—today stands sentinel on a
beach along the bay, directly in front of Jim and Barbara Miller's
Southold home. Like all of Bessin's wildlife sculptures, the heron is
both a tribute to the natural world and a reminder of our collective
responsibility to protect what's left of the earth's wild places. The
steel heron's journey to its present-day home, meanwhile, was
fraught with its own, purely human, perils, mainly in the form of
lawsuits and rancorous neighbors.

Jim's telling of that journey, however, makes it sound like a lark.

His own adventure with the heron sculpture began in the 1990s. Jim says that he and the sculptor, Roberto Bessin, had "known each other for years. I can't remember when I met him, exactly, or under what circumstances—but I knew him, and he knew me. We were both waterfront people, you know. Spent a lot of time around boats.

"Back then, in the mid-nineties, there was a big shot in Port Jefferson who got in trouble with the law. His name was John McNamara, and he owned a high-class restaurant and hotel by the water and a big Buick and Pontiac dealership in town. Turns out, he was also defrauding General Motors out of hundreds of millions of dollars."

Specifically, in one of the largest cases of corporate fraud in American history up to that time, over the course of a decade McNamara somehow finagled loans amounting to more than $6 billion from GM's financing arm, General Motors Acceptance Corporation, to pay for hundreds of thousands of conversion vans that, strictly speaking, never existed. He pled guilty in a sweetheart deal with prosecutors, but after testifying in court against public officials who, he claimed, accepted bribes from him (the officials were acquitted), McNamara served not one day in jail.

"In the midst of these criminal shenanigans," Jim says, "there's this enormous heron sculpture standing out there at the end of the restaurant's pier. That sculpture had been out there for a while and had sort of become part of the Port Jefferson community. But as McNamara's house of cards began to fall apart, the artist who made the sculpture, Roberto, came to me and asked me if there was anything I could do to help him get it back. McNamara was only renting the artwork—rent that he hadn't paid in six months—and Roberto was worried that it might be seized or forfeited or something with the rest of McNamara's assets. He knew that you couldn't get land-based equipment out there to move the sculpture, and he also knew that I had marine equipment, so he asked me if there was anything I could do to help. He said, 'I can't pay you, Jim. I don't have any money for that right now.' But I said, 'That's all right, I'll go play the repo man. That ought to be fun, to go out there and repossess a forty-foot piece of art.'

"We had a landing craft with a crane. We show up one morning at eight o'clock and announce to the people on the dock that we're going to repossess the artwork. There's a big commotion. 'What? How're you gonna do that? It's bolted down. How're you going to lift it? It's an impossible task. We're going to stop you.' Blah, blah, blah. So I say, 'Well, you're not going to stop us. We're going to repossess it.' A couple of bolts? Some welds? That's no big deal. I tell my guys on the boat to give me a torch, and we cut the welds, pick up this big bird, and take it away. We have the artist right there with us. He owns it. Those guys on the dock don't own it, so it's going away with us.

"We take it off the dock and put it on the landing craft, and I ask Roberto what he's going to do with it now that he has it back. He says he doesn't know and asks me if there's someplace we can store it until he figures something out. I tell him that Steve Clarke, who owns the Greenport Yacht & Ship Building Company, is a good buddy of mine, and I can always store something there. I call Steve, and he says, 'Sure, bring it out. Stick it out on the end of the dock, and it won't bother me.' On the way down the Sound, as we're transporting it, I'm looking at this thing in the hold, and I'm saying to myself, 'You know, this is a pretty ingenious piece of art. All the bends in it are realistic, it's really beautifully done, and the welding is first-class. This is a unique work of art we have here.'

"I had recently purchased my own home in Southold, on the waterfront, and I ask Roberto what he thinks the chances are of getting this thing approved to put in my backyard. 'Oh,' he tells me, 'it's no problem. Nobody ever objects to artwork. You can just put it there.' But I'm thinking that in Southold, there are probably some rules you have to follow. I know there's a consultant in Southold who makes a living getting permits for people who want to do something like this. I contact the guy, and he makes a sketch of the artwork and submits a series of permit requests. He sends letters to the Army Corps of Engineers because the sculpture would be erected in the marine environment. He sends letters to the New York State DEC, to the town trustees, to the aeronautical people in case the sculpture is too high. Everybody and anybody who might be interested or might have a say in permitting it. The Corps of Engineers suggests moving it fifty feet up the beach, instead of having it standing in the water. 'If it's above the high-tide mark, it's fine. You don't need a permit from us. Go ahead and do what you want to do.'

"So we go back to New York DEC and tell them we'll be putting it on the beach, and they say the only thing we need is a permit to put in six pilings. So we go to the town, and we get a permit for the pilings. We have permits from the New York State DEC and the town trustees for the foundation, and there's no objection to putting up the artwork. Boom. It's done.

"One day, we put in all the pilings. The next day, we float the bird in on the landing craft, pick it up, and set it on the beach. And the next day, the crap hits the fan. I mean, there's been some talk back and forth that this is a bad precedent, it's going to be bad for the community, it's going to degrade the real estate values—all sorts of stuff. But regardless of the comments, the town approves the permit for this sculpture on my property, and it's 100 percent legal, as far as I'm concerned.

"That weekend, a group of neighbors come over to my house. 'Jim,' they tell me, 'you're new to the neighborhood, and we want to be up-front with you. You have to take the bird down, or we're going to sue you.' That's when I get a little bit irate. I really do not like the idea of these people barging into my house on a Sunday afternoon, when I have guests over, and announcing that they're going to sue me. I tell them, 'Okay, go ahead.' If they think they're going to order me around, so be it. They march off and hire an attorney, and on Tuesday, I'm served with papers to respond in court. Ultimately, their suit is based on the fact that in the town building code, it says that if you build anything that remains in place above ground after the construction, it needs a *building* permit. They claim that it's a structure and that it has to conform to the rules and regulations for an accessory building.

"I respond by saying that it's not a building, it's a piece of art. And nobody in the history of Southold has ever gotten a permit for a piece of art. In court the judge rules that, in fact, it is a structure. It requires a building permit, and since we don't have a building permit, it has to be removed.

"I take it down. I bring it back to Greenport, where it sits out on the end of the dock at the shipyard. I appeal the judge's decision . . . and I lose again. At that point, it really looks like the bird ain't coming back. It's history. That is, until I go and read the building code for myself. That's when I discover that accessory structures are allowed on your property for secondary use, and the exception to that rule involves monuments and steeples, which don't have to conform to the eighteen-foot height restriction set forth in the code.

"So I ask, 'What is a monument?' We do our homework, and we find out that monuments are artworks, structures, or stoneworks installed to commemorate a person, event, or place of importance and worthy of special respect. I say, 'Peconic Bay has recently been admitted into the federal EPA's National Estuary Program. New York's Department of Environmental Conservation deems the Peconic "special waters." We need a monument dedicated in honor of the Peconic Bay.'

"We do a little more homework on who is allowed to name a monument, and it turns out it's basically anybody, as long as there's a dedication ceremony attended by dignitaries and political figures and respected members of a community. If a plaque is placed, it is recognized as a monument. So we have a cocktail party, and we invite the local dignitaries and politicians and media, and the sculpture goes back on the beach. One morning, it just appears. And people get bent out of shape *again*.

"See, my neighbors are among the wealthiest guys in town. By their standard, I'm a newcomer. I'm a Johnny-come-lately. They're the old-timers who have lived there for decades. The rest of the community, on the other hand, is offering us all kinds of support. I have people calling me, telling me not to let these guys push me around. They love the heron. After a while, we have bumper stickers made up with a silhouette of the bird, and it reads 'Southold is the home of the heron.' Suddenly there are hundreds of cars driving around Southold with these bumper stickers. We're getting support from art societies and regular citizens. It's a movement.

"Anyway, the heron is back on our property for the second time. I put it in on Monday, and on Tuesday, I go back to the building department and say, 'Okay, you gave me a building permit on Monday. Now, I want a certificate of occupancy. Send the inspector down. I've met all your requirements.' So I get a certificate of occupancy for the bird as an identified accessory building, but exempt from the height restriction because it's a monument. And there it stands, on the beach in front of my house.

"Around that same time, it's reported that the two attorneys, our side and their side, are up at the local bar having a drink and giggling between themselves about all the fees they're racking up in this fight between these neighbors in Southold. 'I got a sports car out of it,' one says. 'Hey, I got a sports car, too,' says the other one. 'You think we can get these idiots to go for a ski lodge?'

"Gradually, though, the battle subsided. People have grown old and left town. Nobody who sued me remains in the community.

They're all gone. But the heron is still here.

"As a matter of fact," Jim says, a kind of mischievous pride evident in his voice, "over the years, the heron has become something of an emblem for the Millers and our business ventures. Almost like our trademark. We've commissioned Roberto to reproduce the heron many times over, at a smaller scale, and we've placed them at many of our buildings and facilities in different parts of the community here on Long Island, in upstate New York, in New Jersey. That one big bird has spawned a whole series of chicks."

Then, in what sounds like an almost rueful acknowledgment of the passing years, Jim notes that the later heron sculptures were not made of steel, like the forty-foot original, but in bronze. "When Roberto built that first, tall heron, he was a young, strong bull and could cut and bend that three-eighths-inch steel. He could make it do whatever he wanted. As he aged, he's lost some of that strength in his hands. The later, smaller herons are sculpted in bronze. They're still beautiful, though."

("I've had the opportunity to build monuments on three continents," Bessin told *The New York Times* in 2001, discussing the Peconic Bay heron ordeal, "and I have never encountered this sort of silliness.")

Summing up a key lesson of the entire battle to keep the heron on his land, Jim notes that sometimes "you've got to read the law yourself. You have to look at how you can get things done. Think of it this way: I've never had anybody come in for a job interview and give me a list of all the things he can't or won't do. The only thing we're really interested in, whether we're looking at a new hire or facing a challenge like those lawsuits against the heron, is when and how we can get something done. Everything else is just noise."

In the midst of this tale, it becomes increasingly clear that the original heron sculpture was, from the beginning, far more than just a way to pay tribute to the beloved Peconic Bay. For Jim, who appreciates and prizes the ability to design and to build, the heron sculpture possesses an aesthetic power far greater than any utilitarian or monetary value it might have in the marketplace. It is, at heart, a feat of the imagination, wrought in steel—and in that sense, it has a worth all its own.

"I was really struck," Jim says, "that day on the boat, when we were taking it to Greenport, by the level of workmanship—the skill and the imagination and the vision—it takes to create such a piece of art. The gentle bends in the steel that looked like feathers, and like wings. The way the artist made the legs really look like heron legs and the level of detail right down to the toes. But then to have the ability to put things in scale! When you have a bird that's really four feet tall, how do you expand that and keep everything in perspective when you re-create it, in steel, at ten times the size? What size do the eyes need to be? And the feet? And how does that relationship between the different parts of the sculpture evolve? I just found it to be an amazing artwork. You're looking at 4,000 pounds of steel, and it looks like it's made of feathers. That's quite a transition for your mind to work through, don't you think?"

Throughout his story, Jim returns to the resistance his Southold neighbors showed to the sculpture from the very start, and how that resistance—especially the way in which it was first voiced—brought out the fighter in him.

"I didn't welcome the battle with the people who opposed the sculpture," he says. "I wanted to be a neighborly kind of a guy. But you can't allow somebody to come in and tell you what to do just because they happened to be living there before you. They tried to push me around, and you can't do that to me. But beyond that, they were telling me that the bird is ugly, it's an eyesore, it's going to attract the wrong kind of people—whatever the hell that means. Did they think there were going to be boats congregating out in the bay to see this thing, or hordes of people would be marching down the beach to take a look, up close and personal? Or that it was a hazard? That it was going to get blown off the beach and fly through the air and penetrate their house and hurt their children? Whatever their arguments were, I wasn't buying it. And as the years pass, people have grown to love it.

"I'll tell you a little story. A few years ago, some friends and I, maybe six or eight of us, are down in Panama for a week of fishing. We're in a very remote area in a lodge that accommodates maybe sixteen or twenty guests, and one night, here comes a new group of fishermen. Americans. As the evening goes on, we start chatting with them, the way you do on these trips. 'How're you doing?' 'Where're you from?' 'New Jersey? Oh, that's nice. We're from Long Island.' And as soon as we say we're from the island, one of the guys from the other group says, 'Oh, man, I go out to Long Island every spring to go striped bass fishing. But I got a secret spot out there. You wouldn't believe the striped bass I caught out in this little, remote community out on the North Fork, in the bay, of all places. You're from Long Island, so maybe you'd know it. It's adjacent to this place they call Cedar Beach.'

"'Cedar Beach?' I say. 'That's right down from my house.' 'Oh yeah?' he says. 'Well, you wouldn't believe where I caught this fish. You park in this little lot out there, and you walk about a half mile down the beach, and some guy's got a giant friggin' bird standing right there in front of his house. Biggest damn bird I ever saw in my life. But you go out, and you fish right alongside of his dock, and that's where I caught the biggest damn striped bass that I've ever seen in my life.'

"I told him it wasn't really a secret to me," Jim said, "because that's my backyard, and that's my bird. We had a good laugh over that. But that's the way of things, sometimes. You go halfway around the world, and wherever go, you've got a story to tell."

CHAPTER 26

If You Have Your Health . . .

No life fully lived is without its struggles. For Jim Miller and his wife, Barbara, some of those struggles have been titanic. In later years—even as the constant financial worries of their early marriage receded—much of the pain associated with those struggles was of the sharpest, most debilitating kind.

After all, it doesn't get much more debilitating than cancer.

Barbara was struck with an especially aggressive form of brain cancer when she was in her early seventies. During a trip to the Northwest to see some of Jim's cousins, she suddenly suffered a feeling of enormous foreboding. It was not a quantifiable physical pain. She was not feverish. Instead, she was enveloped by a sense of impending doom. All she could say to Jim to describe this paralyzing feeling of dread was that she felt—no, she *knew*—that something awful was coming.

When emergency tests at a hospital in Portland indicated that a massive tumor was spreading with frightening rapidity in her brain, Jim contacted the same oncologist who had treated his lung cancer at Sloan Kettering in Manhattan a few years before (more on that in a bit), finagled a bed in the cancer ward at the hospital, and flew Barbara back to New York that very day. What followed in the coming months and years—radiation, chemo, surgery (during which a significant portion of her brain was "scooped out," as Jim puts it), more tests, more chemo, and endless prayer—was the sort of cruel, winding journey that uncounted families have embarked on together through the centuries, with no certain destination at the end of it. In Barbara's case, she came through largely in one piece, having beaten astronomical odds; changing her doctors and her treatment regimen more than once; and having as a comrade another member of her church who, incredibly, had been diagnosed with the very same, extremely rare form of brain cancer—and who, like Barbara, was living not only months but years past his doctors' most optimistic estimates for his life expectancy. (That man, a friend of Jim and Barbara's named Gary Rose, died after a long, brave fight. Upon his original diagnosis, doctors had given him three months to live. Six months, tops. He lived for five years.)

Barbara had also been involved in a horrific car wreck years before and had endured brain trauma then as well—trauma severe enough to bring on seizures and make driving a car an impossibility. Had that brain injury sparked the tumor's hellishly fast growth decades later? No one can say for sure. But one thing is certain: Barbara Miller is a fighter, with a will as tenacious and resilient as her Christian faith. Today, she still occasionally endures some very rough times—days and weeks when she is depressed, reclusive, simply not up to seeing anyone or leaving the house. But she is alive. She has her faith, her husband, and her family. That is a victory.

In Jim's case, the cancer was in his lungs. After decades of heavy smoking, construction work, and, especially, spackling and sheetrocking homes for a living in an era when safety concerns and such protective gear as the simplest of filter masks were nonexistent, the diagnosis was hardly a surprise. But that didn't make it any less devastating.

Jim, too, was in his seventies when his cancer erupted. Like many people hit with the disease, he had stopped smoking years before. But it found him anyway.

"I stopped smoking when my daughter Barbara was in medical school," he says. "She came home, and she was smoking. But she said, 'Dad, we're doing something in school. I dissected a guy's lungs. A West Virginian. He had black lung disease. My God, it's horrible. And smoking isn't any better. We're both going to die from this thing.' Well, I stopped. Twenty-five years ago. When I decided I was going to Africa to climb Mount Kilimanjaro with Mark, I went to my local doctor and asked, 'What shape am I in, really? Is this mountain-climbing trip idiotic, or should I be able to do it? I'm sixty-two years old, and I've got this cockamamie idea that I want to train and go climb Mount Kilimanjaro. Am I going to kill myself, or what?'

"So he says, 'I don't know. Let me check you out.' He does a sonogram, and he comes back and checks the pictures. 'Uh-oh. See that? See a little bulge right there? That's an aneurysm, but it's very early. It shouldn't be a big deal. They grow very slowly, and you probably won't have to address this for two or three more years.'

"He's the doctor, so off I went to Africa, climbed Kilimanjaro, and came home feeling fine. It was a great adventure. Then we monitored the aneurysm for two years, and the doctor said, 'Okay, it's time. You've got to take care of this now.' I went to Presbyterian Hospital, and at that time, they were just starting to use stents. They wanted to fix it with a stent. I said, 'No, you've got to cut it out, and do it the right way.' They did. They cut me open and took my guts out and did what they had to do and dumped everything back in again. Your guts find the way back to where they want to be after something like that, but for three months or so, they're definitely gurgling.

"Anyway, they monitored me for a while, until some guy said, 'I think there's a little spot on your lung. I'm not sure what it is, but you ought to have this checked.' Nobody wants to hear that. But I got it checked, and they told me, 'Yeah, that looks like a bad thing. You have to have surgery to get it out.' We went to Rhode Island—I had my son-in-law arrange that, and there was a guy up there who was really good at this special arthroscopic surgery, where they went in and took all of the lymph nodes out of my chest, checked them, and said, 'Okay, you have a pretty good chance. It doesn't seem to have metastasized in the lymph nodes.'

"Then we transferred the information to Sloan Kettering, and they said, 'We really believe that you should probably have full surgery, just remove the entire thing. It's going to hurt you more, it's going to take you longer to recover, but if we're successful, you have a better chance of survival.' We went with Sloan. They cut a third of the lung out, stapled it closed, and that was it—except for the chemotherapy and all the crap that goes with it. It was a tough chemotherapy regimen. Three months or so, and one bizarre side effect was that it killed all the nerves in my fingers and my toes. One morning, I woke up, and it felt like somebody had hit my fingers with a sledgehammer. They were black and blue, just terrible, painful. Same with my toes. The doctors asked, 'You want to stop? We have another five treatments. You've had fifteen, and the whole thing is twenty. See, we don't know. Maybe you're cured already. Maybe the next five are all unnecessary, but maybe the next four will do the trick. Your choice. We just don't know how much you can take.'

"I stayed with it, completed it. It was stage-3 cancer, and it was gone. This all happened long after I got back from Africa. Kilimanjaro was a memory. That," Jim says with a smile, "was when I was young."

For Mark Miller, meanwhile, the scary, painful cancer interlude is a critical part of his dad's story "because it's the best example, I think, of all of his qualities meeting. His decisiveness, his way of analyzing a problem, and his overall desire to go through life with the attitude that he's always had. It's all exemplified by his experience with cancer. For me, it's just this confluence of everything about the man. . . .

"Let me explain what I mean. I was with him the day he was diagnosed. I drove him into New York. We were there. The doctor came out, and he wasn't holding back. 'Mr. Miller, I'm sorry to tell you this. There's no way around it. You have stage-3 lung cancer, and it's got a 90 percent mortality rate.'

"Then my dad said one of the most amazing things I've ever heard. It's not like he rehearsed this. There was about five seconds of quiet, and then he stood up and said, 'Doc, too bad for those nine other guys.'

"We were driving back home, and he was quiet then. After about a half hour, he said, 'You know, I just have to deal with it the same way I've dealt with everything else in my life. There's no such thing as a bad thing happening; you just have to look for the opportunity. This is a tough one. I don't know where the opportunity is in this, but there's an opportunity, and I'm going to let you know when I find it.' Sure enough, four days later, I got a phone call. 'I found one of my opportunities, Mark.' I said, 'What's that, Dad?' He said, 'I just got off the phone with Nicholas,' who is my brother Glen's son. He was fifteen years old at the time. Dad said, 'Nick and I were on the phone for two hours. If I didn't have cancer, I would never have had a two-hour conversation with my grandson like that. Isn't that great?' I said, 'That's great, Dad.'

"Fast-forward another couple of months. 'I got another opportunity.' This was around Valentine's Day. He said, 'I always knew that I knew a lot of people, but I didn't know that I had a lot of friends. I never knew that. But I have a lot of friends.' I said, 'Where's this coming from? What's behind this, Dad?' He said . . . sorry, excuse me . . . " Mark chokes up a bit at this point in the telling. And who can blame him? "He said, 'I just got a Valentine's Day card. A *huge* Valentine's Day card. The damn thing is three feet tall, and it's signed only by men. These are the men that I've traveled the world with, fishing. I don't even know who was responsible for it, but this card has gone everywhere, and it's been signed by all of these men, and they come right out and say *I love you*. Wow!' he said. 'What a great opportunity in life to know that you have friends who love you!'

"This was his attitude. And he had humor the whole time. You know, we still have lunch pretty often, but back then, we had lunch together every single day. We were out at some restaurant, and this is when he was deep into his treatment. He had the chemo, and he just looked awful. He'd lost weight. He was pale. He looked like that weird guy in the Great Adventure commercials on TV. The bald guy in the suit with the glasses? He looked just like that guy. Anyway, we were at lunch, and he would always wind up coughing because he couldn't breathe properly. He started coughing, and then he would hiccup, which was a side effect from the chemo. He was just a wreck. He was laughing, hiccupping; his body was just racked with coughs. 'What's that about?' I asked him. 'What? What's so funny?' And he said, 'I never realized I was such a vigorous tooth brusher.'

"*What?* I said, 'Dad, I don't know what the hell that means.' I thought maybe the chemo was affecting his brain. He was hallucinating or something. But then he said, 'This morning, I was brushing my teeth, and my eyebrows fell out.' He just couldn't stop laughing about that.

"Even in the midst of all this, he came to work every day. While he was going through this treatment, he was in the office every day.

Sick as a dog. I think that he felt it was paramount for him to set an example to anyone who wanted to see it, that you don't have to be sick if you have cancer. You can fight this, and you can win. And this is how you do it. He felt like a missionary. I think any day he was not in the office, he felt really bad because it was screwing up his . . . project, I guess you'd call it. The thing that was important to him was to let everybody know that you don't have to just stay at home and die. And I have to tell you that he's impacted so many people. He became like a counselor or something. Anybody who got cancer, if one of his friends or even some distant connection had cancer, somebody would say, 'You have to talk to Jim Miller.' I remember people coming in for years afterward, coming to talk with him and leaving invigorated, like they had this religious experience. It was fascinating.

"In the end, so much of that behavior stems from the fact that he's very, very competitive. Whether he's competing against himself, competing against death, or competing against an expectation people have of what's possible or not possible. He has to win. After his lung surgery, the doctors said, 'Okay, on this day, you need to get out of the bed, and on this day we expect you to walk to the bathroom, and then on this day, maybe you can make it down to the nurses' station. But by the third day, he had already calculated what the length of the hallway was and was doing the multiplication, and he was proud of himself, telling me, 'I did three miles today.' Three miles! He was only supposed to be making it to the nurses' station and back, and he was walking farther than most healthy people walk in a day."

CHAPTER 27

"They Cared about You"

Linda Meyer worked with Jim Miller for twenty-one years, from March 1978, when she and a few other part-time employees shared space in the Miller's home garage/office in Terryville, until June 1, 1999, when she decided she was going to spend more time in Florida. (Since 2008, she and her husband have lived in The Villages, one of the largest planned retirement communities in the country.)

Linda's recollections provide invaluable insights into the day-to-day decisions and the values that helped shape the fortunes of so many during that two-decade span, when the Millers' business ventures—Jim's as well as that of several of his children—grew from small and precarious to huge and thriving. But what clearly strikes Linda most forcibly about her long association with Jim Miller is how little he changed, in the fundamentals of his life and his outlook, despite the outward signs and symbols of his many successes.

"Jim Miller has made a lot of money," Linda says. "But all through the years, he shared it with his employees. As just one example, when I worked with him, we had a Christmas party, and everyone got a bonus. You got $100 for every year you worked at Miller Environmental. Even if you started in June, you'd get $100 for that year. If you'd worked there five years, you got $500. He began this tradition not right away, when I started, but maybe five years in. And by the end, when I left in 1999 after twenty-one years, the last Christmas I was there I got $2,100. That's not bad.

"In fact, one time we tackled so many oil spills and did so well that Jim announced that we were going to have Christmas in July, and everyone's Christmas bonus was duplicated in July. He always, always shared."

It wasn't only about the money, though. Again, as with so many stories about Jim Miller, the notion of fairness, of treating people fairly, is never far from the conversation—and often is the very center of a story's message.

"One day, Jim called me into his office," Linda recalls, "and said that he had heard that an employee's father had passed away. He said, 'Why don't we send a big arrangement of flowers to the funeral parlor?' So I said, 'Well, you heard about that employee's trouble, but two weeks ago, so-and-so's mother died, and I don't think we did anything then.' So we both agreed that we shouldn't do anything this time either because that wouldn't be fair to the other employee. We always tried to be fair with everybody—whether they knew we were being fair or not!"

Perhaps unconsciously, Linda also echoes a Miller family mantra in the midst of her reminiscences: "Jim never said no to a job," she says, without any prompting. "He would always say yes and then figure out how he could accomplish it. He always said that we would figure out a way—and he always did the job because he was always looking to build the business. We learned from the very beginning that when there wasn't an oil spill, we'd have to rely on another part of the business, like his launch service, his boats and transports, when the tankers came in. That business might perk up when the other one died down. He realized, I guess, that you have to have more than one business. If you narrow your eyes and do only one thing, and if that one thing slows down or stops, you're out of business. He was always looking for other ventures that would complement what he did for a living.

"But when I was there, his biggest worry was that if it got slow, he might have to lay somebody off. All the years that I was there, across two decades, we never had to say to the guys, 'Look, we have to give you a couple of weeks off. The business has gotten slow.' We always managed to make it through, and we finally got bigger. Jim used to set goals. 'Let's make a million dollars, let's make $5 million,' and he'd be so happy when we got there."

And then there are the seemingly little things that, in retrospect, loom so large and take on a special significance in Linda's memories.

"I remember when he said that he bought a building out in Calverton," she says, referring to the current Edwards Avenue headquarters of Miller Environmental. "We were in East Patchogue before that, which was much closer to my home. Now, I was never a good driver in snow. I'm a fair-weather driver. But all the time we worked in Calverton, which was maybe twenty-five minutes, a half hour from where I lived, every single time it snowed, I got a phone call in the morning. One of the supervisors—or Jim's brother Dave, who lived close to me—would pick me up and take me to work, so I would not have to drive in the snow.

"That's the kind of office we had. It was caring. They *cared* about you. If Jim knew you were vulnerable to something, he would help you out. He'd say, 'Listen, I don't want you to drive.' Or if I had driven in on a day when it was clear in the morning, the minute he saw snowflakes come down, he'd say, 'Linda, why don't you get in your car and go.'

"But what's really amazing is, I've been out of there for sixteen years, and Jim and I still talk. Who talks to their boss, when you haven't worked for them for sixteen years? It's unheard of. I might not talk to him for a year; then one day, he'll call me. 'You know that Rolodex that you made for me? Well, all of a sudden, a card fell out on the floor, and it was yours. I took that as a sign that I have to call Linda.'

"You know, we had a good time during all those years. I did very well there, and I moved from part-timer all the way up, and Jim would rely on me for a lot of different things. We would talk over everything. He and I used to sit and talk about raises for the entire office staff. He would ask me my opinion. He valued it, I think. When I retired, I was president of the company, but I never considered that my title. In corporations when they need two signatures, Jim Miller was vice president and secretary, and so I was named president. He said, 'You work with me every day, and we need papers signed,' so I said that was fine. But the title that I really believe was mine, and the one that I felt I really worked under, was administrative vice president.

"You know, I've been thinking about those days a lot lately, and what I really remember, after all this time, is how Jim Miller treated his employees and how he genuinely cared. I think about the Christmas parties—how he thought about the people who worked for him and with him, and how he always bought them presents for Christmas. Everybody there knew that if you did a good job, Jim was a very fair guy, and he rewarded you for it. And that sort of thing goes a long, long way, because lots of times, your boss hardly knows your name."

What Linda doesn't mention, but what anyone who's ever spent any time in the workforce knows with painful certainty, is that quite often the people who put their heads down and do the work, and do it well, sometimes go unrecognized, while those who make the most noise—and underperform—often get the promotions, the laurels, and the bonuses. Jim Miller, on the other hand, was the sort of boss who was keenly aware of who was doing the work—perhaps because he was able to surround himself with people who knew what they were doing and who enjoyed both the work and the company of their colleagues.

On top of all that, Linda says, "Jim was a perfect example for everyone else because he worked as hard at the beginning, when we were just starting out, as any of the employees there. They respected him for that. He wasn't someone who sat in an office and barked out orders. He was out there himself, doing the work. If a crew was doing a cleanup job in Long Island Sound or pulling cables out of the mud, he was out on the boat, working just as hard—and usually harder—than any of them."

CHAPTER 28

Jerry Coogan:
One Career, Many Hats

"Like most men skilled at their work they were scornful of any
least suggestion of knowing anything not learned at first hand."

—*from the Cormac McCarthy novel* ALL THE PRETTY HORSES

An awful lot of people have worked for Miller Environmental
Group over the years. That's what happens, after all, when
you're in business for five decades with a company that keeps on
growing and finding new ways to remain relevant: Employees come
and go. But to a striking degree, that traditional reality of turnover
and change is just a little bit different at Miller Environmental.

At MEG, it seems, the employees come and stay.

And while one could walk pretty much anywhere in the offices,
around the garage, or on the several acres—filled with trademark-
blue trucks and machinery—behind the Calverton complex and
bump into someone who's been working there for years and years,
few employees' stories feel more representative, somehow, of what
Miller Environmental has always been about than the one told by
forty-six-year-old Jerry Coogan.

Coogan started with Miller Environmental a quarter century ago, and over the years, he has worked his way up from a laborer to his position today as the company's VP of operations. What that journey ("quite a ride," as Jerry puts it) epitomizes is not just the mutual loyalty that MEG feels and demonstrates toward its employees—and vice versa—but the premium that Jim and his son Mark, as president and CEO, place on life experience and problem-solving skills, above and beyond college degrees and knowledge gleaned solely from books. As Jim is fond of pointing out, an education is a wonderful thing, but if that education doesn't provide a person with the ability to deal with the sort of practical and often unique (and uniquely hazardous) problems that Miller Environmental faces on a daily basis, then a college degree isn't going to be a selling point for someone seeking a job at the company.

"I favor people with life experiences over people with formal education," Jim says. "Too much education, in some circumstances, can be a detriment because it seems to replace or crowd out common sense. In our business—and in most businesses, I think—we have a need for people with simple common sense who can apply practical applications to problems. I respect someone like that a lot more than a guy who has a fancy degree, or a number of fancy degrees, but has no practical experience or common sense."

Jim's preference for experience over a string of letters after someone's name makes perfect sense. After all, just because you're qualified on paper can often mean little out in the field, when—in some circumstances—the success of a project and even the safety of your colleagues might depend on a decision that you alone can make.

In Jerry Coogan's case, his long, steady rise to his current role as a key figure on the company's senior management team was driven in large part by his ability to handle pretty much any task thrown his way. And over the years, his personal life has become inexorably enmeshed with his professional life. He is not just an employee but a friend to both Mark and Jim—and to countless other men and women in the Miller Environmental family. During his time with MEG, he has married and started a family of his own. (He and his wife have twins.) But perhaps what is most evident, when speaking with Jerry about his twenty-six years with the Millers, is his own acknowledgment that he has in a sense grown up alongside Jim and Mark—and alongside Jim's older brother Richie, who at eighty-five still heads into the office in Calverton every day, where he brings a lifetime of deep and disparate talents to bear on a huge variety of projects.

"I left college early," Jerry says, "when I was in my teens and my father passed away. I came home here to the North Shore of Long Island to help out the family, and I worked for a couple of different companies, started my own small landscaping business—that sort of thing—for a few years until I got turned on to Miller Environmental." (Jerry and his family live in Mount Sinai, New York—a hamlet of around 12,000 people located in the town of Brookhaven—but as he points out, "I always just tell people 'Port Jefferson' when they ask where we live, because nobody outside of this area has ever heard of Mount Sinai, except as a hospital. But man, I love it here.")

While Jerry knew that Miller Environmental was a solid, reputable business on the North Shore—the company had made a name for itself responding to some of the largest and most highly publicized spills of the 1970s and 1980s (the *Seaspeed Arabia* spill off Bayonne, New Jersey, the landmark *Exxon Valdez* disaster in '89, and others)—Jerry had another career in mind.

"I was home, and I was working various jobs, but I knew I needed something solid. A friend of mine worked at Miller Environmental, and I interviewed here. Back in the late eighties and early nineties, the job market wasn't great, so I was pretty thrilled when they offered me a job. I took it. My problem was that I wanted to be a New York City cop. That was my goal—to be a police officer. But after I was already working for the Millers for a little while, I got word that I was accepted to the police academy. So now I had to make a choice. Either I stick with the job I had, or I go into the academy and take the chance of something going wrong—getting injured or whatever—and not making it through, and then I'm out of either job. It was a tough decision, especially as I was just a laborer at the time. Steady work, but the money was so-so. Still, I made the decision not to go to the academy, and I stayed here. And as things turned out, that was a good call. It has definitely worked out for me over the years."

Still, even if the decision was the right one in the long run, did Jerry ever regret that he didn't take a chance at becoming a cop?

"It's strange, you know. That is what I always wanted to do when I was younger. I always wanted to be in the police department. But after I'd been with Miller Environmental for a while, I started to realize that a life on the water—working in a marine environment and working on the sort of emergencies we get to respond to—that sort of career had all the challenges and excitement and camaraderie anyone could hope for. I certainly don't regret my decision not to go to the academy. Not for a second. I definitely feel like I made the right choice. I wasn't really sure at the time—how could I be?—but after a while, I realized that Miller was involved, in one way or another, in pretty much every major disaster, all over the world. And I came to understand that it was a big deal to be working for a company like this. I also came to realize, at twenty years old, that I loved what I was doing, and I really liked and respected the people I was doing it with. 'Why mess this up?' I thought to myself. 'I can make a career here.' And I did."

Over the years, as Jerry moved up through the company, holding a slew of positions of ever-increasing authority, he's never completely abandoned or forgotten his earliest role and its responsibilities. And that, too, is by design.

"I tell everybody I speak to about Miller Environmental—and especially when I'm interviewing potential employees—that we all have to wear different hats during our time here because of the nature of the work we do, but you're never allowed to remove the hat you were initially hired to wear," he says. "In other words, just because you're transferred to another task or granted a new title, that doesn't mean that you're no longer responsible for the little things we do around here—or what might *seem* like little things. And this keeps everyone in mind of where we started from, as a business and as individuals. I started off here as a laborer, and at the time, there were a lot of people working here who had been here for a while. Like I said, the job market was tough, there was a long list of people trying to get into the company, and there just weren't a whole lot of new people being hired. So when I came on board, I was the new guy for quite a while. Like, quite a few years. I was a laborer for seven or eight years before I became a foreman, and it was a few more years before I was moved up to supervisor. And like so many others who work for Jim and Mark, I had a hand in designing equipment for specific projects or tasks. The whole time, I was learning from my colleagues—really smart, talented people."

("I favor those who have some skill in construction, or plumbing, or fishing," Jim Miller says of his own approach to hiring. "I find that these are thinking people—they have practical skills. They make better employees and are usually more creative than people who don't have to solve problems all the time. For years, we've had to design our own equipment, and sometimes we build prototypes right here, to see if our ideas translate to the real world. I always say that the best design table I've ever used is a plot of dirt in the backyard and a sharp stick to draw with. If it doesn't look right, you just use your foot to erase it and draw it differently, and then if you have a couple of guys with a welding torch, well, you put it together and see what happens. Halfway through, somebody might say, 'No, that's not going to work.' So you hit it with a hammer, knock it apart, and start all over again. Eventually, you might have a prototype for a piece of equipment that you'll use for years, on all sorts of jobs.")

"I moved up to project manager at Miller Environmental," Jerry says, "and not long after that, we were contracted to design, build, and operate decontamination facilities at Ground Zero after 9/11. We built some automated truck washes, and all the trucks, equipment, and people on the site had to go through us before they could head out into the streets of the city. I ran that project for about four months, and during that time, the manager of our Calverton location decided he wanted to move on and do other things, and they asked me to take his position as manager of the main branch. I became a regional manager, and then, around 2010, I was promoted to my current position, where I oversee company operations—including health and safety initiatives—at all of our facilities."

As for the rarity—perceived or real—in today's corporate culture of someone starting off as a laborer and rising to vice presidency of a multimillion-dollar company, Jerry notes that family-run companies of considerable size are becoming harder to find. "They're bought up by larger conglomerates, or by raiders and hedge-fund types who hope to flip them and turn quick profits, so the emphasis isn't on the employees anymore.

"But at Miller Environmental, as long as I've been here and, I'm sure, long before, that's always been the focus. It's been drilled into me by the Millers, both Jim and Mark. We look at our employees—really look at them, and we work beside them—and decide who belongs where, who's going to grow with us, and, sometimes, who would like to just stay where they are. I think what keeps us as strong as we are is the company's emphasis on its employees and its emphasis on family. I can't even tell you all the times something happened to an employee—an unexpected expense, something terrible happening to someone's family—when Mark took care of the whole bill or Jim paid for someone's funeral. And they do it quietly. They don't make a big deal about it. So many things happen around here like that, and 99 percent of the company never hears about it."

There is one story of Jerry Coogan's, however—a story not about Jim's generosity but about his unique approach to mentoring—that much of the company *has* heard. It's an amusing tale, but it also says something conclusive about Jim's philosophy of on-the-job training—a philosophy that might be styled "There's no such thing as a bad time to teach someone a lesson."

"It's a funny story," Jerry admits, "and sometimes when I tell it, I think that the telling doesn't really do it justice, because it was one of those times when you really had to see the look in people's eyes when it was happening. . . . Anyway, it was early on in my career, and I guess I was twenty-one, maybe twenty-two years old. I had worked with Jim on the boats many times, and on all types of things. He's still hands-on today, even though he sold the company to Mark years ago, but back then, he was *very* hands-on. He ran a lot of the boats, especially for certain customers because they were very delicate jobs—which is what this one was. At the time LILCO had submarine power cables running along the seabed from Long Island to Connecticut, and they bought and sold power back and forth with United Illuminating, CL&P, and other utilities. Those cables sometimes failed and leaked oil—when there was a fault or blowout, and the cable sheath was breached—and we were always hired to fix those. We would bring divers out, drop them down, bring the cable up on board, repair it, and put it down again. That's the dumbed-down version of a very technical job that sometimes took months.

"One particular day, I was running late to the boat. Just plain and simple, running late. I drove to the dock as quick as I could, parked my car, and I could see that the boat was still there. I was running down the dock, and I could see that Jim was there on the back of the boat. You know, the average person who didn't know the rules about this sort of thing would have seen the boat still sitting there and said, 'Okay, I have nothing to worry about,' and they might have just walked the rest of the way, thinking the boat would wait for them. But with Jim, the general rule was that if you're not fifteen minutes early, then you're late. And he would not tolerate that. So I was running for the boat, hopeful that I could get on board before he realized I wasn't there."

(Another aside: Jerry Coogan is hardly the first person to mention the importance of punctuality in Jim Miller's life. Steve Gordon, Jim's friend and accountant for twenty years, tells the story of the time he and his then-teenage son were a few minutes late to the boat when they'd been invited on a fishing trip. "My son doesn't have the same idea about time that I have," Steve says. "He's not bad, but his attitude is sort of like, 'Eh, we're within ten minutes. It's okay.' But when we got to the dock that morning, at 6:04 or something like that, Jim is standing there, waiting, like a gatekeeper. And he says to my son, 'You're lucky. You're getting a free pass this time. But you are to never, ever do this again.' And when my son tried to make excuses, Jim made it plain that he didn't want to hear it. 'Don't give me that,' he says. 'If you're not here at six o'clock, you're not on time. You're late. Period.' And he meant it."

Ken Murphy, who has known Jim Miller since he himself was a boy and has worked with him for years, echoes Steve's tale. "I've never known Jim Miller to be late for anything," Ken says. "Not once." And, like Steve, he says that spending time with Jim over the years has taught him all sorts of things—including the value of punctuality and the fact that one way of showing respect for another person, and of earning that person's respect, is by considering his time as valuable as yours.)

"So there I was," Jerry continues, "running for the boat, and Jim, of course, already knew that I wasn't there. The boat engine's running, everything is ready to go, and as I'm running, I could see him look right at me, and he just gives this hand wave that he used to make, letting the other guys on the boat know they should release the line. By the time I got down there, the boat was about five feet off the dock, and I stood there with my head down, my bag in my hand. His plan was to make a big production about bringing the boat back just to get me, which he did, and I got the message loud and clear. I got on the boat and didn't say a word, and Jim just kind of stared at me. If you're late for the boat, he used to say, you're late for the job, and we don't need anybody late around here, because you're costing the customer. I knew the speech. In fact, that was pretty much the way my father had raised me, too, so I got it. I wasn't somebody to cry about it. I owned it. It was my fault.

"We went about our day. It was cold out there on the water. I mean *cold*. It was one of the last days of the job, we were wrapping everything up, and there was a buoy in the water that we weren't really sure about, because the cable company had dropped it originally to mark the spot where the oil was coming up from the blown-out power cable. We didn't know what was on it, and Jim came up to me and said, 'You know what? You were late, you can pull it up.'

"Typically, you put something like that on a winch, or a couple of guys would grab it to figure out what it was, get a handle on how heavy it was, and then pull it up. All we knew was what kind of line was on whatever was there on the bottom, but we didn't know what the line was attached to. We assumed it was a concrete block, or a couple of concrete blocks. But we really had no idea of knowing. Anyway, the line running into the water was quarter-inch line, which is kind of like parachute cord, not much bigger than a shoelace. Most people don't realize this—and there's no reason they should—but two cinder blocks, 140 feet deep in a running current, on a quarter-inch line, I can't really explain what it takes for one person to get that up to the surface. Your hands, man. You pull up three feet, and two feet of line flies back into the water. It feels like it's hundreds of pounds, so by the time you get ten or fifteen feet of line in, your hands feel like you've had arthritis all your life. I started to pull it in, and Jim is standing right there with a big smile on his face, just waiting for me to give up. That was the plan—to see me give up, and then move on and bring the blocks up the way we normally would.

"But I kept at it, kept pulling and pulling, and it was taking forever. After a little while, Jim started to realize what I was doing, and he asked me, 'Do you understand? About being late?' And I said, 'Oh, I understand.' But believe me, I wasn't talking that much just then. I was out of breath. Jim asked another guy to take over, but I said no, no, I'd finish it. He told me to let go, I was going to hurt myself, but by that point, I was determined to finish—even though I could barely get the words out to tell him so. But I kept saying it, and pulling on that line, and eventually I got the blocks up on the boat, and Jim looked at me for a while and shook his head. Then he said to me, 'Well, you'll never do that again, will you?' And I told him absolutely not. I said I would never be late again. And what's funny, all these years later, is that I've always remembered the captain on the boat, who only worked for us for a short period of time, and the look on his face. He was just so taken aback by the fact that someone would make somebody else do hard labor in order to teach a lesson. He was shocked by that. But I grew up with a father who was very hard and who made it clear, from the time I was young, that you do what you have to do, or you suffer the consequences. It was all about teaching me the right thing to do, the right way to be, so I respected it and I got it.

"The next day, Jim came over to me, and he said, 'You know, I have to tell you, I went home last night, and I told my wife that I might have met the most tenacious son of a bitch I've ever met in my life.' So it became something of a bonding experience for us, rather than mere punishment. I learned a lot about him, he learned a lot about me, and I think I can point to that experience as the time when my career with Miller Environmental really started. And later on, I came to realize that with the kind of work that we do, if you can't be like that—if you can't bounce from one thing to the other and let it go and then get back to it when you have to—you won't survive in this business. You just won't.

"But what's really funny about that story is that it grew and became almost legendary, until it's kind of this commonly under-stood joke within the company. We had a company fishing trip once, not too long ago, and the human resources rep had just started with the company. I was on the boat with some other guys and with Jim, and we were waiting for her because she was late. She finally showed up, and Jim just kept looking at her. Finally he said, 'Okay, let Jerry tell you what happens to people on the boat when they're late.' I didn't tell her right then, so she didn't really understand what the big deal was. I said, 'Don't worry, you will.' When she went back to her office the next day, there in front of her door were two cinder blocks with parachute cord tied on them and a buoy on the end. I told her the story then, and it's become a bit of folklore within the company."

In the end, though, what has made Jerry's quarter century at MEG so much more than just a job is the enormous respect that he has for Jim and for Mark and the respect he has earned from them through the years.

"You know, the Miller family has been very good to me. We work well together, and we've done great things together. Jim and Mark—these are guys who get it. By that I mean I can go into one of their offices at any time and explain something, and they'll listen even if they have a completely different understanding of how something should be done. I will always have time to give my side, my point of view. They may change their mind, or they may not, but they're open to listening to new or opposing ideas about pretty much anything. What sort of equipment to buy, where we should spend more money. To have people trust you with their business and their finances, it's a huge honor.

"Obviously, Jim has been a tremendous mentor to me for my whole career. He's more than just somebody to work for. He's a tremendous human being. Maybe the most unique thing about him is that it doesn't matter if you're his employee, his competitor, his customer, or somebody doing business with him in real estate, he is *always* mentoring. He takes control of a conversation, and he brings you in, and he explains his philosophy in life, but his method of mentoring is also by getting you to talk to him, not just him talking at you.

"Jim will walk into my office and ask me a question that I know damn well he knows the answer to. But he doesn't want his answer, he wants my answer. He wants to know, first of all, do you think like him? And second, if you don't think like him, how do you think? And is it maybe a better way of thinking? He'll take the simplest question and turn it into an hour-long mentoring session when you think he's just having a conversation. It happens all the time at work. I see him walk out of someone's office, and while it's not exactly clear what just happened, you can see by the look on that person's face that he or she just learned a whole lot. He's still smart enough to keep an open mind, and I challenge you to find somebody with that much knowledge in his head but who still can listen to your point of view objectively and say, 'You know what? You might be right.' It's an amazing quality. It really is. And I'm incredibly fortunate to have experienced it, day in and day out, for so much of my life."

CHAPTER 29

Idea Man

Having friends, family, and colleagues vouch for one's ingenuity is all well and good. And after spending even a little bit of time with Jim Miller, it's pretty clear that if no one *but* his friends, family, and colleagues ever sang his praises or spoke highly of his approach to challenges large and small, he'd be okay with that.

This is not a man who requires a great deal of affirmation from the world at large in order to know his own worth.

Then again, there is certainly something satisfying about legitimate, sanctioned, codified evidence that, yes, as a matter of fact, one does have a creative, problem-solving cast of mind. Tributes and awards from local civic associations and governmental agencies, for example: Jim Miller has a slew of those hanging on the walls in the offices of Miller Environmental in Calverton in the form of proclamations, plaques, and the like.

But few things say *inventor* or *problem-solver* quite like a government patent, and Jim Miller has a couple of those, too.

"The two patents are for two different functions," he says. "One is a patent for an oleophilic disc skimmer. In layman's terms, *oleophilic* means a material or a plastic that oil will adhere to. A disc skimmer rotates downward through an oil film, and the oil sticks to the polypropylene disc. As it comes up, the oil is scraped off and separated from the water. We improved on that concept and put it into a multi-disc configuration, making it an oil-spill-recovery device, separating the oil and the water at the site of a spill. In the past, on a waterborne spill, you might vacuum or otherwise pick up huge amounts of water along with the oil. Maybe 5 percent of the total volume of what you were dealing with was oil. With the multi-disc skimmer, that ratio was basically reversed, so 95 percent of what you ended up with was oil and the other 5 percent was water. It was so much more efficient.

"All of the technology for this sort of approach had long been known. What we patented was the application of the technology in a new way. We never even really went into production for sale of the device, or anything like that. It was really for our own use, and it still works today. In fact, we've never protected the patent, so its use has become common all over the world."

Why, one might ask, would Jim not protect a patent on an application that has global appeal in his own industry?

"That just wasn't the business that we were in. We're not manufacturers, and frankly it wasn't worth the effort to try to protect it. With fairly minor modifications, anyone could circumvent the patent anyway. The other patent I have, though, is more unique. That's an application of a whole series of technologies—an accumulation of different techniques of removing polychlorinated biphenyls, or PCBs, from pipelines. And everybody knows that PCBs are powerfully toxic environmental contaminants. Years and years ago, when natural gas was being transmitted across the country, there were layers of sulfur and corrosive components in the gas as it moved through the pipes. In order to keep their compressors from failing because of these corrosives, the natural gas companies would inject lubricating and corrosion-fighting oil into the compressor stations—oil that routinely contained PCBs, which could then leach into the soil, the groundwater, all sorts of places.

"On top of all that, injecting the lubricants into the compressors meant that they often mixed with the natural gas, in a mist form, and the natural gas with PCBs was distributed throughout the United States. Maybe somebody one morning is sampling some guy's house a hundred miles from the source of the natural gas he uses to heat his home or whatever, and all of a sudden, 'My gosh! There are PCBs in these pipes. Where the hell is that from?'"

Polychlorinated biphenyls have a long half-life, and they also accumulate in the food chain. They impact fish and all kinds of creatures, and ultimately they can affect human beings. In the 1970s, laws were put into place banning domestic production of PCBs in the United States—but there were still thousands of miles of contaminated pipeline in the ground that would have been extremely difficult and outrageously expensive to remove, dispose them as a hazardous material, transport them to another location, and bury them in a secure landfill. The whole nine yards.

"The system we concocted to deal with this problem utilized a high-pressure wash," Jim explains, "a jet that we could push down through a pipeline, wash it out, and then recover and process the liquid. We separated the PCBs from the wash, and at the end of the day, we could certify that the pipeline no longer contained any PCBs whatsoever. We used a vacuum system to recover the wash in tank trunks that we designed.

"And again," Jim notes, "all of the technology—the pump, the chemicals in the wash, the vacuum mechanism, all of it—was already out there. But we invented the system of utilizing all of that technology for this particular purpose. In fact, we're the only company in

North America with an EPA license to certify that a pipeline that's been treated utilizing this system is clean of PCBs. So *that* particular patent is one we protect because it's become a key component of our business enterprise, and it's valuable. It's very valuable."

CHAPTER 30

Teach Your Children

It doesn't take long, after meeting just a few of the Millers, to get the sense that here are men and women who are going to be competent at whatever task they choose to address or whatever path they elect to follow (or forge) in life. So many of us spend our lives searching for a career that is meaningful, provides us with a living, and is, for lack of a better term, fun. Not frivolous. Not silly. But something that buoys us—or, at the very least, something that doesn't drag us down.

Many of the Millers, though, seem to have gravitated toward pursuits that not only are meaningful or gratifying, but are also ones at which they excel.

"What I've tried to teach my children," says Glen Miller, who for more than thirty years has run one of the largest, most successful marine-launch businesses in the United States, out of Staten Island, "is that they should avoid doing anything—for a living, I mean—that they don't like. Do things that you're passionate about, because then chances are good that you'll automatically be great at it. I love what I do for a living. And honestly, I don't really understand people who complain about their work. I just don't get it. If you don't like it, change it.

"What Dad instilled in all of us was the true American dream, the entrepreneurial spirit that should live in everybody and that in turn has offered up so many opportunities—because you could make money doing anything. That's something he showed us early on. It doesn't mean that it's going to be easy. It's just that you can figure things out to make money. You don't have to do things the way that everybody else does them, or has always done them.

"When I was, I think, six years old, I remember going to the woods with my dad, chopping down a tree. I mean, how much was I really helping him? But I was getting the lesson of my life. We were chopping the trees down to bring them home and turn them into lobster traps. And that whole process: 'Look, there's a free tree there. You can make money just by some energy spent, and next spring we're making money out of that tree.' How do you teach that? And what's worse is that I think it's so hard to get those sorts of opportunities nowadays.

"Of course, a parent can tell a child until his or her face turns blue, 'Work hard, be creative, be original, be imaginative, find opportunities!' But unless you show a child—especially a young child—that you're able to embody those traits yourself, then the lesson rarely sticks. And even if the lesson does take hold, it's often the case that the actual meaning of the lesson—the truth, or the kernel, of the lesson—is only grasped later. One gets the lesson, gets the meaning behind it, down the road a piece. It's a bit like comedy, really. What's the point of explaining a joke? If somebody tells you a joke, and then immediately after delivering the punch line, they blurt out, 'Now let me tell you why that's funny,' it sort of kills the humor, doesn't it?

"When I was young," Glen says, "there were situations I was put in that, if anyone were to try that sort of thing today, somebody would be yelling, 'You're endangering the life and welfare of that child!' Well, you know what? Thank God my dad 'endangered' me. I mean, that's a funny statement, but I can remember at a very young age doing a salvage job with Dad. It was dangerous, but I then got to experience that you have to take risks. You do have to *do* things.

"How dangerous was it really? There was danger, yes, but you know that level of success comes with risks, even if that is a very difficult thing to explain to a child unless you throw them in harm's way a little bit. Let Mother Nature smack them around some. 'We're gonna go out and catch these critters, but there's a cost to this. The sea is in control, and you're not. But you're in control of your own destiny—kind of.'

"I think back to the lessons he was giving us. Was it the intentional, or was it the unintentional, consequences that were produced? I think maybe it was both.

"Throughout my life, it's always been these unexpected lessons from Dad that I didn't understand until later on. I can remember when he bought a payloader, which was a gigantic machine that moves dirt. He showed me how to use it. Maybe I was fourteen years old. You know what fourteen-year-old boys are like. They're all over the place. But he was willing to show me how to use this thing—and then he said, 'Okay, I'll see you in a couple of hours.' There was a mound of dirt, and he says, 'Move that mound of dirt from over here to over there.' I did that like I was eating candy. I almost turned the machine over a bunch of times. I got in trouble. It ran out of fuel. Lots of things happened that made me ask myself, 'How do you fix this? Or how do you do that?' And the lessons came.

"The next year, I'm running the same machine on a real job. Here I am, fifteen years old, driving a machine on Jones Beach in the middle of the winter with fifteen thirty-year-olds. They're working for me. I'm the machine operator in a heated cabin, and they're outside in the cold shoveling oil into a bucket."

CHAPTER 31

From *Exxon Valdez* to NRC

By any measure, the March 1989 *Exxon Valdez* oil spill remains one of the most devastating environmental calamities in history—a monumental, human-driven catastrophe that not only forever altered one of North America's most pristine natural habitats but also transformed the way that industry and governments respond to such disasters.

Today, more than a quarter century later, it's still easy for countless people around the world to close their eyes and immediately conjure the signature images of the spill. The massive tanker itself, aground and spewing crude into the formerly clear waters of Prince William Sound. Miles and miles of coastline covered with a toxic black sheen. Oil-covered seabirds, seals, otters, and other wildlife. While there have been larger spills and, of course, far larger oil-well blowouts over the years, for many people, the *Exxon Valdez* is still the perfect—and perfectly horrific—emblem of the sort of hell on earth than can result when humanity's bottomless thirst for oil collides with humanity's inevitable fallibility.

In the wake of the disaster, meanwhile, government regulators, watchdog groups, environmentalists, outdoorsmen, and even many in the oil industry realized that the spill in Prince William Sound wasn't just bad PR for one of the world's biggest companies. It was a frightening and long overdue wake-up call. For Jim Miller, it also launched one of the single greatest business adventures of a life that was already filled with memorable ventures both large and small. This is the story of the National Response Corporation—a remarkable, and remarkably successful, enterprise that most people have never heard of.

"When the *Exxon Valdez* happened in the late eighties, there was outrage by the environmental community, government, and everybody else," Jim Miller recalls. "In the opinion of many people, the response to the *Exxon Valdez* was inappropriate and inadequate, mainly due to a lack of equipment, manpower, technique, and whatever else might have been needed to address a catastrophic spill of that size in the United States. At the same time, as government often does, the feds said, 'Well, we'll have to fix that,' and their proposal at the time was that we have to organize a new level of government to address oil spills.

"'We're going to build an organization within government,' they said, 'in order to respond on a national basis to clean up oil spills. We'll have it like either the Coast Guard, or the state militia, or some other body that has the capacity to respond. And certainly, if we're going to have to incur these tremendous costs in order to build this organization to respond to events that are caused by oil companies, we should devise a tax so that those companies have to pay their share of this enormous expense.' The oil companies heard about this, and they said, 'We think that private industry can do the job much better than government. We recognize that industry should create the capability to respond to these catastrophic oil spills, but government is the wrong entity to use to do it. Private industry is the correct way to go.'

"So . . . to show that they were serious about meaningful change, some of the world's biggest oil companies—Gulf Oil, Standard Oil of California, Texaco, which is now Chevron, and others—banded together and made an announcement that they would fund an oil-spill-cleanup organization capable of addressing the worst-case events that could happen when it came to oil spills. They were going to absolutely exclude government and fund this thing and create it as a private entity, to respond to these catastrophic events, but without the interference of the government and governmental bureaucracy.

"They also said that to demonstrate their good faith in this effort, they would put up seed money to get the organization started, and they proposed contributing, collectively, $1 billion to establish this organization. They named it at the time the Petroleum Industry Response Organization, PIRO. They established this fund of $1 billion, and then they hired the people who, in their view, were the most capable. They said, 'Why don't we hire the Coast Guard admirals who are now retired, because they know all about oil spills?' And they began to build out the organization itself.

"As it evolved, they proposed that the foundation of their new company would be to build sixteen newly designed vessels to respond to catastrophic oil spills along the coastlines of the United States. These specially designed oil-spill-recovery vessels were to be built at a cost of about $12 million apiece, and they were going to build sixteen of them. Then they would research and buy the best spill-recovery equipment and the smartest personnel that they could get.

"Along the way, it became clear to me—as a guy who responded to oil spills myself—that this company was going to be gigantic.

And I thought, 'If this organization that they're trying to build functions in reality, they're going to displace *my* opportunities,' so we made a proposal that we at least become their subcontractor. When there's a catastrophic oil spill, since I had some equipment, I either could be a first responder in my area, or supplement with equipment and manpower. But at that time, just getting off the ground, they weren't really interested in that sort of operational model.

"Now, just by chance, Charles Fabrikant owned a supply boat company down in the Gulf of Mexico, and he made a proposal to them at the same time when he heard that they were going to build sixteen new vessels. 'Look,' he said, 'I've got vessels already in existence that'll do the same work that your new vessels will do. Why don't you hire me to modify my existing fleet to do the same job at a very much reduced cost?'

"But again, that did not fit into the way that PIRO envisioned itself operating, so nothing came of that."

Charles Fabrikant, it should be noted at this point, is hardly a minor player in the watery world. Several decades ago, he and some other investors took over NICOR Marine and adopted the name SEACOR—primarily, Fabrikant once wrote (perhaps only half-facetiously), "because it was less costly to paint over two letters than the entire name."

These days, SEACOR Holdings has a hand in a vast variety of businesses—many of them still associated with the marine service industry, others that are nowhere near salt water. It owns and operates tankers, barges, and helicopters (which work not only in the oil and gas field but also as transportation in medical emergencies, in firefighting efforts, and in other realms). Like Miller Environmental, it also works in the environmental-cleanup business—as with the Deepwater Horizon disaster in the Gulf of Mexico a few years back.

In other words, Charles Fabrikant is now, and was back in the early 1990s, a formidable figure by any measure.

But again, to the men behind PIRO, his expertise—and his ships and other equipment—were not necessary. The message to his offer remained, "Thanks, but no thanks."

"I had not yet met Charles at that point," Jim says, "as he was based in Manhattan, but his operations were headquartered down in Morgan City, Louisiana. He had a salesman by the name of Al Wood, and he told Al, 'Do some research, and find out what the deal is with cleaning up oil spills. Is it a real high-tech business? What does it take to really be an expert in oil-spill cleanup?'

"He sends Al out, and he's checking around, looking to see who the main contractors in the country are who clean up oil spills and have first-class reputations. By chance, he comes across MEG on this list that he's developing. He reports to Charles and says, 'Well, there's a company up on Long Island that looks likely, and Shell Oil said positive things about them. You live in Manhattan, and you have a summer place out on the island. This company seems to have a pretty good reputation, and it's a small, privately owned operation. Why don't you go talk to them?' So Charles tells Al to call MEG and see if maybe the owner wants to sell his company.

"So he calls up and talks with Mark. It turns out that Mark has been tracking developments of the Oil Pollution Act closely, and Al Wood was, too. Al finally asks Mark if we want to sell the company, and I tell Mark, 'No, not really. I'm happy running my business the way it is. I'm doing fine, it's going nicely, so thanks, but nah, I'm not going to sell my company.' Al says, 'Well, would you talk to my boss? He wants to know about the business, and maybe there's something we can do together because he's got a fleet of work boats down in the Gulf that he's looking to put to work. Maybe you can collaborate somehow.' So I say, 'Well, if he's going to pay for the lunch, I'll eat it.'

"We accept the invitation. Al says, 'His sister has a house out in the Hamptons, and he comes out on Friday afternoons, so why don't

I organize a Friday afternoon luncheon?' We go to a local restaurant, and Charles, his wife, Sara, Mark, and I sit down and have lunch.

"We chat about OPA 90 and the issues with PIRO, and whether we'd be able to participate going forward if there's any way we can get business from them. Charles says he'd made a proposal that was declined, and I say we'd been talking with PIRO and getting nowhere. He says, 'Well, maybe we can get a little competition going. Maybe they'll hire us just to get rid of us.'

"Lunch started at about eleven that morning, and we didn't stand up from the table until around six o'clock that night. And when it was over, we had a concept that maybe we could put up a program to compete with this huge company. We thought we could at least put on a good enough show that they would have to stop and think for a minute that maybe these guys actually have some capacity and that we could be of use."

Charles Fabrikant, meanwhile, remembers his initial involvement with Jim and Mark Miller and the founding of the National Response Corporation with a mixture of pride at what they accomplished together and fondness toward Jim and his family.

While the Millers and Fabrikant have not remained in especially close or frequent touch with each other since those early years—NRC was sold to the private equity firm J. F. Lehman & Company in 2012, effectively severing Fabrikant's association with the company—Fabrikant stresses that the infrequent contact "is not because there isn't a high degree of both respect and affection on my part. It's simply that, as our commercial areas of interest diverged over the years, I've been busy doing my thing—and, as I would put it, wallowing in my sometimes miserable and at other times quite interesting life. People's paths go in different directions, you know. But I distinctly remember meeting Jim, who's only around ten years older than I am, and thinking that he seemed a *lot* more experienced. I was in my forties, and he was in his fifties, but for some reason, that seemed like a huge age difference back then. Regardless, we hit it off very quickly. I was bowled over by a number of things about him—the work he'd already done in the oil-cleanup field, his strong connection to his family, and especially Mark's and his can-do attitude. You know, Jim's refusal to say no to anyone who came to him with a job—which was something I witnessed from the start—was extremely impressive. But what's equally impressive is that he actually figured out a solution to any problem that he agreed to tackle. The world is full of people who say yes but who fail miserably when it comes to execution. From what I saw, Jim could not fail. He refused to fail."

Unbidden, Charles Fabrikant then offers up some high praise, indeed—especially coming from someone who has moved in the rarefied circles that he has known, socially and in business, for much of his life.

"I've never known a finer family than Jim's," he says. "And I've never dealt with a finer human being. That might sound sycophantic, but I really mean it. Jim Miller is someone for whom I have enormous respect. You know, I was more than aware of Jim's . . . I wouldn't say struggles, but challenges. In my own case, I was fortunate to have a good education—not that that's the only key to success, by any means—and I came from a family of comfortable assets. Most of my career and what I did with my life was a product of choices without much pressure. His road was much more difficult than the one that I had to traverse. If anything, my respect is enhanced by that. And finally—but certainly not least—he's a man of his word. When you shook hands with him, you had a deal. You didn't require a twenty-page contract. And if you *did* have a twenty-page contract, you didn't have to look at it."

Above and beyond the deep respect and liking that both men had, and still retain, for each other, the Fabrikant-Miller partnership was, in a number of quite practical ways, a perfect fit.

"With Charles's fleet of boats and ships," Jim points out, "and with my experience and capabilities with oil spills—and I had pretty good relationships throughout the industry—we conceived an idea of establishing a network of independent contractors to respond to disasters, rather than owning all of the equipment and hiring thousands of employees ourselves. We thought that maybe we could make an association of contractors and create the capability to respond throughout the United States. You know, we knew people in the industry, and we'd been around for twenty years already, and we were pretty well recognized. We were considered one of the top-line contractors, with a reputation for paying our bills and having a moral standard. A handshake was a handshake. We honored that. That's the way it was going to be. There was already a national trade association of contractors, and I knew most of the people in the industry. If there was an oil spill in an area that was near one of my customers, I could call a contractor nearby and get an initial response and get the job going and then say, 'Well, I'll be down in the morning, and we'll see where it's going to go.' So there was already a loose working relationship with contractors all over the country.

"But you know, we really didn't believe at that early stage that we were going to be forced to compete toe-to-toe with PIRO. We thought they would capitulate and say, 'Aw, maybe it's easier if we just hire these guys.'

"At any rate, we conjured up the plan, and we knew, to do it correctly, we had to write a true business plan. How much equipment? How much manpower? How could you set up this network of contractors? How could you really put some real meat on the bone to make this thing happen? There's a lot of work to be done to design a company that's going to respond on a national scale.

"Charles and my son Mark and Charles's wife and I—the four of us agreed to put a true business plan together, and we agreed it would probably cost about $100,000 to set it up. We decided at that lunch meeting that if we were going to go this way, we would offer our services or our potential services not to the major oil companies, not to the big guys that were already establishing their own group, but to the next tier of oil companies and the traditional, industrial-size users of petroleum. The public utilities, the power companies, the small oil distribution companies, and the independently owned barge and oil tanker companies—because the talk was that whoever transported, dealt, or traded in oil would have to demonstrate the ability by contract that they could respond to their own specific worst-case situation. If they had a tank that held 100,000 barrels of oil, they had to demonstrate that they would have the capacity, by their own in-house resources or by contract with somebody else, to clean up and respond to a 100,000-barrel oil spill in adverse weather. These were the guidelines that people were talking about having to deal with. The law hadn't even been written yet outlining exactly what these regulations or requirements would look like, but at that first meeting with Charles, we agreed that we would make a presentation to the middle-tier oil companies and ship owners, we would hold it in Manhattan in a fairly exclusive office tower   in the offices of one of the highly reputable New York law firms—and we'd put on a first-class cocktail party to present the proposal.

"Now, one of the conditions of attending that cocktail presentation would be that each company would send an executive who could sign a $10,000 check in the field, if needed. There are plenty of vice presidents in oil companies who don't have the authority to sign a check: 'That has to be reviewed by the board.' 'It's got to go to purchasing.' 'I can't make that deal.' 'I can't spend $10,000 of the company's money.' And we said, 'Well, we want decision makers. If you can't spend $10,000, we're sorry, but there's no reason for you to be there.'

"We had quite a lot of pushback, but that forced it up the line to a real vice president who could really spend $10,000 in the field. We had this fancy cocktail party in Manhattan, and we had a pretty good group of people show up from the various oil companies, electric utilities, and vessel owners. They were all anxious to see the arrogance of these upstarts who were demanding that they had the ability to sign a $10,000 check. They were really not sure what the hell to do with us.

"We tell them that we're going to propose an alternative to PIRO—which by then has evolved and has been renamed the Marine Spill Response Corporation, or MSRC—and they say, 'Well, that's ridiculous. Who the hell is going to compete with MSRC? They're funded with $1 billion. Who are these two characters?' But they think maybe it's worth an afternoon's entertainment and some free drinks to hear us out.

"Charles is an elegant speaker, and we have a pretty good presentation prepared. He begins by mentioning that MSRC plans to build their organization focused on the sixteen ships that they're building. But we think that's inadequate. Sixteen ships is really not a fair representation for all the coastal waters of the U.S. The steaming times are not sufficient to get you on-site to clean up. There are, we feel, shortfalls in their approach.

"We tell everyone that we think that it's more likely that around fifty vessels would be appropriate—and now everybody in the audience is looking around at one another, as if to say, 'Okay, this guy is drunk. Doesn't he realize that these ships that they're building cost $12 million apiece, and he says that sixteen of them ain't *enough*? These guys are crazy, because all of the shipyards in the United States have already been under contract to build the sixteen ships for MSRC. There are only a few shipyards that could build these things, and they're already on contract.'

"Charles just continues with his remarks, going on to say that in addition to the sixteen ships that they're going to build, which are truly inadequate, we think that an operational time frame of ninety days is much more realistic.

"Now they're thinking that this guy is really wacky. 'He's got to build fifty of these things. What is he going to do, make them out of rubber balloons and blow them up?' But you know what? By now, a few people are sneaking out of the room, making phone calls to friends and colleagues. 'Who the hell are these two characters, Fabrikant and Miller? This presentation is entertaining, but it's also bizarre.'

"They come trickling back, and there's a buzz in the back of the room, with people telling one another, 'Hey, this Charles Fabrikant is not a flaming idiot. He is a very real deal. He owns in excess of fifty ships already, and he already has them deployed in the North Sea, Africa, the Gulf of Mexico. It's just a matter of redeploying his ships for this new venture, so this time frame of ninety days is actually not at all unrealistic.'

"At that time, Charles was not a giant, like he eventually would become, but he had put some safety ships out in the North Sea, and he was a pioneer in that part of the industry. He was a dynamic young fellow and a Harvard grad, an attorney, and was recognized by everybody who knew him or knew of him as a really, really smart guy who got things done.

"Then someone asked us about MSRC planning to have hundreds of full-time employees. What did we propose?

"'Well,' said Charles, 'we believe one very productive and efficient way to address a spill is by using a network of existing contractors that are already cleaning up oil spills on a daily basis as part of their businesses. Since they're already cleaning up spills, they're operational right now, as we're having this meeting. We can respond to a spill today if need be. As a matter of fact, a tanker truck just capsized two hours ago on the Sunrise Highway and dumped 9,000 gallons of gasoline, and Miller has a team responding to that spill as we speak.'

"That got everybody's attention. Charles ended the meeting saying that this was an opportunity to create a viable alternative to MSRC. And when people asked, 'Since we don't know how much the MSRC costs are going to be for our industries, how are you going to compete against that?' Charles's response was that we certainly believed that because we were using existing vessels and existing systems and everything else, we were going to put a program together that would necessarily be less expensive for our members than theirs would be.

"Then Charles ended the presentation with the reality of this proposal and the reason we had asked everybody to the meeting in the first place. 'You had cocktails and hors d'oeuvres, and you had an interesting presentation, and we can all go home and be happy. We're not going to carry this thing any further, because right now we need approximately $100,000 to put together a business plan, and we're not going to incur that cost on our own. We need to see that you people here in the industry understand that this is a real thing and that you're anxious to take the next step. There's a bowl on the table. Anybody here in the room who said they have the capacity to write a check for $10,000, they can do it now. At the end of the evening if there is $100,000 in the bowl, we'll write a business plan and share it with the people who contributed. If there are not sufficient funds, we'll send the checks back and say, 'Thanks, it didn't pan out, and see you around, guys.'

"When all was said and done, there was $180,000 in the bowl, and we were in a position to write a full, legitimate, professional business plan for this new business venture, which became the National Response Corporation."

CHAPTER 32

NRC: The First Test

As it turns out, the first spill that NRC responded to was something of a model test case for how both NRC and MSRC might handle, separately or together, a catastrophic event in the new world of highly public, highly scrutinized, and occasionally highly politicized oil disasters. In August 1993, three vessels—the jet-fuel-filled barge *Ocean 255*; the barge *Bouchard 155*, carrying five million gallons of No. 6 fuel oil; and the phosphate freighter *Balsa 37*—collided in the waters off Tampa Bay, Florida. Fuel from the *Ocean 255* caught fire, while more than 320,000 gallons of oil spilled from the ruptured barge *B-155*. Oil eventually fouled an estimated fourteen miles of beaches, resulting in the now-familiar litany of injuries and deaths to birds, fish, sea turtles, and other wildlife, and polluting mangrove habitat, salt marshes, shellfish beds, and other natural gems.

For Jim Miller and NRC, it was showtime on a huge stage—without a moment's rehearsal.

"In Tampa Bay," Jim recalls, "there was a collision between an outbound phosphate ship, an inbound barge with jet fuel on board, followed by an oil barge. Through some miscalculations, miscommunication, or some other major mishap, the phosphate ship hit the jet-fuel barge, which blew up and burned. The freighter was now out of control, ricocheted off the jet-fuel barge, and had a collision with the black-oil barge. He was ruptured and bleeding six oil into the bay. The freighter continued out of control and finally ran aground and began to sink. So you've got three events taking place right there at the entrance to Tampa Bay. This was on August 10, and on August 18, we were supposed to be operational with the National Response Corporation. MSRC was our competitor. One of the barges involved, the black-oil barge, was a customer that was negotiating with us to be enlisted with NRC. The jet-fuel barge was MSRC's client, so they were the responding contractor on that.

"So here we were, both of the major, national companies, responding simultaneously to the spill. One was a nonprofit, and one a for-profit company. It was eight days before the law went into effect, where we *had* to respond with this capacity to address a catastrophic spill. But as it happens, at that very moment, we were delivering our equipment to our network of contractors. NRC had organized a network of contractors throughout the United States; instead of having our employees stage and man and operate the equipment, we did it through our contractors all over the country. So instead of having employees ship out or fly out to get to a disaster, we had contractors who were basically on-site wherever anything might happen. Mark got the phone call about the Tampa situation directly from the owner of the barge, we had people on-site within hours, and we began our response. During that same time frame, we were distributing all of our equipment throughout the United States from various manufacturers. Part of our concept was that our equipment was all going to be staged on flatbed trailers—forty-foot flatbed trailers—in order to give us mobility and an immediate response wherever we might be needed, anywhere in the country.

"Now, these flatbed trailers weren't customized for the gear that was going to ride on them. They were just forty-foot flatbed trailers. In the creation of NRC, we were on a budget, while our competitor had a billion dollars. We organized the flatbed trailers to carry all of our equipment. We hired a local guy. We told him, 'We're going to need about a hundred flatbed trailers. We want you to go out and find a hundred secondhand roadworthy flatbed trailers, with good suspensions and good rubber.'

"We gave him a budget number to buy the trailers, and we told him he had to paint them all blue. Timmy Cropper of Island Transportation, a local business in the trucking industry, was charged with that responsibility, and he did it at modest cost. I don't remember the exact number—maybe $6,000 apiece for the forty-foot tractor trailers, all of them secondhand, all of them roadworthy, all of them painted blue and licensed.

"They were all empty, so we had to deliver them to the factories to load the equipment, tie it all down, and cover it with tarps so it was safe for transport. At the time of the spill, we had trucks all over the United States, coming, going, to a factory, from a factory, or to a contractor. We got the phone call that we'd got a catastrophic spill on our hands. But we'd got our equipment scattered all over the country. It was everywhere. It was nowhere. It was someplace. Nobody had cell phones then, of course, and communication was poor. The employees that we had at NRC—I think we had sixteen or eighteen employees in total—one of them was a logistics guy who had retired from the military. He went to work for us. He was charged with arranging those 100 trailer-loads of supplies and getting them to Tampa. He came up with the idea of making the federal alert to all of the police departments in the country: 'If you see a blue flatbed truck with NRC on it, stop it and tell the driver he's got to call his office *immediately.*' Within a very short amount of time, we contacted every single one of the guys driving trailers and redirected them to Tampa. *Everything* was heading for Florida.

"We also alerted all of our contractors that we were diverting to Tampa and that they should make arrangements to be there when the equipment got there. In addition, if *they* had equipment, they should bring it, too. We were not only going to have a hundred trailer loads of NRC equipment, we were also going to have hundreds of pieces of equipment from the independent contractors' network. Within twenty-four hours, there were traffic jams of blue. Blue equipment, blue trucks, blue, blue, blue. The Coast Guard was saying, 'We never believed that this type of equipment could ever be amassed that quickly.' We had hundreds of thousands of feet of oil containment booms, trailer load after trailer load of oil containment booms. We organized a response capability. We hired staging areas and cranes. We had barges. We had all kinds of equipment. We responded to a catastrophic spill. Within a day, we were there, on-site, and everything was in operation.

"Now, if this event in Tampa had happened, say, six months before—forget it. It would have been impossible to organize a response that looked anything like what we had in August. Be that as it may, the jet-fuel barge was on fire, but it didn't sink. Ultimately, the phosphate freighter didn't discharge anything. It just grounded. Somebody took care of that. The black oil and the jet fuel were all commingled now, and there was collaboration between all of the people on the job site, because many of the contractors who worked for us were also hired for MSRC. Really, there was tremendous integration, and a spectacular, cooperative response. I mean, within twenty-four hours, we had *fifteen hundred* people on-site, tractor trailers, equipment, boats, manpower. We had a ton of stuff. I think the first day's billing—our first day of business as NRC, in the field—was in excess of a million dollars. That was our debut."

Charles Fabrikant—a man not easily impressed—was also on-site for a few days early in the Tampa spill response, and today, so many years later, he turns to a striking, and perfectly apt, literary reference to help convey the scale of what he witnessed:

"To be honest, it reminded me of a scene out of *War and Peace*. Granted, my memory is a little loose, because I used to read that book between exams when I was at law school as pleasurable relief—if anyone can believe reading Russian novels is pleasurable relief. And this spill struck me as being very much like the war scenes in Tolstoy's book. All of these generals racing around, sending and receiving reports, and no one *really* knows what's happening. It's just chaos, basically, and while the generals in the book think they have control over the battle, in reality it's not clear that they do. That was my first impression as I was watching there in Tampa. People running around like chickens without heads, drawing maps in the sand—which reminded me of drawing football plays when I played touch football as a kid. It seemed that no one could coordinate with anyone. But there were Mark and Jim, cool as cucumbers, and of everyone there, they seemed to have things in hand."

(As it turns out, one of the more famous lines from *War and Peace*, concerning victors and vanquished, might also be applied to the approach—strategic, logistical, philosophical—that the Millers have always brought to their jobs. "A battle," Tolstoy wrote, "is won by the side that has firmly resolved to win.")

As colossal and complex as the Tampa Bay spill was, Jim Miller—who never focuses on the obvious but instead takes what might be termed a holistic view of any problem—offers a surprising observation on that inaugural NRC operation.

"Maybe the most challenging part of that entire scenario," he says, "was setting up an accounting department. We didn't have a billing program yet. Everybody was working with yellow pencils and writing handwritten worksheets and trying to record what the hell we were doing, with thousands of people all over the place. We were still ramping up the corporate infrastructure and had yet to fully develop the internal systems for tracking and recording finances, resource movements, all of that stuff. Just getting the logistical support in place was really, really tough, because the staffing of NRC was not yet full-strength. We had one or two people in the accounting department. It was just way beyond what they could handle—what any of us could handle—so we had an outside accounting firm come in. They were CPAs, and they were going to set it up like CPAs would. It was a complicated program and really hard to get it settled down.

"But there were some very shrewd maneuvers made during the process as well. My son Mark was the president of NRC. I was the principal of Miller Environmental. I was a subcontractor to NRC, and I was a partner in NRC. And I clearly remember one of the moves I made involved a supplier of oil-absorbent materials, Sorbent Products in New Jersey, run by a friend of mine, Mr. Clancy. When I recognized the magnitude of this project, I called him up, and I asked him what his production was on a daily basis. He said he could produce a tractor trailer in a half a day. Something like that.

"I said, 'Okay, whatever your production is, I want it for the next thirty days. All of it. Whatever you can produce, I am now your only customer. You can't sell it to anybody else. I'm it. I will commandeer everything that you have for thirty days. As fast as you can make it, load it on tractor trailers, and send it down to me in Tampa.'

"We had a handshake agreement and an understanding between us that we would run this project. Within the first few hours, all of the contractors ran out of absorbents. Nobody was geared for the magnitude of this kind of a spill. We set up what we called, later on, Central Supply. We coordinated all of the absorbent purchases and supplies, and then we made arrangements with other suppliers to supply us with worker protection and rakes and shovels—that sort of thing. Because in the first twelve hours of something like this, you walk into a hardware store, and you say, 'All those shovels are mine. Every single one. I want all the shovels. I want all the rakes. Put 'em on the truck.'

"That was the magnitude of the operation. We were equipping a thousand or two thousand people. We set up a central supply, and we set up our own hardware store."

And how does a company like NRC—fresh out of the gate—house and feed one thousand people on twenty-four hours' notice, and make sure that workers have a place to go to the bathroom, and handle all of the other logistics that have to be addressed and locked down in such a chaotic, fluid situation?

"We downsized it by passing it to our subcontractors. That became their responsibility. 'You're sending us fifty guys? Take care of them. We're not going to take care of your guys. You take care of your fifty guys. You do what you've got to do. We don't really care how you do it. We want to know that it's done, but we don't need to hear about the nitty-gritty.'"

In the end, while the 1993 spill remains a bleak memory for countless longtime Tampa Bay residents, the fact remains that it very well might have been far, far worse. Wind and tides initially pushed at least some of the enormous spill away from the shore, while the appearance of thousands of cleanup workers—along with backhoes, oil booms, and other critical cleanup equipment—within hours of the three-ship collision felt almost providential.

National Response Corporation, conceived at a long, long lunch meeting on Long Island less than two years before, was not only alive and well but off and running.

CHAPTER 33

Steve Candito:
A Life Redirected

Like the vast majority of the people in this book, Steve Candito was born and raised on Long Island, and, like the Millers, he has more than a little salt water in his veins. When he was young, his summer jobs usually involved digging clams on the Great South Bay. Later, he attended the U.S. Merchant Marine Academy after thinking to himself, 'Hey, if I can go to college and still be on the water, I'd sure like to do that.' And that's what happened: For five years after graduating from the academy, he went to sea, sailing as an engineer on board oil tankers.

After a time, though, Steve realized that the seagoing life was not something that he necessarily wanted to do for his entire career. He went to law school (Hofstra) while still employed full time by Exxon. After a few years of not-very-inspiring legal work for the oil giant, he was hired in the mid-1980s by what at the time was the most prominent maritime law firm in New York City, Haight, Gardner, Poor & Havens. In 1990, an 800-foot tanker, the *BT Nautilus*, ran aground in the Kill Van Kull waterway near Staten Island, spewing

260,000 gallons of No. 6 fuel oil in one of the worst spills in the history of New York Harbor. Allegations of intoxication and possible negligence on the part of the crew flew fast and furious in the days following the accident. And it's at this point that Steve Candito first makes the acquaintance of the Millers.

"I was working on the *Nautilus* spill as a junior attorney," he remembers. "There was a senior partner there, too, and we were doing things that attorneys do in those circumstances—interviewing witnesses, gathering up logbooks, getting ready for all the litigation that's going to come out of it. The DA's office in New Jersey was looking at some kind of criminal prosecution. The authorities did a drug and alcohol test on the captain and the chief mate, and lo and behold, the chief mate failed the breathalyzer test. All of a sudden, there was a big criminal investigation, and it was all focused on this chief mate. Now, the chief mate who failed this breathalyzer had nothing to do with causing the spill. The ship had run aground while it was being docked, and the chief mate was on the bow. The captain and the pilot, who were in charge of maneuvering the vessel and had caused the grounding—they passed their drug and alcohol tests, but the whole focus of the investigation was now on the chief mate. That's important because the senior partner I was working with then got sucked into the criminal investigation and defending the chief mate, and as a junior attorney, I was now left to deal with all of the Coast Guard issues and the actual cleaning up of the oil spill. Jim, Glen, and Mark, who were the main cleanup company on the spill, recognized that I was kind of green. I had some experience as a lawyer, but I really had no experience cleaning up oil spills. I had technical experience; I had worked as an engineer in my job with Exxon, on the tankers, so I had some idea of the technical aspects of the spill. But that was about it.

"Eventually, though, because of a whole bunch of personnel changes and other complications with the insurance claims, I was left to run the spill. Jim, Glen, and Mark were physically doing the work, but they had to interact with me and with the Coast Guard to make sure that this thing went well, and pretty quickly we developed a great relationship. From day one, really, we seemed to understand each other, and we trusted each other. And because of the good working relationship that I developed with the Millers, we cleaned up the oil spill efficiently and cost-effectively. We all got good marks for what we did, even though I was completely green and there was all sorts of turmoil around it."

Professionalism on both sides certainly eased the relationship along and allowed Steve and the Millers to hit it off quickly. But to another, quite significant degree, there was also common personal ground—a shared vernacular that arose not only from everyone's maritime background but also from Steve's engineering capabilities, which the Millers immediately respected.

"We were simpatico, I guess," Steve says. "I certainly told them about my clamming experiences early in my life, during one of the late-night conversations we had. On jobs like this, you're together basically twelve, sixteen, eighteen hours a day in that emergency phase. Yes, you're busy doing what needs to be done, but there are also times when you're just chatting and sharing experiences. You're kind of getting the measure of the other person, and if there's animosity or even just a lack of personal connection, these things can sometimes go badly: A spill doesn't get cleaned up well, or it does get cleaned up, but the cost is astronomical because there's no cooperation between the cleanup company and the insurance company and the Coast Guard and everyone else. That sort of messy, costly nonsense didn't happen here, because we worked well together.

"After the spill was over, the Millers went back to doing what they did, and I went back to lawyering. We did stay in touch, and in fact, I believe that they actually sent me some work, a small matter but one I appreciated, because they recognized that young lawyers need to bring in business for the firm.

"About a year later, they're getting NRC up and running with Charles Fabrikant. I'm now a seventh-year associate, and this is the year that, normally at least, at Haight Gardner you would be up for partner. I'm married, and we have just had our first child, my older son. The partner that I was working for has always assured me that, 'Hey, you're the top associate in your group. You're going to be the one. Don't worry about anything. You're going to be a shoo-in when the time comes.' I'm working hard and doing all the right things, and everything, according to my performance reviews, is perfect. And then the partnership decision comes back, and it turns out they don't make anyone partner that year. We'll all have to wait until next year.

"Law firms are sort of notorious for that, where they tell you you're going to make partner, but they string you along for a while. And even if you eventually get frustrated and bail, at least they get another couple of good years out of you.

"I've stayed in touch with Mark, and when I tell him that I'm not really happy with what just happened and that I'm thinking about maybe making a move, he says to me, 'Listen, Steve, it's a start-up, it's very uncertain, but why don't you come work for NRC?'

"I start talking this over with my wife. We've just had the baby, we're living in Brooklyn Heights, and I'm doing this very short commute into Lower Manhattan every day. But we're starting to realize that if we're going to raise children in New York City, the expenses associated with that are pretty heavy. Maybe we should move out to the suburbs, to Long Island or New Jersey or Westchester? We're really struggling with this decision. I talk to Mark again, and he says, 'Why don't you come work for us? I know it's risky, but I'll tell you one thing: You can move out to Long Island and work out here, and you'll have that nice backyard and the swing set for the kids. Give it a chance.' And then Jim starts weighing in. 'Listen, it's a start-up, so you've got to do a little bit of everything, because we're all just pitching in to get this thing going. But we also need to go out and get clients. Those clients are going to be ship builders and insurance companies. You can speak to both of those sorts of people, Steve. Think about the insurance company on the *Nautilus* spill; they were very happy with how things turned out. You could approach them about using this new company, NRC, on their projects.' And that's what I did. My first job with NRC was not really a legal position; it was going out there and building up that customer base."

And just like that, Steve Candito went from being a lawyer in Brooklyn Heights to being a salesperson out on Long Island. And his wife, Marianne? Well, it also worked out perfectly well for her, professionally. A lawyer in her own right, she told Steve that she felt the move would be great because, as Steve tells it, "when we got out to Long Island, she could continue to do per diem work for the New York firms, but she could also set up her own little law firm and be a hometown lawyer, doing real estate closings, wills— anything that people in the community needed done. That's exactly what she ended up doing for twenty years, very successfully. That's just one reason why we're so indebted to the Millers, because they gave both of us that opportunity."

Steve ended up at NRC for twenty-two years. He was the CEO of the corporation—taking the reins when Mark left to run Miller Environmental in the late 1990s. Steve resigned from NRC in the summer of 2015—but he has taken the lessons he learned from both Mark and Jim with him throughout his entire career.

"As businessmen, the Millers see the big picture," he says. "They want to run a successful business, or a number of successful businesses, but they want to be fair to people along the way. They want to take care of their employees and help them to grow with the company. It's not that I didn't have tough decisions to make when I was the head of NRC—letting people go in slow times, for example. But I learned by watching the way Jim ran his own company, and the way Mark ran both NRC and then MEG—that there's a balance, and you don't *always* have to make a decision based purely on what the numbers seem to indicate. You have to take people into consideration.

"You know, one last thing I want to stress is that my first impression of Jim, which was so positive to begin with, has only strengthened over time. When I think about those first meetings and the late-night talks we'd have, way back on that *Nautilus* spill, I think first of Jim's unassuming personality. He didn't come off as a know-it-all. He didn't pound his fist on the table, saying that this is the way we're going to do things. What came out very early on was that he was trying to be fair. He was trying to be reasonable. 'Hey, I want to make some money on this, but we can do the right thing here as well.' I very quickly saw the fairness in him, and that made him trustworthy, somebody I could go back to and ask for advice, somebody I could rely on over the years. And that's exactly what I've done."

CHAPTER 34

No Such Thing as
Small Details

Sometimes a company's quieter, seemingly smaller actions during a rescue-and-recovery operation can help define the company's reach as well as, or better than, the larger, more impressive capabilities that come into play on a major disaster site.

In NRC's case, the horrific—and still controversial—explosion and crash of TWA Flight 800 off southern Long Island in July 1996 showcased the company's ability to handle the overall disaster as well as seemingly obscure minutiae that arose from the calamity. Two decades later, communities in that region of Suffolk County—and specifically the Moriches—still bear the emotional and psychological scars of the Flight 800 crash. As with 9/11, the *Challenger* space shuttle explosion, and other epic, shattering events, everyone in that part of the world remembers where they were when they learned that a 747 had exploded in midair just minutes after takeoff from JFK and that not one of the 230 people aboard had survived. And like those other disasters, the Flight 800 crash generated its own cottage industry of alternate theories about what brought the plane down. Federal investigators determined that the most probable cause was a fuel-tank explosion sparked by a short circuit. But an awful lot of people—including many who do not routinely don tinfoil hats and see conspiracies everywhere they look—believe that a U.S. Navy ship might have accidentally shot down the plane or that it was, in fact, a terrorist attack. At least one retired U.S. Navy officer and some members of the International Association of Machinists and Aerospace Workers (IAMAW) who were party to the National Transportation and Safety Board's investigation concluded that the fuel-tank-explosion theory was tenuous, at best. That what really happened on that July night over the ocean might never be known only adds to the grief and, in many cases, the still-smoldering anger of so many of the victims' friends and families.

For the Millers, word of the explosion and crash came quickly—as did the decision to respond.

"We immediately became aware of the misfortune," Jim recalls, "because Miller's Launch in Staten Island maintains a twenty-four-hour-a-day monitoring system for marine activities in and around New York Harbor. The dispatcher on duty that evening heard captains of vessels talking about seeing an explosion in the sky over the Atlantic."

Mark Miller, who was running NRC by that time, got a phone call within a half hour of the plane going down from the vice president of TWA.

"He activated us [NRC] initially to respond to the jet-fuel spill," Mark remembers, "because they still didn't know very much about what had happened. No one had yet grasped the magnitude of the disaster. Nevertheless, TWA wanted NRC to handle the response. I activated my nearest contractor in the NRC network—which happened to be Miller Environmental Group—and we immediately went and set up a command post at the Moriches Coast Guard station. Miller Environmental was obviously a big part of that critical first response—and for weeks and even months thereafter."

"By this point," Jim says of the hours immediately following the plane's disappearance from the radar, "boats out on the water are reporting debris fields, oil on the water is burning—there are fires on the surface of the sea—and it's clearly turning into a giant event. The New York State Department of Environmental Conservation is involved, regulatory agencies are coming out of the woodwork, the FBI has a presence on the scene, TV trucks are arriving. It's becoming something like a military operation in scale.

"At the same time, that part of the Moriches quickly becomes a limited-access area. The Coast Guard's Captain of the Port is on his way from New Haven to take charge of the overall site, and we have a working relationship with him. We know who he is, and he knows who we are, so in pretty short order, an established group of people is in control of the site."

As he does in so many of his stories, Jim quickly switches from the general to the particular in order to emphasize a point—as well as to inject some humor into what could very easily be an unrelievedly bleak narrative.

"Let me tell you very quickly about something else that evolved from the chaos around this disaster. A day or so into the response, a multitude of regulatory agencies are setting up, the police department is putting restrictions on where people can and can't go, and the media is camped outside the perimeter with radio towers and satellite dishes and everything else. At some point, someone sets up a helicopter landing pad for the mayor, the governor, congressmen and senators, the Navy brass, and others who are flying in, and they have some guy out there directing the helicopters to the landing site. He's got a bullhorn and flags in his hands, and he's directing aircraft to come in here, get over there, clear the site, get out of the way so this helicopter can land. He's a lieutenant colonel with the U.S. Army Reserve, and he's taken control of the helicopters' comings and goings. 'I've got a bird coming in. Clear the site!' He's got the lingo and seems to know what he's doing. This goes on for a couple of days, and by now, we're established enough that there's a morning meeting with everybody who's responsible for some key part of the operation. We discuss site security, protocol, who's in charge, what we're doing, what are the boundaries of the search area. And this guy—who by then has been appointed by the Coast Guard as the director of Air Traffic Control at the site—has always got something to say. 'You guys have to understand that I'm landing these birds, and they have priority over everybody else on the site, because when the copter's coming in, he's carrying these dignitaries, and he can't deviate from his position.' Blah, blah, blah. We understand where he's coming from, and we accept that he has a role to play.

"About the third day, when he's berating everybody for not cooperating, not clearing the pad quickly enough, an FBI guy finally does a check on this guy. All along, he's claimed that he's an Army Reserve colonel or something, but the FBI determines that the guy with his uniform and his bullhorn and his flags and everything else is a fraud. He just walked onto the site and took over. He has no authority, no responsibility, no nuthin', but he's run the damn place for about three days before he gets arrested. Turns out he's been convicted in New Jersey *the day before* the crash for fraudulently posing as a doctor. That should give you an idea of how chaotic these emergency-response scenes can be in the first day or two after a disaster.

"But the story that comes to mind about just how broad our responsibilities were, from the largest job down to the smallest necessity, took place on the seventh or eighth day. They've defined the search area and found the wreck, and now they have divers down there. We get a phone call at around eleven o'clock on a Saturday night that one of the things they're starting to desperately need on the site is Vicks VapoRub, and they need it by the next morning. Most drugstores, at least those out on the island, are closed. So we dispatch a couple of guys to the mall and shopping center to find any all-night drugstores and buy as much VapoRub as they can get their hands on. We call one of our branch offices in New York. We call upstate. Now we have guys from three or four offices looking to buy VapoRub in the middle of the night.

"By the early hours of the morning we have a couple of cases of Vicks that we have to get to the site by dawn. And we make it. We get it there.

"We later learned that in order to keep working in those conditions, with bodies being brought out of the water days after the crash, these guys were smearing VapoRub under their noses to mask the smell of the corpses."

Eventually, Miller Environmental leveraged its relationship with colleagues at the old Grumman airport in Calverton and gained access to one of the hangars as a location for reassembling the plane. And it was there that, over the coming months, investigators reconstructed TWA's 747 from the wreckage—ranging from bits and pieces that could fit in a thimble to aviation parts large enough that they were carried to the hangar on flatbeds and in tractor trailers. In another part of the hangar, workers deposited suitcases, charred pieces of clothing, toys, oil-soaked stuffed animals.

As the investigation proceeded, Miller Environmental maintained the hangar for close to two years. They handled hazardous waste and electronics recovered from the seabed and parts of the fuselage that fit together like grim, enormous jigsaw-puzzle pieces. The company worked closely with the FBI Evidence Recovery Team and even provided site security. They billed the government hundreds and hundreds of thousands of dollars—and earned every penny. They stayed on the job until their services and equipment and people were no longer needed. And throughout it all, the company ran as smoothly as it ever had, responding on a daily basis to other disasters—of all shapes and sizes—in other parts of the country and other parts of the world.

For Jim, the Flight 800 job, in all its complexity, was one of the most significant and—in a solemn way—most satisfying of his career. By that point, Miller Environmental was a national and international force in the cleanup industry, having responded to major disasters—and been the lead contractor—across the U.S., in the Caribbean, and beyond. The company was also constantly growing and developing new businesses (waste disposal, training and compliance certification, alternative and sustainable energies). And incredibly, all of this was accomplished without accumulating any debt. In Jim's eyes, running a debt-free enterprise that paid its bills on time not only showed sound business sense; it was also a moral imperative. ("I don't understand people who are buried under credit card debt and are mortgaged to the hilt and are burdened with car payments and everything else," he says. "Spend money before you've earned it? I think that's an immoral way to live.")

But today, twenty years after the Flight 800 disaster, it's not only the huge, impressive accomplishments that Jim recalls with pride. When he takes the time to tell the story of dispatching a dozen guys in the middle of the night to seek out jars of Vicks VapoRub—because the people he had shaken hands with on a job had asked for it—it's clear that, to Jim's way of seeing, there is no such thing as a detail that's too minor to bother with.

In the wake of a disaster, there's no such thing as a small request.

CHAPTER 35

Growing Up Miller:
A Granddaughter's Tale

As unusual (in the best possible ways) and as unique as it might be growing up a Miller—especially in recent years, when the family is so well known on the North Fork and, indeed, on much of the rest of Long Island—it would be less than candid to ignore the fact that bearing the Miller name might occasionally be more burden than blessing. After all, it's hard enough coming of age in *any* family, in any environment, in light of the emotional, psychological, and (let's face it) hormonal challenges that accompany adolescence and young adulthood. Add a high-profile family name to the mix? Well, one can see why Jim and Barbara's daughter Tracey put it the way she did: "No one who is part of this family is invisible. That's just the way it is."

For Mark's daughter Emily, the oldest of Jim and Barbara's (thus far) fourteen grandkids, the Miller name has long since ceased being a millstone around her neck. Or rather, as she has gotten older (she's in her late twenties and works as a public defender for the Suffolk County Legal Aid Society), Emily has embraced the responsibilities and complications—as well as the undeniable privileges—of being part of such a spirited and noteworthy clan.

"There are still times, even now, when it feels as if my siblings and I, and our cousins, are under a microscope," Emily says. "And it can be hard to know we're being judged by people outside of our family simply because of our name. Growing up in a small town on Long Island, everybody kind of knew everybody else. And I've been in situations where people who never met me before assume that I'm just like everybody else in my family. And that sort of preconceived idea about who I am has sometimes made it hard for me to maintain my identity as an individual.

"That's one reason—but not the only reason—that I went away for college. I went out of the state, to the University of Miami. There, I felt like I could be my own person and develop my own identity because no one knew who I was. Believe me, I know that sounds horrible, but it's not because I'm ashamed of who I am or where I'm from. I could not be more proud to be a Miller. But sometimes it's important, when I'm meeting people for the first time, for them to understand who I am first, as an individual. After that, perhaps they'll find out who my family is, and maybe they'll have some kind of connection to my parents or grandparents in some way. And as proud as I am of my family, I hope I'll have established who *I* am before a new acquaintance or friend judges me for being a Miller.

"It's obviously complicated. But I've gone through the stage of, 'Wow! I don't really want to be a Miller, because I want to be my own person,' to the point where I am now, where I can say, '*Yeah,* I'm part of this family, and it's so great. I can be my own person and still be a Miller.' At the same time, I've come to understand that, for example, in the course of business, my grandfather and my father have had to make tough decisions that might have resulted in the loss of a job for someone, and it's difficult to know that someone who was perhaps let go from Miller Environmental might hold our whole family responsible for that. It's unfair, but it's a reality we deal with."

Despite the fact that Emily loves her job, she also mentions, a bit wistfully, that "if I could do volunteer work for the rest of my life, I probably would. I volunteered overseas, helping the victims of the sex trade, and I've worked in children's hospitals. I just love that sense of giving back. It's where I feel most happy. That's one of the main reasons I took the Legal Aid Society job when it was offered to me. It offered a way for me to help people. It's also a job where I can get a lot of experience in a short amount of time, and one that I think can open possibilities for me in the future. Getting some fundamental ligation experience was crucial for me. When all was said and done, though, when it was offered, I knew it was an opportunity, and I sure as hell wasn't going to miss this one."

What comes across so powerfully when speaking with Emily about her life is that, as much as she has accomplished, and as far as she's likely to go in any career path she chooses to follow, she's perfectly aware that she is not alone—not by a long shot.

"I'm sure that any Miller would say this, but the fact that our family is so close is unbelievably important to me. Of course, my sister and brother and I went through phases where there was a lot of sibling rivalry. Now I'm extremely close with all of them. *Extremely* close. And then there are the more tangible benefits, like having the opportunity to do some really amazing things because of the financial position we're in. My education was basically taken care of. I didn't have to worry about paying off student loans. I'm so, so grateful for that!"

(As a matter of fact, not one of Jim Miller's grandchildren needs to be concerned about leaving school burdened by student debt. He has set up college funds for all of the grandkids, whether they graduate from a four-year school, go on to post-grad work, or pursue other educational paths. Tuition, room, and board at any college or university in the world—it's paid for. Of all the things that Jim Miller has been able to do for his family, paying for his grandchildren's educations makes him especially proud. And, as he constantly points out, his grandkids have made him proud, too.)

"Or when I think about the network of people that my family knows and how connected we are," Emily continues, "it's just astounding. I remember my father once telling me that between him and Pops, anywhere in the world I happened to go, I would have somebody that I could reach out to. It's almost unfathomable sometimes to really try to understand how many connections my family has made and maintained over the years."

As for the nature of Emily's—and by extension, the other grandchildren's—relationship with her grandfather, affection and respect seem to fight a constant, friendly battle for preeminence. And, as with many memorable events in the Miller family history, some of Emily's most profound lessons were learned (grudgingly) on or near the water.

"I remember being young and going on fishing trips with just my grandfather," she says. "He would pick me up early in the morning, and we'd drive out to the charter boat we were taking for the day. On the way there, he would try to teach me things—even though I didn't realize he was trying to teach me anything. He would be talking, and he would have different sayings that would stick out. Like, 'Nothing bad ever happens, only missed opportunities.' He would tell me these things over and over, and because I was young and didn't understand, I was like, 'Pops, I've already heard this.' But he never gave up and never missed an opportunity to teach us something. When I was younger, I thought they were ridiculous little lessons. Now, looking back, I realize that not a day goes by when I'm not using some of the phrases that he taught me. Talking to clients, I'll use the 'missed opportunities' one. When discussing politics with a friend, I'll use the 80/20 rule—which, Pops said, means that 20 percent of the people or 20 percent of any given company usually causes 80 percent of the problems. But for me to sit there and try to listen to that when I was in sixth grade?"

Emily laughs, and it's clear that the humor lies in the memory of her younger self trying to absorb her grandfather's lifetime of wisdom—and, at the time, having no idea what her Pops was going on about.

"Now, everything he taught me makes so much sense. In fact, it's become second nature to me, and to all of my siblings and cousins. Oh, and I can't forget my grandmother, either. She had a saying that was so great and that I will always keep with me. We call it the 'the good, better, best' rule. It goes like this: 'Good, better, best, never let it rest, till the good gets better and the better gets best.' I think that really sums up everything that my grandfather and the rest of the family care about. Good is good, good is all right—but it can always be better. If you strive to be better, don't let that be your best. Keep going until you can't anymore, because it's worth it. You put in the effort, and you reap the rewards. Like when I went to law school and got my law degree and Pops was at my graduation and then came to my swearing-in ceremony for the bar. He started to see me as an intellectual and somebody he could respect, and not just a grandchild he loved. That meant so much to me, and it still does, and it came about because I put all that hard work into getting that degree. Our relationship now is better than it's ever been. Part of that is definitely because I'm so appreciative of everything that he does for all of us, and maybe I wasn't that appreciative before.

"I don't know how else to express it, other than to say I feel extremely blessed to be part of this family—despite the times I kind of bowed my head and kept walking and tried not to be associated with the Miller name. Now, after all this time, I honestly could not be more proud."

CHAPTER 36

Still Going, and Going . . .

In the years since Jim Miller surrendered the reins at Miller Environmental—or rather, since he sold the company to Mark, who became president and CEO in 1999—he has hardly rested on his laurels or settled down into a sedentary retirement. This is a man, after all, who is very good at a great number of things. Doing nothing is not one of them.

"I spend more time in real estate now than I did earlier in my career," he says, "even if I occasionally had a hand in it from way back when. You know, I think back to the time my brother Richie and I bought a house together, as an investment, in Port Jefferson when we were in our twenties, and when you put the economics in perspective, the numbers are so out of proportion to the realities of today's market that it's almost humorous. You're talking about rents of fifty and sixty dollars a month for an apartment back then in the late fifties and early sixties. You might buy a whole property for $6,000. Those were just completely different times. But in recent years—in fact, for the past twenty years or so—I've partnered with my friend Paul Elliott on various real estate projects. Paul is the president of the Soundview Realty Group in Farmingville, and we originally became partners in a building in Riverhead. I knew him already, but he called me one day and said that he had an interesting project in Riverhead village, an old three-story telephone company building that had been vacant for several years, and it was rumored that there was a tremendous amount of environmental risk attached to the property. A banking company in Texas had held the property for a while; then they went bankrupt, and the building, with a mortgage of several million dollars, was coming up for auction. Paul had a feeling that it was probably going to go pretty cheap, and he asked me to come down and take a look to see if there was a real environmental risk, or was it just something that people were saying—a rumor, of sorts, maybe to scare off potential buyers.

"I went down and examined the building, and I came to the conclusion that the environmental risk was fairly insignificant. It had a fuel tank that was above ground, which was not a substantial risk at all, and there was asbestos exposure in the building, which, in my view, wasn't monumental or insurmountable. I was pretty comfortable buying the building, even with that minimal environmental risk.

"At the auction there was a very, very small group of interested parties, and the bidding opened at $1 million. There were no takers. The auctioneers knocked it down to $750,000. No takers. Eventually it got down to about $100,000, and I said, 'I'll buy it.'

"As soon as I said that, somebody else put his hand up, and it became a bidding contest for a little while, but that quickly faded away because this was a COD auction. If you won the auction, you had to be prepared to write a check for it. We wound up paying something like $200,000 for a building that was originally mortgaged for several million.

"At some point, some guy sued us because he claimed he wasn't aware of the bidding, and if he was, he would have been there at the auction, and he tied us up for six months. We eventually won in court and proceeded to renovate the entire structure and invest maybe a million dollars in it to complete the renovation. During the renovation, it became clear that there weren't sufficient parking spaces for the building as an office complex. The property came with a parking field a block away, but that was kind of a sketchy neighborhood, and we didn't believe that people would—or that they should—walk from there to the building.

"We debated a long time whether to use the first floor as office space, but without sufficient parking. We looked it over, and looked it over, and looked it over, and finally we said, 'How about if we just abandon the first floor? Let's finish the top floors and leave the first floor vacant. In fact, why don't we just turn *that* into parking?' We finished the basement off as a parking area beneath the building. Within a year we had finished the upper floors and had 100 percent occupancy in the building. Title companies, the local sheriff's union's offices, a couple of law firms. We had class-A tenants, and we finished the building off in style.

"Within a year of full occupancy, a guy calls up praising us to the sky—he loves the building, he loves the parking underneath. The cash flow, he says, justifies a purchase price of $4 million, and he would love to buy it from us. We sold it to him and reaped a very, very nice profit from it. We rewarded ourselves with distributions from that money and established a very solid working relationship. We also subsequently bought an eleven-acre property in Calverton, next door to the Miller Environmental offices. We've developed that over the years by building a gas station and convenience mart and a rental building for Allied Supply. That was quite profitable for us as well, as we recently sold a four-acre piece of that property for $3.5

million. So real estate is something I've been involved with for a while, and it's certainly been rewarding—financially, of course, but also in terms of learning as much as I can about a new business.

"But our real estate ventures, at this point, are really not for our own, personal benefit anymore. Instead, they're for my children's and Paul's children's trust funds. Mark has joined us as well, as a 30 percent partner. In 2012, we purchased a six-story, 52,000-square-foot building, well known in the area as the former Teachers Federal Credit Union headquarters in Farmingville. Paul and I bought it in the name of the trust funds. That building, which we named the Heron Professional Center"—there's that heron again!—"is 100 percent occupied, and we continue to develop it and manage the building. We created it as a condominium-office complex, and we've sold off one floor and reaped the benefit from that sale by reducing the mortgage. Then came an opportunity to sell a lease for space on the roof. We had a lease, renting space for cell towers that was generating something like $30,000 a year in income, and when a guy offered to buy that from us for $650,000 or $700,000, we did the math, and it made sense. We sold that lease but continued to maintain additional space for potential users down the road. We still have space available, and we're in negotiation with somebody else to lease the rest of the roof. So," Jim says with a smile, "in that sense, maybe we can say that the building is 110 percent occupied.

"The fundamentals of all this is that we're financed in such a way that we're never forced to do anything we don't want to. We're capable of carrying the mortgages. If every tenant walked out of the Heron building tomorrow, that wouldn't bankrupt us. We could maintain the building, regardless, and that gives us a certain level of confidence. If you radiate that confidence, people gain confidence in the building, and it becomes very, very attractive.

"All in all, this is a unique part of my life, and a big part of that is because for most of my career, my business ventures have been conducted debt-free, but when you're in real estate, you start borrowing money and leveraging it. There are tremendous tax ramifications when you own a building and sell it, but if you own a building with cash flow, you can actually borrow money and remove capital tax-free. If the cash flow is sufficient to cover the mortgage, you're better off maintaining ownership of the building. For my part, I'm forced to do business in a different way than I would in other circumstances. But it's interesting because I'm managing a business that is not aimed at my direct benefit anymore. It's for the next generation, and when you start doing estate planning and looking into the ins and outs of wealth transfer and that sort of thing, it becomes a quite complicated and fascinating evolution."

Throughout these conversations about savvy real estate investments and the financial windfalls that he and Paul Elliott have reaped from their smart business decisions, it gradually becomes evident that one of the central, driving motivators for Jim in all this is not just the thrill of making a profit. Of course, that thrill, along with the satisfaction of building something—in this case, a very impressive real estate portfolio—plays a role. But there's something more at work here. Call it a kind of quiet vindication for a man who, in his earliest years, wasn't given much of a chance by people who never took the time to find out what he was really made of.

"I often think back," Jim says, "to the experience we all had in school, when they sent you to the guidance counselor. Most of us were told, 'You've got to decide if you're going into a vocational program or if you're going to try to go to college someday.' In my case, as far as guidance counselors and teachers were concerned, being on track for college was out of the question, because I was a lousy student, and I wasn't going to amount to anything. But kids grow up because of what you tell them, or in spite of what you tell them. For my own part, I think I grew up in spite of everything."

CHAPTER 37

A Short Chapter on Big Subjects

Like most people who have lived long and lived well, Jim Miller is not easily pigeonholed. For example, while he might be a publicly acknowledged "environmental champion" for his designing and building a fish passage for alewives, no one should make the mistake of considering him an environmentalist—at least not in the contemporary sense of the term.

"That sort of vocabulary doesn't fit me," Jim declares, with perhaps a little more heat than he brings to most conversations. "I reject that label. I mean, I'm not a tree hugger. Yes, much of my career has been in oil-spill cleanup, but I do that to make money. You know, it's an interesting conversation we have with new employees. 'Why did you come to work for us?' we ask them. And every once in a while, someone might say something like, 'Well, I feel good working for an environmental company. It's so nice that you do all of this work to save the environment.' And I'm the first one to tell them, 'Listen. We do this to make a living.'"

Still, while the primary aim and directive of, for example, Miller Environmental Group is to turn a profit, to keep people employed, and to have a viable business that grows at a sustainable rate, is there any element of the company's mission that has room for "environmentalist"—with a lowercase *e*—aims or goals? To Jim Miller's way of thinking, focusing on the health of the business is, in and of itself, a boon to the environment.

"I believe we have a tremendous environmental impact," he says. "We employ people, we give them an opportunity to enhance their careers, to support their families, to live a life. That to me is an environmental success. Hugging trees and picking up trash? That's make-believe stuff. In the end, it has nothing to do with the environment—but it might make the people doing it feel good about themselves. I guess we see things differently, as a business, than the local Sierra Club chapter might.

"It's like the way people get an idea of what a farmer does for a living, when they think to themselves, 'I want to be a farmer because I love animals.' Well, I have news for you. You're going to raise those animals, and you're going to slaughter them."

The briefest of pauses, and almost as an aside, Jim then engages in a bit of rare self-labeling. "Generally speaking, I'm a conservative economically. Socially, I'm a liberal."

Conservative, liberal, libertarian. Whatever unique melding of those particular denominations he might have attained over the course of his life, there's one particular characteristic that family and friends alike comment on when discussing Jim Miller—a characteristic that both encompasses and transcends convenient political labels: generosity.

Jim Miller's particular brand of generosity, meanwhile, is not limited to his family or to those he works with. Certainly some of the gestures he's made through the years are seen and noted by the general public: the 9/11 memorial sculpture in Southold, for example, the funding for which was raised through a collaborative effort of Miller family members, business associates, and friends—with Jim and Barbara acting as prime movers in the effort. Or the aforementioned fish ladder, which evolved into a permanent fish passage system at Grangebel Park in Riverhead. Jim and the late Bob Conklin designed the passage, which Jim funded, to help alewives—a type of small herring—migrate from fresh water to salt water, where they're an essential link in the food chain and timeless prey for species like fluke and striped bass.

Of the fish passage, Jim once noted that the success of the project "has reached a magnitude beyond our belief. We had fantasized that maybe some tens of thousands of fish could possibly migrate. We are now of the belief that it's hundreds of thousands. It could actually impact entire fisheries on the East Coast of the United States."

In May 2013, both Jim and, posthumously, Bob Conklin, who taught science at Riverhead High School for years, were honored as "Environmental Champions" by the North Fork Environmental Council for their work on the fish passage.

Above and beyond Jim's forays into civic betterment, or his lifelong involvement with volunteer fire departments on eastern Long Island, there are countless other, anonymous acts—some of them quite large, others so small they might make only a slight ripple in the fabric of a community. Both Jerry Coogan and Linda Meyer, for example, mentioned how Jim and Mark might anonymously foot the bill for an entire funeral for an employee or a neighbor whose family was in dire straits.

But even more telling, perhaps, are the smaller, lower-profile gestures that seem to give Jim the biggest thrill.

"Say I'm at the supermarket, shopping on a Saturday morning," Jim says. "Ahead of me, in line at the cash register, there might be a little old lady with a shopping cart filled with food, but she can't afford the last two cans of soup or whatever. Before she can put them aside, and before she can get embarrassed, I might call over a store manager or employee and say, 'You see that lady right there? I've got her entire bill. I'll pay it. Tell her that she's the one-hundredth customer of the day or something, and as part of a store promotion, all her groceries are free today.' The old lady never knows that I paid for her groceries. She doesn't have any need to know. But it gives me such a charge to be able to do something like that every once in a while."

When the conversation shifts—quite naturally, as it turns out—from the importance of playing a positive role in one's community to the even larger question of what he sees when he looks back over his more than eight decades (when he stops working long enough, that is, for such self-indulgence), Jim is as straightforward as can be.

"I'm not afraid to die," he says. "I have had an unbelievably wonderful career and a wonderful life."

When asked about his attitude toward death, his response brings the focus back, once again, to the life he's led, rather than what might await him in some unknown and ultimately unknowable future.

"When the time comes," he says, "there's no way I'll look back and say, 'I was robbed. I didn't have a decent life. I didn't have an exciting time.' Maybe the best way I can express how I feel about my own life is to say that I'm very sorry for those who have led different lives than I have."

Asked about people who recall so much of their own lives with regret, Jim mulls that for a while, the look in his eyes suggesting that he will never be able to fathom that sort of temperament or frame of mind.

"I can't regret my life—even with all the hardships I faced. Or maybe I can't regret anything *because* of the hardships. I look back at the opportunities, the successes, the challenges, all the people I've met and been privileged to know, and I'm just amazed. Don't get me wrong," he adds, raising both hands as if to ward off the very notion that he's somehow getting ahead of himself with all this talk of death and dying. "I don't plan to check out any time soon. But I would not trade my life for anyone else's. It's been a dream beyond dreams. It really has."

Epilogue

In October 2015, a lively, companionable group of men and women gather at a beautiful, many-windowed house perched high above Long Island Sound. Set back from the edge of a bluff on the island's North Fork, the house overlooks the very waters that two generations of Millers worked as fishermen and lobstermen forty and fifty years ago.

On this particular fall morning, sunlight shines on low waves that stretch north toward the Connecticut shoreline—a wavering, dark line on the horizon. Jim and Barbara Miller are there at the house, sitting at the kitchen table with some of Jim's siblings and their spouses. Dave Miller is there with his wife, Sandy. Jim's sister Loretta is there, too, with her husband, Bob, visiting from their home in Milledgeville, Georgia. Jim's sister Marguerite is in bed, having taken a fall the day before. Her husband, John, shuttles between the bedroom, where he checks on his wife, and the kitchen, where he sits in on the conversation for a while before heading to the bedroom for another look at Marguerite to see if she needs anything.

Richie, recovering from cataract surgery, could not make it this year. Nor could Tom, the author of a warm, lighthearted memoir of his own, titled *The Miller Boys*. Dialysis treatments several times a week kept him close to home in Pennsylvania, where he lived with his wife of sixty-one years, Rosemary.

(A Navy veteran of the Korean War, a father and grandfather, a lifelong outdoorsman, a woodworker and painter, a longtime volunteer ESL teacher, a charter member of the North Merrick Fire Department Drum and Bugle Corps, and a master plumber for more than forty years—Tom died on Christmas Eve, 2015. He was eighty-three years old.

"I've had what I consider a really good life," he said just a few months before he passed away. "I'm not a rich man. I don't really desire to be rich, but I am rich in one sense because of the people I've known and the experiences I've had. All in all, it's been a wonderful life.")

While some of her siblings are missing, Jim and Barbara's daughter Tracey is there, if only for a quick visit before she heads back out to her countless errands and meetings throughout the day. She checks her phone, tells jokes, refills the coffee mugs of anyone who asks, teases her mom—all at the same time.

The men and women around the table make up part of what has come to be called the Old-Timers Club, or the OTC. Every October for many years, the Miller siblings—those who can attend—have gathered for a week-long reunion of the OTC, marked by good meals, news of the kids and the grandkids, and countless shared memories.

This is a morning filled with stories, most of which have been told so many times that everyone in the room can fill in any blanks that might arise, or supply names and dates that might have been forgotten by the others around the table.

Barbara describes how Jim taught the kids to swim by tossing them off a barge into Port Jefferson Harbor, and by the tone of her voice, it seems the passing years have not eased her indignation at that singular pedagogical method. ("They learned, didn't they?" Jim asks, cheerfully.)

Loretta and Jim tag-team the story—clearly a Miller family classic—of how as a teenager he and Kenny Meyer tied a dead shark to the halyard of a flagpole in downtown Freeport, hoisted the shark to the top of the pole, tied it off, and then cut the lower half of the rope so the shark would be hanging up there for a good long time. ("Otherwise, they would have just lowered it down again," Jim says. "That wouldn't be any fun.")

Other tales of mischief involving young Jim Miller, Kenny Meyer, and dead sharks follow in the flagpole story's wake. A shark propped up in the driver's seat of a car—maybe dressed in top hat and tails, maybe not. A shark set up for drinks at a bar.

"Sharks," Jim explains, "played a role in a lot of our pranks."

The stories are passed around the table: shared, examined, appreciated like family mementos. Laughter echoes through the house. The morning hours pass. Lunchtime comes and goes, and the stories roll on.

During a rare lull in the hubbub, Barbara speaks up. It's clear from the tone of her voice that she's not about to launch into yet another often-told story.

"Isn't it amazing?" she asks, and just like that, she has everyone's attention. The room is quiet. "After all this time, after everything we've been through, we can sit here together in this beautiful house and share these stories. Better yet, we can *laugh* about them. And isn't it wonderful that we can remember all the people who can't be here, just by including them in the stories we tell?"

While it seems such a simple sentiment, the way that Barbara phrases her questions transforms the words into an affirmation of sorts. The answers, even when unspoken, are perfectly clear.

For the Millers, everything comes back to family.

Family is all.

Family is the ship, the buoy, and the anchor.

Outside, while the brilliant October sunlight streams down, the air is growing cool. Winter is coming—one can almost sense it, right around the corner—but on an afternoon like this, it's easy to imagine that there are plenty of warm days yet to come.

— AUF WIEDERSEHEN —

Luck and Choice

I t's certainly true, as the old saying has it, that you can choose your friends, but you can't choose your family. What the old saying fails to mention, however, is that there's absolutely no guarantee that you will end up being friends with your family.

I have had the great fortune to be born into a family that has, collectively and for as long as I can remember, treated life as a great adventure. In fact, in many ways, the Miller family itself *is* a great adventure.

At the core of this adventure, there has always been my father and my friend, Jim Miller—a great dad in every imaginable way. He did not have a "father knows best" parenting style; that's not the kind of home we grew up in. Instead, he was an unconventional parent: sometimes incredibly tough, often showing a soft side, and always, always fair and anchored by his rock-solid system of beliefs and his philosophy toward life and work.

He has been a terrific business partner, a trusted advisor, a debate provocateur—always challenging my ideas—a longtime neighbor, a regular lunch partner, and my hero. His unswerving consistency in standards, personal conduct, and business practices established a touchstone of enormous significance that has helped light my own way along my life's journey. His unbounded wisdom and confidence in how to live often made me wonder if he was on his second or third go-around here on earth. On top of it all, he has been an extraordinary grandfather to my children and to my many nieces and nephews.

It is for this next generation, and the generations to come, that my wife, Içim, and I embarked on this book project: Put plainly, his story had to be told. The voice of Jim Miller and much of his full, bursting-at-the-seams life is captured—as much as any life of such variety and sheer, improbable fun can be captured—in these pages. For those lucky enough to know my father firsthand, this book serves as a reminder and repository of a number (but certainly not all!) of his amazing recollections. For those unfamiliar with Jim Miller, please know that this book serves as a fond, strong portrait of a truly exceptional life.

This singular, intensely independent man persevered despite enormous obstacles—both early and late—and a sea of challenges. In spite of possessing only an eleventh-grade education, throughout his life, my father has always evolved. His inquisitive mind led him to the study of abstract mathematical theories and treatises on economics, and it brought him into conversations and discussions with countless people from all walks of life on topics ranging from philosophy and faith to the workings of the natural world. Whether talking to a fellow fisherman, a colleague at Miller Environmental, or his neighbor and friend who happened to build Albert Einstein a telescope as a gift, he has always asked "the next question" in order to fully understand anything that caught his attention and was worth learning about.

Forever a tinkerer and an idea man, he holds patents for two inventions—one of which has generated millions of dollars over the years—and has had a hand in designing and implementing count-less improvements, large and small, in the equipment he's worked with throughout his career, from his lobstering and fishing boats to apparatus and machinery we still use today at Miller Environmen-tal. (There's a reason my father's license plate reads MEG ONE: He's had a hand in more of the innovations at MEG than anyone else associated with the company.)

As he grew more and more successful in business, he continually mentored and taught those who were willing to listen and to learn, yet he was always prepared to change his position on almost any sub-ject or issue if a compelling enough argument was presented to him.

He has always been deeply compassionate and empathetic. He has quietly and charitably helped innumerable people over the decades. Complete strangers have often benefited from my father's kindness and his generosity. He has always stood up and been pre-pared to fight for what he believes is right, and he has ferociously protected and provided for those he loves.

To my mind, he is the literal embodiment of the American Dream.

Above all, though, he is my dad. On his eightieth birthday in 2015, I could not think of a more fitting way to celebrate his life and to thank him for all he has afforded our entire family than to com-mission this book. I want to express my humble thanks to all of our friends and family who so generously took time to share your memories.

Thanks, too, to Ben Cosgrove for so respectfully and beautifully capturing Jim Miller's voice and his story.

Finally—and especially—thanks, Dad. For everything.

MARK MILLER
Southold, L.I., January 2017

The Martha R. Ingram—*the first Integrated Tug/Barge Unit (ITB) —in Port Jefferson Harbor, January 1972. An ITB was integrated by a system of hydraulic rams in the bow of the tug that fit into a deep notch at the stern of the barge. When connected, the two functioned as a single vessel. The* Martha R. Ingram *split in two while leaving the dock after off-loading fuel oil. "I heard this huge, awful noise coming from the harbor," recalls Jim Miller, who was at his house in Port Jefferson Station when the accident occurred, "and even from miles away I could feel this enormous vibration under my feet."*

Miller Environmental Group's very first vacuum truck, 1976.

The 648-foot container ship Seaspeed Arabia, *pictured in the mid-1970s, grounded in Newark Bay in July 1979, spilling 120,000 gallons of diesel and heavy fuel into New York's Upper Harbor. Working on this spill, and setting up a base of operations on Staten Island, established Jim's company as a major player in the harbor and beyond.*

Miller Environmental crews work the Seaspeed Arabia *spill in the summer of 1979, preparing to deploy an oil containment boom. Mark Miller is on the right, in a T-shirt, on the boat in the foreground.*

Jim Miller with his three sons—Jim Jr., Glen, and Mark—in 1988.

Miller Environmental Group's box trucks in 1992. Today, the company operates a fleet of hundreds of vehicles of all shapes and sizes, serving multiple purposes.

In 1990, an 800-foot tanker, the BT Nautilus, *ran aground near Staten Island, spewing 260,000 gallons of No. 6 fuel oil.*

"A spill doesn't get cleaned up . . . when there's no cooperation between the cleanup company, the insurance company, the Coast Guard and everyone else. That sort of costly nonsense didn't happen here, because we worked well together."

—Steve Candito, lawyer for an admiralty law firm at the time, future CEO of NRC, and a longtime friend of the Millers

In August 1993, three vessels—a jet-fuel-filled barge; a second barge carrying five million gallons of No. 6 fuel oil; and a phosphate freighter—collided off of Tampa Bay, Florida. Oil eventually fouled an estimated fourteen miles of beaches. The cleanup was the first major test of the newly formed National Response Corporation. Note the thick, black band of oil on the beach at the water's edge.

In January 1994, a 300-foot single-hull barge, the Morris J. Berman, *hit a coral reef and lost nearly 750,000 gallons of heavy-grade oil in the waters near San Juan, Puerto Rico.*

A Miller Environmental crew pulls a Northeast Utilities Service Co. (NUSCO) cable from Long Island Sound in 1996. "Those cables sometimes failed and leaked oil—when there was a fault or blowout and the cable sheath was breached—and we were always hired to fix those," says Jerry Coogan. To this day MEG continues to be actively involved in submarine cable projects.

In September 1996, the Julie N. slammed into the Million Dollar Bridge in Portland, Maine, ripping a thirty-foot hole in the tanker's hull and spilling almost 180,000 gallons of heating oil into the Fore River.

Jerry Coogan works from the back of a Miller Environmental Group vacuum truck in the late 1990s.

The partially reconstructed wreckage of TWA Flight 800 in a hangar in Calverton, New York, months after the Boeing 747-100 exploded and crashed off of Long Island in July 1996, killing all 230 passengers and crew. Miller Environmental played a central role in the recovery effort.

Miller Environmental Group's decontamination station near Ground Zero after 9/11. The company had crew and equipment on the ground in Lower Manhattan for twelve months after the 2001 terror attacks.

The Harry Miller *crew boat in New York Harbor, 1999.*

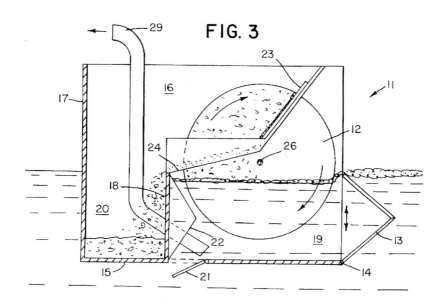

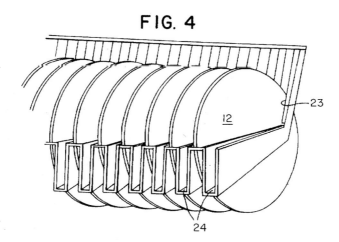

Two drawings from Jim's patent for the Weir Disc Oil Spill Recovery Device.

(12) **United States Patent**
Davey et al.

(10) Patent No.: **US 6,604,536 B1**
(45) Date of Patent: **Aug. 12, 2003**

(54) **APPARATUS FOR REMOVING PCBS, CONTAMINANTS AND DEBRIS FROM GAS TRANSMISSION LINES**

(75) Inventors: **Jim Davey**, Calverton, NY (US); **James C. Miller**, Calverton, NY (US)

(73) Assignee: **Miller Environmental Group, Inc.,** Calverton, NY (US)

(*) Notice: Subject to any disclaimer, the term of this patent is extended or adjusted under 35 U.S.C. 154(b) by 0 days.

(21) Appl. No.: **09/366,350**

(22) Filed: **Aug. 2, 1999**

(51) Int. Cl.^{7} **B08B 9/02**

(52) U.S. Cl. .... **134/104.2**; 134/166 C; 134/169 C

(58) Field of Search .... 134/104.2, 166 C, 134/169 C, 168 C, 166 R; 15/302, 321, 320

(56) **References Cited**

U.S. PATENT DOCUMENTS

918,091 A	*	4/1909	Roche
1,328,726 A		1/1920	Dezendorf
2,259,644 A	*	10/1941	Kling
2,356,254 A		8/1944	Lehmann, Jr. et al.
2,800,134 A	*	7/1957	Merritt
3,010,853 A		11/1961	Elliott
3,039,477 A	*	6/1962	Harbo
3,084,076 A		4/1963	Loucks et al.
3,182,670 A	*	5/1965	Howell
3,536,081 A	*	10/1970	Riess
3,600,225 A		8/1971	Parmelee

3,658,589 A	*	4/1972	Shaddock
4,134,174 A	*	1/1979	Flynn et al.
4,199,837 A	*	4/1980	Frisco, Jr.
4,206,313 A		6/1980	Cavoretto
4,234,980 A	*	11/1980	DiVito et al.
4,549,966 A		10/1985	Beall
4,922,571 A		5/1990	Driear
4,935,984 A	*	6/1990	Bryant et al.
4,995,914 A		2/1991	Teter
5,007,444 A	*	4/1991	Sundholm
5,107,875 A	*	4/1992	Sundholm
5,296,039 A		3/1994	Cooper
5,341,539 A	*	8/1994	Sheppard et al.
5,737,709 A		4/1998	Getty et al.

FOREIGN PATENT DOCUMENTS

DE	286594	*	2/1913
GB	1188517	*	4/1970

* cited by examiner

Primary Examiner—Frankie L. Stinson
(74) *Attorney, Agent, or Firm*—Hiscock & Barclay, LLP; Somendu B. Majumdar

(57) **ABSTRACT**

An apparatus and process for removing and recovering contaminants from a pipeline while containing and preventing the contaminants from spilling or leaking into the environment during said removal comprising. Specifically, the apparatus and method effectively and safely remove PCBs from a gas transmission pipeline. The apparatus and method implements a unique coupling system the prevents dangerous contaminants from escaping into the environment. Furthermore, the apparatus and method implements and system for recycling cleaning solution for continuous treatment of the pipeline.

19 Claims, 4 Drawing Sheets

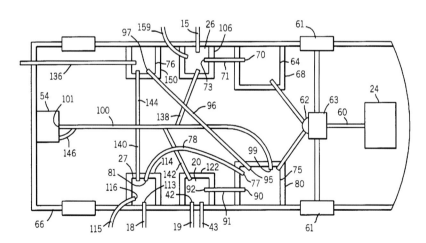

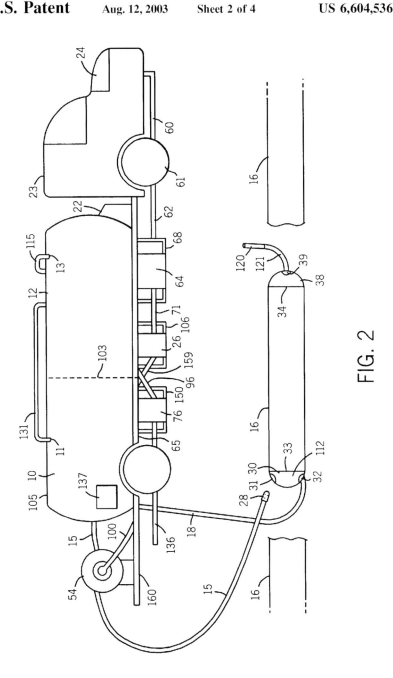

FIG. 2

Jim Miller's patent for the Envirojet.

Jim and Barbara's home in Southold, on Long Island's North Fork—just a few minutes' walk from Mark and Içim Miller's house, overlooking Peconic Bay.

Artist Roberto Julio Bessin's forty-foot-tall, two-ton steel heron—crafted of gracefully bent, three-eighths-inch steel bars—stands sentinel on the beach in front of Jim and Barbara Miller's home.

Jim and Barbara with their six kids—counterclockwise from top left: Jenniffer, Tracey, Mark, Jim Jr., Barbara, and Glen—during their fiftieth wedding anniversary weekend at their home in Southold, Long Island, 2005.

The older and, for the most part, wiser Miller boys, July 2012. From left: Jim, Rich, Tom (d. December 2015), and Dave.

Jim and Barbara's grandchildren (left to right): Megan, Rachel, Rana, Evan, Samantha, Erin, Abigail, Joel, Nicholas, Julia, Rob, Jessica, James III, and Emily.

Jim and Barbara Miller in 2009, seated in a restored 1950s Plymouth Belvedere convertible—a mint replica of the car they had when they were married—presented to them on their fiftieth wedding anniversary by their children.

A quiet moment for Jim doing some freshwater fishing on the pond at daughter Jenniffer's home in Maine, New York, 2002.

Index

MATTITUCK INLET
Scale 1:10,000

L O N G   I S L A N D   S O U N D

G R E A T   P E C O N I C   B A Y

Last Correction: 7/25/2014. Cleared through:
LNM: 2914 (7/22/2014), NM: 3114 (8/2/2014), CHS: 0614 (6/27/2014)

SOUNDINGS IN FEET

LOGARITHMIC SPEED SCALE

SCALE 1:40,000